PERSONAL MEMORIES

SOCIAL, POLITICAL, AND LITERARY

WITH

SKETCHES OF MANY NOTED PEOPLE

1803—1843

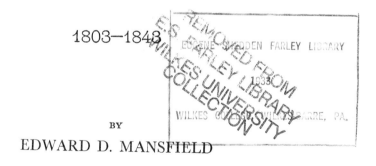

BY

EDWARD D. MANSFIELD

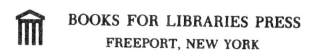

BOOKS FOR LIBRARIES PRESS
FREEPORT, NEW YORK

First Published 1879
Reprinted 1970

INTERNATIONAL STANDARD BOOK NUMBER:
0-8369-5559-5

LIBRARY OF CONGRESS CATALOG CARD NUMBER:
72-133527

PRINTED IN THE UNITED STATES OF AMERICA

PREFACE.

I HAD no such vanity as would have induced the publication of this book. It was urged upon me by others. Several years ago a number of gentlemen in Cincinnati sent me a written request to publish my reminiscences. After that my children made the same request. Not liking personal publicity, I paid, at first, little attention to the subject. Subsequently I began writing my memories in a series of letters to my children. In this form they had more of personality and of personal address than perhaps a printed book should have, but the reader will no doubt make allowance for that.

One reason for my publishing these personal reminiscences is, that I remembered I was always interested, and I think others have been also, in this kind of narrative. Human-nature is always interested in itself, and each individual looks with curiosity on the progress of others in the journey of life. This common interest in each other is my best reason for this publication, a small contribution to the history of human nature. It will satisfy the curiosity of some, inform others upon the social events of my time, and record some portions of unwritten history now almost forgotten, and which would otherwise remain unknown.

One other thing ought to be mentioned. Many persons of whom I might be expected to speak are not named, and of the large commercial class, among whom I had many friends, little is said. For this, I think, there are sufficient reasons. First, the period to which I limited myself—1803 to 1841—excluded most of them; and secondly, while I was so limited, I excluded, as far as possible, the living. If I should be encouraged by the public, or my strength will permit, I may add a second volume, which would bring the memories of my time through the War of the Rebellion. Such a thing would be pleasing to myself; but, like all human events, is in the hands of Divine Providence, which ordereth all things right, and to which we should submit with patient and humble resignation.   E. D. M.

YAMOYDEN, *March*, 1879.

CONTENTS.

CHAPTER VI.

CHAPTER VII.

CHAPTER VIII.

CHAPTER IX.

CHAPTER X.

CHAPTER XI.

CHAPTER XVIII.

CHAPTER XIX.

CHAPTER XX.

PERSONAL MEMORIES.

By E. D. MANSFIELD.

*My Father—Appointed Surveyor-General by Jefferson—
Marietta in 1803—Society—Madam Blennerhasset—
Her Lament—Pioneer Survey of Indiana—Wild Animals of Ohio—Prevalence of Intemperance and Infidelity.*

THE reader of "Personal Memories" must desire to
know something of the writer, and of his qualifications to interest the public.

My father's family came from Exeter, in England,
landed at Boston in 1634, and were among the first
settlers in New Haven, in 1639. They were upright,
intelligent people, who, with their descendants, have
continued from that time to this—a period of two
hundred and forty years—without reproach; always
in respectable situations, and some of them in public
life. My father, Jared Mansfield, was, all his life, a
teacher, a professor, and a man of science. He began
his life as a teacher in New Haven, where he taught
a mathematical school, and afterward taught at the
"Friends' Academy," in Philadephia, where he was
during the great yellow-fever season, and went from
there to West Point, where he taught in the Military
Academy, in 1802-3 and in 1814-28. In the mean-

time, however, he was nine years in the State of Ohio, holding the position of Surveyor-General of the United States. The manner of his appointment, and the work he performed, will illustrate his character and introduce a small, but interesting chapter of events.

While teaching, at New Haven, he had several pupils who afterward became famous, or rather distinguished men. Two of these were Abraham and Henry Baldwin. The first was afterward United States Senator from Georgia, and the second, Judge of the Supreme Court of the United States. These boys, as may be inferred, had decided talents, but were full of mischief. One day they played a bad trick upon my father, their teacher, and he whipped them very severely. Their father complained, and the case came before a magistrate; but my father was acquitted. It may be thought that the boys would have become my father's enemies. Not so; they were of a generous temperament, and knew their conduct had been wrong; this they acknowledged, and they became my father's fast friends. Judge Henry Baldwin told me that nothing had ever done him so much good as that whipping; and the brothers were warm in their friendship to my father, both in word and act.

While teaching, in New Haven, he published a book entitled "Essays on Mathematics." It was an original work, and but a few copies were sold; for there were but few men in the country who could understand it. The book, however, established his reputation as a man of science, and greatly influenced his after life. Abraham Baldwin was, at that time, Senator from Georgia, and brought this book to the notice of Mr. Jefferson, who was fond of science and scientific men. The consequence was, that my father became a captain of engineers, appointed by Mr. Jefferson, with a view to his becoming one of the professors at the West Point Military Academy, then established by law. Accordingly, he and Captain Barron, also of the engineers, were ordered to West Point, and became the first teachers of the West Point cadets in 1802. He was there about a year, when he received a new appointment, to a new and more arduous field in the West.

Mr. Jefferson had been but a short time in office, when he became annoyed by the fact that the public surveys were going wrong, for the want of establishing meridian lines; for the accuracy of the surveys depended upon establishing meridian lines with base lines at right angles to them. The surveyors of that time, including General Rufus Putnam, then Surveyor-General, could not do this. Mr. Jefferson wanted a man who could perform this work well, necessarily, therefore, a scientific man. This came to the ears of Mr. Baldwin, who strongly recommended my father, as being, in fact, the most scientific man of the country. My father did not quite like the idea of such a work, for he was a scholar and mathematician, fond of a quiet and retired life.

He foresaw, clearly, that going to Ohio, then a frontier State, largely inhabited by Indians and wolves, to engage in public business involving large responsibilities, would necessarily give him more or less of trouble and vexation. He was, however, induced to go, under conditions which, I think, were never granted to any other officer. It was agreed that while he was engaged in the public service in the West, his commission in the engineer corps should go on, and he be entitled to promotion, although he received but one salary, that of Surveyor-General. In accordance with this agreement, he received two promotions while in Ohio, and his professorship at West Point was (on the recommendation of President Madison), subsequently, by law, conformed to the agreement, with the rank and emoluments of lieutenant-colonel.

I mention this, to show the confidence that Presidents Jefferson and Madison had in him, and the respect which, in those days, was paid to men of science. Alas! that it should not be so now. I do not think my country has, on the the whole, gone backward; but it is in vain to say, that worth, virtue, or talent can any longer expect either the reward or recognition which they received at the hands of the early administration of the government. In these days *office* is the reward of partisan services. It is true, that occasionally a literary man is appointed to office; but I do not remember a single man of science, who, in the last twenty years, has received office at the hands of the government, as a reward or recognition of his distinction *as* a man of science. Irving, Bancroft, Motley, Bayard Taylor, and Lowell have been appointed to foreign missions, probably from their distinction as literary men; but where is there a man of science who has received from the government any recognition of his services? Professors Henry, Agassiz, and others have been distinguished in public service, but never at the hands of the government.

My father, so far as I know, was the only man ap-

pointed to an important public office solely on the
ground of his scientific attainments. This was due to
Mr. Jefferson, who, if not himself a man of science,
was really a friend of science.

My father's removal to the West, which took place
in 1803, required in those days a long journey, much
time, and a good deal of trouble. The reader will
understand that there were then no public convey-
ances west of the Allegheny. Whoever went to Ohio
from the East had to provide his own carriage, and
take care of his own baggage. At that time there
was really but one highway from the East to the
West, and that was the great Pennsylvania route
from Philadelphia to Pittsburg. It professed to be a
turnpike, but was really only a passable road, and on
the mountains narrow and dangerous. It was chiefly
traversed by the wagoners who carried goods from
Philadelphia to the West. A private carriage and
driver, such as my father had to have, was the abhorrence of the wagoners, who considered it simply an
evidence of aristocracy. They threatened, and often
actually endangered, private carriages. My mother
used to relate her fears and anxieties on that journey,
and, as contrasted with the mode of traveling at the
present day, that journey was really dangerous. Arrived at Marietta, Ohio, my father established his office there for the next two years. At first, some
trouble arose from differences of political opinions at
Marietta. Political excitement at the election of Jefferson had been very high, perhaps never more so.
General Rufus Putnam, my father's predecessor as
Surveyor-General, had been a Revolutionary officer
and a Federalist, while my father was a Republican

(now called Democrat), and supposed to be a partisan of Jefferson. This political breeze, however, soon passed over. The people of Marietta were, in general, intelligent, upright people, and my father not one to quarrel without cause. The Putnams were polite, and my parents passed two years at Marietta pleasantly and happily. I, who was but a little child of three or four years of age, was utterly oblivious to what might go on in Marietta society.

Two things, however, impressed themselves upon me. They must have occurred in the summer and spring of 1805. The first was what was called "The Great Flood." There is a good deal said, every little while, about extraordinary cold, heat, or high water, but all these things have occurred before, and nothing of natural phenomena has happened in the last half century which has not happened before. The impression on my mind is that of the river Ohio rising so high as to flood the lower part of Marietta. We lived some distance from the Ohio, but on the lower plain, so that the water came up into our yard, and it seems to me I can still recall the wood and chips floating in the yard. However, all memories of such early years are indistinct, and can only be relied on for general impressions. My mother insisted that she could remember Colonel Sabin riding through the streets of New Haven with a drawn sword, crying, "Turn out! Turn out!" on the invasion of the British Tories under Tryon and Arnold. This was in 1779, and she was only three years old. It is said that old people decay in the memory of recent events, but my mother had no loss of memory. It was the same to her whether the event was a year or seventy years old. As I was four years old at the time of the Marietta flood, it is probable that my impressions of it are correct.

The other event which impressed itself upon my mind was the vision of a very interesting and very remarkable woman. One day, and it seems to have been a bright summer morning a lady and a little boy called upon my mother. I played with the boy, and it is probable this circumstance which impressed it on my mind, for the boy was handsomely dressed, and had a fine little sword hanging by his side. The lady, as it seems to me, was handsome and bright, laughing and talking with my mother. That lady soon became historical—her life a romance, and her name a theme of poetry, and a subject of eloquence. It was Madame Blennerhasset. Although the main facts in her history are known, perhaps a brief account of her may interest the reader. Blennerhasset was an Irishman, of good family and education, but of fanciful and visionary ideas. His wife was an accomplished lady of high family. From some idea of adventure or romance, Blennerhasset moved to Ohio, and bought and improved what is known as Blennerhasset's Island. It is about twelve miles below Marietta, and is held by a patent received by Patrick Henry. There he built an elegant house, had a fine library, a philosophical apparatus, and a beautiful garden. Of these nothing now remains. Blennerhasset was one of the victims of Aaron Burr—became involved in his wild schemes, was driven from the island, which was left in ruins, the house burned, and the garden destroyed. The Virginia militia, who came in from Wood county with lofty patriotism on their tongues, were alike indifferent to beauty or to culture. The public history of Blennerhasset and Burr is well known, but that of Margaret Blennerhasset is more interesting than either. It is seventy years since Wirt, in the trial of Burr, uttered his beautiful and poetic description of Madam Blennerhasset and the island she admired. Poetic as it was, it did less than justice to the woman. An intelligent lady who was intimate with her, and afterward visited the courts of England and France, said she had never beheld one who was Mrs. Blennerhasset's equal in beauty, dignity of manners, elegance of dress, and all that was lovely in the person of woman. With all this she was as domestic in her habits, as well acquainted with housewifery, the art of sewing, as charitable to the poor, as ambitious for her husband, as though she were not the "Queen of the Fairy Isle." She was as strong and active in body as she was graceful. She could leap a five-rail fence, walk ten miles at a stretch, and ride a horse with the boldest dragoon. She frequently rode from the island to Marietta, exhibiting her skill in horsemanship and elegance of dress. Robed in scarlet broadcloth, with a white beaver hat, on a spirited horse, she might be seen dashing through the dark woods, reminding one of the flight and gay plumage of some tropical bird; but, like the happiness of Eden, all this was to have a sudden and disastrous end. The "Queen of the Fairy Isle" was destined to a fate more severe than if her lot had been cast in the rudest log cabin. Associated with the schemes of Burr, Blennerhasset was compelled to fly. The Virginia militia ravaged his beautiful home, and the island returned to the barbarism from which it had emerged. Mrs. Blennerhasset accompanied her husband to Natchez, where they lived for a time, and thence to Montreal. After her husband's death she returned to England, but came back finally to New York, having declined gradually from splendid fortune to pinching want. While on the St. Lawrence she wrote the "*Lament to the Fairy Isle.*" The following are two stanzas:

> " The stranger that descends Ohio's stream,
> Charmed with the beauteous prospects that arise,
> Marks the soft isles that 'neath the glistening beam
> Dance in the wave and mingle in the skies—
> Sees also *one*, that now in ruin lies,
> Which erst, like Fairy Queen, towered o'er the rest,
> In every native charm by culture dressed.

> " There rose the seat, where once, in pride of life,
> My eye could mark the Queen of rivers flow;
> In summer's calmness, or in winter's strife,
> Swollen with rains, or battling with the snow—
> Never again my heart such joy will know.
> Havoc and ruin, and rampant war have passed
> Over that isle with their destroying blast."

The end of this accomplished woman none can think of without a sigh. Reduced to absolute want in New York, she died and was buried by a benevolent society of Irish women—

> " By foreign hands, thy humble grave adorned,
> By strangers honored, and by strangers mourned."

During my father's residence at Marietta, there appeared in the Marietta paper a series of articles in favor of the schemes of Burr, and indirectly a separation of the Western and Eastern states. These articles were censured by another series, signed " Regulus," which denounced the idea of separating the states, and supported the Union and the administration of Jefferson. At the time, and to this day, the writer was, and is, unknown. They are mentioned in Hildreth's "Pioneer History," as by an unknown author. They were, in fact, written by my father, and made a strong impression at the time. For an account of the society and people at Marietta, I am indebted to my mother, of whom, I will here make such mention as is proper. Her maiden name was Phipps, and my grandfather Phipps came from Falmouth, Maine, to New Haven, Connecticut. He had the distinction—for in a historical sense, such it was—of being an officer in the first naval squadron ever fitted out by the United States. He sailed under Commodore Hopkins, who captured the island of New Providence in the Bahamas from the British; he remained in the navy during his life and was a remarkable man ; he was a strict disciplinarian and a pious Christian. Once, when commanding the frigate Essex, he heard the sailors swearing; he called the men up and said : "Men ! there must be no swearing on board this ship ; I do all the swearing." For some years after the Revolution, the Government having no employment for him, he commanded a merchant ship trading with Holland and Ireland. In his voyages from Ireland, he brought from Londonderry and Belfast a large number of Irish emigrants, among the first who came to this country.

Of my mother's early education, I never could learn that she had had more than that of the common schools, at that time common enough. I have heard her say, that, when a child, her teacher was Mrs. Henry Mansfield, the mother of General Joseph

Mansfield, killed at Antietam. My mother, probably got no other education, in the popular sense, than reading, writing, and, perhaps, geography. But— was that all? If it were, it was pretty good proof that more than that was not necessary to make a very intelligent person; for there were few people so well qualified, either for the duties of life, society, church, or state. The truth was, however, that my mother was brought up in a very religious family, and there- fore had all the knowledge that the Bible and the church can give, and that is not a little. In the next place, she had a strong literary taste, read all the En- glish classics, with the popular literature of the times, and remembered what she read. Her husband being a man of letters and of science, she was always in the best society and acquainted with many distin- guished literary and scientific people. This *social* edu- cation is, perhaps, the best, and, with her naturally strong mind, made my mother a superior woman. She needed none of the forms of schools, nor any fash- ionable accomplishments, to place her in the first rank of educated society. What others had of music, danc- ing, languages, or dress, she more than supplied with the flow of her full, cheerful, and brilliant mind. Gen- tlemen and ladies, young and old people, officers and scholars were glad to visit Mrs. Mansfield, lingering in her society until late hours and parting with regret, from what was indeed a "feast of reason and flow of soul." She had strong views of politics, and was a great patriot; for this, she had, in her experience, good reason. When Arnold and Tryon captured New Haven, in the Revolution, my mother's family suf- fered; some of them fled to the country, and others remained. It was then that her great uncle, Benjamin English, when over eighty years of age, was stabbed in his chair and killed by a Hessian soldier. That incident never faded from my mother's memory, and a warmer patriot or a greater enemy to the English government, than my mother, never lived. Here let me say, that I am indebted for my political opinions to two persons, except so far as they have been modified by my studies and experience. These persons were my mother and Oliver Wolcott, of Connecticut. Of the latter I shall speak again. The reader may ask if I got no opinions from my father. Some, certainly; but not of that positive character and influence which marked my mother's principles and views. He was a philosopher, a student of science, and a teacher; his mind was cool and philosophical, while my mother's was positive, direct, and earnest. She believed in the triumph of Christianity; in the success of the American Republic, the overthrow of the British Government, and the downfall of all oppression. She was lion-hearted, and would have died a martyr to her opinions had it been necessary. Such was my mother, and from her I derived most of my information about the early society of Marietta and Cincinnati. Among her friends in Marietta were the Putnams, the Meigs' family, the Greenes, the Backus' family, and the Stones. Some of these families seem to have disappeared; but some have left descendants. Here let me remark on the society of the past generation, as compared with the present. There is always in the *present* time, a disposition to exaggerate either its merits or its faults. Those who take a hopeful view of things, and wonder at our inventions and discoveries, think that society is advancing and we are going straight into the millenium. On the other hand, those who look upon the state of society to-day, *especially if they are not entirely satisfied* with their own *condition*, are apt to charge society with degeneracy. They see crimes and corruptions, and assert that society is growing worse. Let me here assure the reader that this is not true, and that while we have all reason to lament the weakness of human nature, it is not true that society is declining. No fact is more easily demonstrated than that the society of educated people—and they govern all others—is in a much better condition now than it was in the days succeeding the Revolution. The principles and ideas that caused the French Revolution, at one time, brought Atheism and Free Thinkers into power in France, and largely penetrated American society.

Skepticism, or, as it was called, Free Thinking, was fashionable; it was aided and strengthened by some of the most eminent men of the times. Jefferson, Burr, Pierrepont, Edwards, of Connecticut, and many men of the same kind, were not only skeptics, but scoffers at Christianity. Their party came into power, and gave a sort of official prestige to irreligion. But this was not all; a large number of the revolutionary army were licentious men. Of this class were Burr, Hamilton, and others of the same stripe. Hamilton was not so unprincipled a man as Burr, but belonged to the same general caste of society. No one can deny this, for he published enough about himself to prove it. Dueling, drinking, licentiousness, were not regarded by the better class of society as the unpardonable sins which they are now regarded. At that time, wine, spirits, and cordials were offered to guests at all hours of the day, and not to offer them was considered a want of hospitality. The consequence was that intemperance, in good society, was more common than now, but probably not more so among the great masses of the people. Intemperance is now chiefly the vice of laboring men, but then it pervaded all classes of society. Judge Burnet, in his " Notes on the Northwest," says, that of nine lawyers cotemporary with himself, in Cincinnati, all but one died drunkards. We see, then, that, with a large measure of infidelity, licentiousness, and intemperance among the higher classes, society was not really in so good a state as it is now. At Marietta, were several men of superior intellects, who were infidels, and others who were intemperate. And yet this pioneer town was probably one of the best examples of the society of pioneer times.

I have said that my father was appointed to establish the meridian lines. At that time but a part of Ohio had been surveyed, and he made Marietta his headquarters.

In the rapid progress of migration to the West, his surveys also were soon necessary in Western Ohio and in Indiana. Indiana was then an unbroken wilderness, although the French had established the post of Vincennes. This was one of a line of posts which they established from the lakes to the Gulf of Mexico, with a view to holding all the valley of the Mississippi. There may have been a settlement at Jeffersonville, opposite Louisville, but except these there was not a white settlement in Indiana. It became necessary to extend the surveyed lines through that state, then only a part of the Great Northwest Territory. For this purpose, my father, in 1805, in the month of October, undertook a surveying expedition in Indiana. As it was necessary to live in the wilderness, preparations for so doing were made. The surveying party consisted of my father, three or four surveyors, two regular hunters, and several pack-horses. The business of the hunters was to procure game and bring it into the camp at night. Flour, coffee, salt, and sugar were carried on pack-horses. but for all meat the party depended on the hunters. They went out early in the morning for game and returned only at night. As the surveying party moved only in a straight line, and the distance made in the day was known, it was easy for the hunters to join the others in camp. It was in this expedition that some of those incidents occurred that illustrate the life of a woodsman. One day the hunters had been unfortunate, and got no game, but brought in a large rattlesnake, which they cut into slices and broiled on the coals. My father did not try that kind of steak, but the hunters insisted the flesh was sweet and good. On another day a hunter was looking into a cave in the rocks and found two panther's cubs, he put them in a bag, and afterward exhibited them in New Orleans. Here let me say that posterity will never know the kinds and numbers of wild animals which once lived on the plains of the Ohio. Some are already exterminated, east of the Mississippi, and can only be found on the mountains of the West. A citizen of these days will probably be astonished to hear that the buffalo was once common in Ohio, and roamed even on the banks of the Muskingum; but such was the fact. A large part of

Ohio was at one time a prairie, and the vegetation of the valley very rich. The wild plum, the papaw, the walnut, and all kinds of berries were abundant, so that Ohio was as fruitful and abundant to Indians and wild animals as it has since been to the white man. In the valleys of the Muskingum, the Scioto, and the Miamis, were Indiãn towns where they cultivated corn, as white men do now. Marietta, Chillicothe, Circleville, Cincinnati, Xenia, and Piqua are all on the sites of old Indian towns. The wild animals and the wild Indian were as conscious as the civilized white man that Ohio was an inviting land—a garden rich in the products which God had made for their support. But man was commanded to live by labor, hence, when man, the laborer, came, he supplanted man, the hunter.

The animals most common in Ohio were the deer, the wild turkey, squirrel, buffalo, panther, and wolves. All these were found near Marietta, and all but the buffalo subsequently near Cincinnati. Deer, turkeys and squirrels were very numerous, and I have heard wolves near the present limits of Cincinnati. It is not my purpose, however, to go into the natural history of Ohio. The inhabitants of the woods fast disappeared before the man with the spade. I, myself, saw birds and animals in the valleys of the Miamis which no man will hereafter see wild in these regions. I recollect one bird which made a great impression on me—the paroquet—much like the parrot, its colors being green and gold, but was smaller. This bird I have seen at Ludlow station in large flocks. I was told it was never seen east of the Scioto.

Our residence at Marietta lasted two years. In 1803 Ohio was admitted into the Union, with a constitution, which continued until 1850. The first Constitution of Ohio was, I thought, the best constitution I ever saw, for the reason that it had the fewest limitations. Having established the respective functions of government, judicial, executive, and legislative, it put no limitation on the power of the people, and in a democratic government there should be none. For half a century Ohio grew, flourished, and prospered under its first constitution. It was the best and brightest period Ohio has had. It was the era of great public spirit, of patriotic devotion to country, and of the building up of great institutions of education which are now the strength and glory of the state. In forming educational institutions I had some part myself, and I look upon that work with unalloyed pleasure.

CHAPTER II.

Voyage down the Ohio—The "Ark"—"Keelboat"—Arrival at Cincinnati—General Findley—Fort Washington—Indian Lookout—Ludlow Station—Little Turtle; his appearance, character, and death—Israel Ludlow Sarah Bella Ludlow—John Mansfield.

AMONG the most remarkable characteristics of a country is its scenery. I am now writing on the first day of autumn, and in this region of the country, autumn is the most beautiful of the four seasons. A cloudless sky, a cool but balmy air, the grass green and fresh from recent rains, the foliage still rich and verdant, the distant scene mixed with every element of rural beauty, all unite to make this a lovely and beautiful season. I imagine it was on some such day, though a month later, in 1805, that my father and mother, with their little boy, left Marietta for Cincinnati. There was then neither railroad, steamboat, nor stage. How were they to travel?

There were two kinds of boats on the Ohio, substantially the same, but different in their make. One was called a keelboat, and the body was like that of a small steamboat, but was propelled by poles. Long, strong poles, with iron points, were used by men who put their shoulders at one end of the pole, and by walking the length of the boat, pushing, gained a distance equal to the length of the boat. Six or eight men, by poling, could thus push a boat up stream, and the keelboats were the only boats that could go up stream. Some of these boats had small cabins, well fitted up for families; but I think our boat was not of that kind, but an ark, as it was called, from a supposed resemblance to Noah's vessel. It was simply an oblong boat, made of boards, with a flat bottom. In the one we came in, there was a small cabin at one end fitted up for my mother. The keelboat has disappeared, but the ark is occasionally seen; for it is a cheap conveyance, needing only a steersman to keep it in the channel, and when it gets to the end of its journey is broken up and sold for lumber.

We arrived in Cincinnati, I think, the last part of October, 1805. Here occurs the first memory of which I am absolutely sure. Cincinnati was the first town I had seen, except Marietta, for the various towns now on the Ohio were then not in existence. But what was Cincinnati then? One of the dirtiest little villages you ever saw. Of course, I was not driven around *that* immense town to see its splendors, but the principal street or settlement was Front street, and that I saw. The chief houses at that time were on Front street, from Broadway to Sycamore; they were two-story frame houses, painted white. One was that of General Findley, receiver of the land office. This gentleman belonged to a family in Pennsylvania distinguished in political affairs. One member of this family was governor of Pennsylvania, one was member of Congress from the Chambersburg district, and James Findley, of whom I speak, was receiver of public moneys in Cincinnati, and subsequently member of Congress from the Cincinnati district. The Findleys were all of a popular caste of character. They were sanguine, pleasant, genial men. Belonging to the Democratic party, at a time when that party was dominant in nearly all the states, they were readily promoted to political honors. James Findley may be properly characterized as a gentleman—not so common a character as some persons suppose. He was easy in manner, kind hearted, genial, fond of good living, and a very upright man. The Findleys and my parents were intimate, hence I have described James Findley. We remained in Cincinnati but a few days, when my father removed to "Ludlow Station." You may ask *why* a station? Nobody would give such a name to a house now. In the early settlement of the Miami country, there was much fear of the Indians, less, however, by far, than attended the subsequent settlements in Indiana and Illinois. In fact, and to the honor of John Cleves Symmes, the founder of the Miami settlements, be it said, that he sought, not to destroy and oppress the Indians, but to conciliate them by equity and justice. No general war with the Indians ever occurred in the Miami country, but of course there were some collisions between them and the whites. Between Fort Washington, the original site of Cincinnati, and Fort Hamilton, where Hamilton now is, there were several affrays. In one of them a white man was killed who wore a wig. It is said that, according to the Indian habit, an Indian ran up to scalp him, and took hold of the wig; it came off; the Indian looked up astonished, and exclaimed, "One big lie!" The Indian seems to have understood one principle of moral philosophy very well—that a lie could be acted as well as spoken. These difficulties were over before I came upon the stage, and while Fort Washington was yet occupied as a military post by United States troops. At that time the Indians often came near the fort, especially on the neighboring hills. The wife of Colonel Strong, who was an officer in the fort, told me that she had often met and conversed with White Eyes and other Indian chiefs. White Eyes told her he had often watched what was going on in the fort from what has since been the site of the old Cincinnati Observatory. On the brow of the hill (Mt. Adams), there was then a very large oak tree, which I have myself seen. It was in the branches of this tree that White Eyes concealed himself, looked down upon the fort, and saw all that was going on.

At the time I came upon the scene as a child, in 1805–6, the Indians had almost wholly passed away from this region, and no danger was apprehended from them. The "stations," as they were called, of which Ludlow was one, were originally points of rendezvous and defense. They soon ceased to be of that character, but their names remained on the popular tongue and on the maps almost until the present day. We removed, as I have said, to Ludlow Station. It was built by Colonel Ludlow, one of the original proprietors of Cincinnati. It was then a large two-story dwelling, with wings—the best looking and, I think, the largest house then at Cincinnati. My father being Surveyor-General took one of the wings as his office, and the other was used as a kitchen; a lawn sloped down toward Millcreek, and there was a large garden. This house is still standing in the midst of Cumminsville. This leads me to what I thought a remarkable incident. After the campaign and victory of Wayne in 1795, a treaty was made with the Indians called the treaty of Greenville. The northern boundary of the Indians, one point of which was Greenville, ran through northern Ohio, and had been not quite determined when my father came to Ludlow Station. It was one part of his business to run that line, and it was something in reference to that which occasioned the following incident.

One day a dark man, with swarthy countenance, riding a very fine horse, dismounted at our house and went into my father's office. I wanted to go in and see him, but for some reason was not allowed to. After some time—it was in the forenoon, I think—I saw him come out, mount his horse, and ride rapidly away. I was struck by the man, and asked my mother, "who is that, ma?" She said it was "LITTLE TURTLE," the great Indian chief. And here I will extract from my discourse on the pioneers, which is founded on the best authorities and will give you some idea of one of the most remarkable men among the aboriginal races of this country. There had been four distinguished Indian chiefs in this country, who were the principal figures in the confederacies, which at different times were formed to suppress the white men, and save the Indian race from destruction. These were " KING PHILIP," in New England, PONTIAC, in the northwest, BRANDT (in the Indian tongue, *Thayendanega*), chief of the Mohawks, and LITTLE TURTLE, chief of the Miamis. It is far from the purpose of these "Memories" to recite the history of Philip, of Pontiac, or of Brandt, but I saw Little Turtle myself, and his name is associated with the early history of the Miami country. When the early settlers arrived on the

Muskingum and the Miamis, they found the Indians friendly. This was a consequence of the wise policy of Putnam and of Symmes; for both had, in their very first intercourse with the Indians, taken measures to conciliate them and show a friendly feeling. This friendship was, however, interrupted by the conspiracy which Brandt was then forming. The spirit and energy necessary to such an organization were supplied by the successive defeats of Harmer and St. Clair, an account of which you will find in the current history of the day. It was just after these Indian triumphs, and with the high hopes, which victory gives, that a conference was held at the mouth of Detroit river, between the commissioner of the United States and those of the confederate Indian tribes. This was a crisis in the Indian destiny. The orator of the Indians was Brandt; and the claim and argument set up were at once ingenious and powerful. They denied the authority of former treaties, and claimed the Ohio as the boundary. They represented themselves as without a country; that no more lands remained for them to occupy, and that all they asked was the country north of the Ohio, and perpetual peace. But the settlements of Marietta and Cincinnati were in the way; and for this, they had a ready reply : " We know," said they, " that these settlers are poor ; now, offer them the large sums of money which you offer us, and they will be glad to return."

The boundary of the Ohio was refused by the American Commissioners, because the country of the Miamis, the Scioto, and the Muskingum, had already been ceded in the treaty of Fort Harmer. The conference broke up, and with that conference the Indian dominion perished forever. The last hope that even a fragment of that race could remain perished there. The Indians shrieked their warwhoop along the frontier, and Wayne sounded his bugles along the Ohio. In Cincinnati, the northwestern army assembled. In was encamped on Millcreek bottom. Its sentinels walked on Fifth street Mound, which stood at the foot of the present Mound street, and is now gone—demolished by the hand of civilization—but was then a remaining monument to races long disappeared, whose history is unknown, and whose very existence is becoming rapidly obscured in the mists of time. Thus, in the summer of 1793, Wayne drilled his troops in all the arts of Indian warfare, and especially in those maneuvers which were suggested by Washington himself, and derived from his early experience. The army was wintered on the Stillwater Branch of the Miami, and in the spring moved slowly forward. It was more than once furiously attacked, but it got to be near the end of August, 1794, before the gathered bands of the Delawares, Miamis, Ottawas, Shawnese, and Wyandots were ready for their last great battle. Then they descended like the northern blast, but only to be broken and dispersed forever. The battle of the "Fallen Timber, at the Maumee Rapids, was fatal to the Indian power, and the victory of Wayne was the last act in the conquest of the northwest.

This last confederacy had been founded by Brandt, but the figure which stands out on the historical canvass, in bold relief, is that of MECHE CUNNAQUA, the Little Turtle, chief of the Miamis. This most acute and sagacious of Indian statesmen was, it is said, even a polished gentleman. He had wit, humor, and intelligence. He was an extensive traveler and had visited all parts of the country, and became acquainted with the most distinguished men. He had seen and admired General Washington. He was presented with a pair of pistols, by Kosciusko, and the Polish Hero told him to use them in defense of his country. He was intimate with the French Philosopher, Volney, who constructed a vocabulary of the Indian tongue from his information. In conversation with Volney, the Frenchman told him that the Indians had come from the Tartars, in Asia. "But," said Little Turtle, "*why may not the Tartars have come from America?*" Are there any reasons to the contrary?

"Little Turtle" commanded the Indian forces at the defeat of Harmer and at the defeat of St. Clair; but, though present and fighting bravely at the battle of the "Fallen Timber," seems not to have commanded. He advised against the attack, and said to the Indians: "We have beaten the enemy twice; we can not expect always the same good fortune. The Americans are now led by a chief who never sleeps. The day and the night are alike to him. 1 advise peace. When defeat came upon him and disaster pressed upon his nation, he was still calm, prudent, wise, and fearless. He signed the treaty of Greenville with the chiefs of ten tribes, and never again appeared on the field of battle. A few years after that event, he came (as I have related above), to my father's house, at "Ludlow Station," to arrange for the survey of the Greenville line. As he rode away from the house, in the declining sun, I might, without any violent stretch of imagination have seemed to see the last great spirit of

the Indian race leaving the land of his fathers, looking, for the last time, upon the beautiful valley of the
Miamis, and bidding farewell to each hill, and wood,
and stream forever.

Thirty years after the treaty of Greenville, he died,
at Fort Wayne, of the *gout* (!)—which would seem
a marvellous fact, did we not remember that the
" Turtle" was a high-liver and a gentleman ; equally
remarkable was it that his body was borne to the
grave, with the highest honors, by his great enemy,
the white man. The muffled drum, the funeral salute, announced that a great soldier had fallen, and
even enemies paid their mournful tribute to his memory. The sun of Indian glory set with him ; and the
clouds and shadows, which for two hundred years had
gathered round their destiny, now closed in the star-
less night of death.

" Ludlow Station" belonged to Col. Israel Ludlow.
ISRAEL LUDLOW was one of the proprietors of Cincinnati, and, under Judge Symmes, the purchaser of the
Miami country, laid out Cincinnati, and was the
surveyor of the adjacent country. The original
proprietors were Denman, Patterson, and Filson
(a schoolmaster) ; but, in an exploring expedition,
Filson was killed, and by a subsequent arrangement,
Ludlow took his place as one of the proprietors of
Cincinnati, and also the surveyor of the Symmes purchase. It is not my purpose to trace the early history
of Cincinnati—of which there are now sufficient
materials—but only those events connected with our
own family. Suffice it to say, that Col. Ludlow having built " Ludlow Station"—then quite a handsome
building—died just before my father came to Cincin-

nati. My father rented the place, at what would now be a very low price. It had a large apple orchard and two gardens—a kitchen and a flower garden. Before we left, Mrs. Ludlow married Mr. Risk, a clergyman, and lived in, or near, Cincinnati for several years. Mrs. Risk (Ludlow) came from Chamberburg (Pa.), and was of the Chambers family. She was a pious, devoted woman, who was thought, by her friends, to be a very superior woman. She was the grandmother of the third Mrs. CHASE, who was a daughter of James C. Ludlow. Mrs. Risk was an occasional visitor at our house, and some of my earliest memories are connected with her daughter. SARAH BELLA LUDLOW (now Mrs. McLean) was quite near my own age. When they left the "Station" for us, the little Sarah gave me, in a keg, a large number of duck's eggs, which subsequently proved a great amusement. I hatched my eggs under hens, and found myself having (I suppose, by selection) a flock of seventeen ducks, all of which were white, without a dark feather. That flock of ducks was my pride and delight. One day I was thrown into a great fright by a very natural, though, to me, a strange incident. Wild ducks were very numerous in the creek, and my white ducks got to associating with them; so one morning the wild ducks took flight into the skies, and my ducks with them. I thought they were gone; but after a while, to my delight, they returned. The little Sarah Bella was one day at our house with her mother, when (as I was recently reminded by Mrs. McLean) we undertook to run a race in the porch. She says that I outrun her, and my looks expressed triumph; but, seeing her mortified, I expressed sympathy. So it is, that the little things of life often make a stronger impression than the great ones; and so is it that the little boys and girls are only miniature men and women.

SARAH BELLA LUDLOW, I can recollect, was then a fair-haired, bright-eyed girl, a perfect blonde. She grew up to be a very handsome woman, and was as brilliant as handsome. She was, as long as I saw much of her, one of the most attractive persons in society. She married a young lawyer from Kentucky, named GARRARD, and had four sons, two of whom (Garrards) were generals in the war, and were active and gallant soldiers. Being a widow, Mrs. Garrard married Judge McLean, of the Supreme Court, and for several years accompanied the Judge to Washington City, where she always appeared as a charming and elegant woman. Again a widow, Mrs. McLean has till recently resided at Fontenac, on Lake Pepin, where she and her sons hold a great estate. She is a pious and fervent Christian, much devoted to the tenets of her own church, believing baptism by immersion an essential point of Christianity. I have thus mentioned Mrs. McLean, not only because she has been a distinguished woman, but also because it is not often we can testify, at the distance of more than sixty years, to those whom we knew in their childhood, and have known during an entire generation, of which nearly all have passed to the grave.

I can not stop to describe, even if memory would permit, the many brilliant, and some of them afterward greatly distinguished, persons who were either members of our family or visitors at Ludlow Station. Among others were John Mansfield, a young man of extraordinary worth and genius; Joseph Totten, who afterward became General of Engineers; Dr. Daniel Drake, the most distinguished physician of the Ohio valley; Judge—afterward Governor—Brown, and others of less note, but equally agreeable members of the social circle. I was too young to take much note of society, but most of them I knew in after life, and many I did not know my mother fully described. Of most of them I shall speak hereafter.

Memories so distant must, of course, be faint; but, it seems to me I can yet see Ludlow Station, where I was a boy, when no railroad was heard of; when no City of the Dead reminded us of generations past; when the wolves' long howl could still be heard; when the paroquet was still seen with his golden wings; when the green lawn stretched down from the "Station," lined with bending trees. Alas! it is gone; and no hand of civilization, with all its art and all its wealth, can replace much that is lost. We boast of "progress;" we talk of civilization; we really think that we are superior, and certainly, if the mechanic arts be the test, we are; but there was much in the old pioneer society which, to say the least, was more agreeable. In proportion to the number of the people, there was was more genius then than there is now; society was fresh; men were more honest; women were more social, and fashion did not exercise so much control. On the frontier, in a new state of society, there are, of course, more adventures, and there was also much more speculation upon the course of events. In one word, there was more that was new, notwithstanding all the mighty doings of telegraph and railroads—I mean more that was new, in the actual doing of things around.

I will close this chapter in the words of my old friend, Gallagher : *

"We liv'd not hermit lives, but oft in 'social converse met,
And fires of love were kindled then that burn on warmly yet.
O! pleasantly the stream of life pursued its constant flow,
In the days when we were pioneers, sixty years ago!"

* W. D. Gallagher, poet and editor.

CHAPTER III.

First Observatory at Ludlow Station—Public Surveys— Society in the Country— War of 1812— Volunteer Companies—Captain Mansfield—General Totten—Traveling in 1809—First View of a Steamboat—Log School House—The Hunters—Earthquakes of 1812.

LUDLOW Station adjoins the present Spring Grove Cemetery, which is a part of the original Ludlow farm. More than thirty years ago, I accompanied a party of ladies and gentlemen to view the ground afterward selected as the site of the cemetery. In my boyhood, I had set quail traps there, but at the time it was selected for the cemetery it was a grass field with a few scattering trees. In the short period which has passed since then, it has become populous with the dead. In the presence of such a reminiscence, one may say with Young—

"'T is greatly wise to talk with our past hours,
And ask them what report they've borne to Heaven—
And how they might have borne more welcome news."

They might, but who can tell? We know the road we have traveled, but not the road we *might* have gone. Some one has said, it is sad to think what *might* have been true; but it might have been much sadder to have known it. For my own part, I would much rather have taken the happiness I've had in the path I actually trod, than to have taken a chance of more in any other path. Then let the might have been rest with the unknown. I have said already, that my father was appointed by Mr. Jefferson for the express purpose of running the meridian lines, on which our whole system of public surveys depend. The astronomical instruments, whose purchase by Mr. Jefferson has been described, were set up in one room at our house, at Ludlow Station. Hence, as I have often said, the first real observatory was established in our house.[1] There my father made such astronomical calculations as were necesssary to his purpose. Besides these, he calculated the orbit of the great comet of 1807, an account of which was published in the " Proceedings of the Connecticut Academy of Arts and Sciences." I was sometimes allowed to look through the telescope, and remember to have been much pleased at seeing, at noon-day, Jupiter and his moons as plainly, and seemingly more beautiful, though not so large, as we see our moon with the un-assisted eye-sight. While my father was in office, he established three of the principal meridians in Ohio and Indiana, and by them were surveyed the great body of lands to the north and west of Cincinnati. In his employment, as deputies, were many young men who became afterward the most successful and distinguished men of the West. Among these were Thomas Worthington, afterward governor and United States senator; Lewis Cass, afterward governor, sen-ator, secretary, and embassador, who was one of his clerks; Ebenezer Buckingham, of Zanesville, subse-quently a very wealthy man ; Governor Ethan Allen Brown; the Rectors, two of whom were Surveyors-

---

[1] See an account of Observatories in Harpers' Magazine.

General in the West, and others whose names I do not recall. He had, at one time, as many as forty deputies having contracts for surveys. To the honor of himself, as well as his generation, I will mention a fact which has seldom its counterpart now. In all the settlements of his accounts with the treasury, he was never once indebted to the government, but the government always to him. He expended very large sums of money, and made his settlements with Mr. Gallatin, then Secretary of the Treasury. Mr. Gallatin was a very exact man, and the correspondence with him, which I have looked over, shows much more exactness and care in public business than is now found.

Perhaps, I may here mention our mode of living, as illustrating the manners and customs of that day. The family were not lonely, although occupying a solitary country house near the then village of Cincinnati. At that time, a gentleman's country house was a semi-hotel. Taverns were scarce, and it would have been a breach of hospitality not to have received and entertained any respectable looking person who came along.

Besides these casual guests, there was a young lady with us, who often entertained friends from Cincinnati, among whom were two or three gentlemen, afterward quite distinguished. My father's office was also the center of a large public business; so, in fact, we saw a good deal of society; the only lonely person was myself, a boy in the country with no other boy to associate with, no school to attend, always with older persons. I was not intoxicated with the levities, frivolities, and fancies of youthful life. On the contrary, I was, of necessity, lonely, timid, and abstracted. The impress of that timidity and abstraction remained upon my character until I had passed the meridian of life. Our family was an interesting one, and two or three of its members were afterward distinguished in public life. The young lady, I mentioned, was Miss Harriet Sisson, my father's niece and adopted daughter. While at Ludlow Station, she married Dr. Daniel Drake, a man of genius and science. My father had in his office two nephews, both of whom were pleasing and even brilliant men. One of these, Captain John Fenno Mansfield, was an older brother of Gen. Joseph Mansfield, killed at Antietam. Captain John F. Mansfield was thought by my parents, who were good judges, to be the most promising man they knew. He was a man of genius, a student of science, and an elegant writer. Some of his articles appeared in "*The Portfolio*," then edited by Joseph Dennie. Anticipating some years following the time of his residence with us, I will here give a sketch of his brief career. In November, 1811, occurred the battle of Tippecanoe, which, although seven months before the declaration of it, was, in fact, the beginning of the second war with Great Britain. The Indians, under the leadership of the " Prophet " and his brother Tecumseh, had for a third time formed a confederacy under the impression that they could drive the whites from the Western Territories. They were assembled at the Prophet's town, near the Wabash, where they were attacked and defeated by Governor Harrison. In all their preparations and in all their subsequent conduct in the war, they were urged on and assisted by the British. Of this, there is no doubt, and it is one of the facts which ought never to be forgotten by those who wish to understand the history of those times. It is enough to say, that in the following spring —1812—the war seemed inevitable. The government ought to have begun its preparations five years before, when a wanton attack was made on the frigate Chesapeake. If the reader will look back seventy years, he will be astonished at the vast change which has taken place in the relations of this country to other nations.

At that time, British cruisers searched American ships and impressed American seamen. What country would now venture to search an American ship or impress American seamen? Or attack an American frigate? Or conspire with American Indians? And yet these things were done by Great Britain. What country would *now* venture to confiscate American ships and property in foreign harbors? And yet this was done by the Emperor Napoleon, who confiscated American ships and tobacco in the harbor of Antwerp. This was all ended by the war of 1812–15. It was the second war for independence, and the last one. Now, all is changed. England paid, because she permitted privateers to be fitted out against us in the Rebellion, fifteen millions of dollars into our treasury. France, which had undertaken to put Maximilian on the throne of Mexico, retreated speedily, when a diplomatic note informed her that America tolerated no intrusion on her ground. All that is past. This great Republic is now beyond the interference, the attacks, or the insults of any other nation upon earth.

I rejoice that from 1765—for that year was the beginning of the controversy—the American people have maintained that controversy, till they have es-

tablished not only their independence, but their power
to influence and direct all the future movements of
mankind. The battle of Tippecanoe occurred, as we
have said, seven months before the declaration of war,
in 1812, but was, in reality, the beginning of that war.
In the spring of 1812, the army, which was to be
commanded by General Hull, began to assemble at
Cincinnati. Governor Meigs called out the First Division of Ohio militia, to meet at Hutchinson's Tavern, on the Colerain road. This was near our house,
and I went with my father to the place of meeting.
The division was drawn out in line, and presented as
motley an appearance as has ever been seen. Some
of the men had rifles, but the greater part only sticks
and cornstalks. As to uniform, there were all kinds
of apparel, from hunting-shirts to butternut jack-
ets. There was, however, an exception. Cincinnati
boasted at that time of two volunteer companies.
One was a company of light infantry, commanded by
Captain John Mansfield, of whom I have spoken.
The other was a company of dragoons, commanded
by Captain Sloane. These were formed on the right
and left of the militia line. When the call was made
for volunteers, it seemed to me the whole division
volunteered. At any rate, these two volunteer companies were received, and made part of the army of
Hull. Captain Mansfield entered upon this campaign
with the zeal and high hopes of a young man, but he
had not advanced far with the army, on the way to
Canada, before he wrote to his uncle, what afterward
proved the truth of history, that General Hull was an
imbecile, from whom nothing but disaster could be
expected.

I need not relate the particulars of that campaign. Hull surrendered his army to the British without striking a blow, to the disgust and indignation of the whole army. Captain Mansfield was surrendered with the others. He was released; but in crossing Lake Erie took a fever. He had barely strength enough to return to Cincinnati, and died at the house of his friend, Ethan Stone, Esq., not of fever alone, but of a broken heart. Another member of our family circle was Joseph Gilbert Totten, my father's nephew, and one of his clerks. He was then about eighteen years of age, a genial, pleasant, and popular person. I will here make a brief mention of his life. At my father's instance, he was appointed a cadet at West Point. From there he was appointed Lieutenant of Engineers, and stationed at New Haven, building the fort at the mouth of the harbor. When the war of 1812-1815 came on, he was sent to the Niagara frontier. He was in the battle of Queenstown Heights, and was distinguished and promoted. The year after the war he married Catalina Pearson. The marriage was a singular one. Miss Pearson's father having objected, solely because Totten was an officer of the army, the lovers ran away, and were married at the house of a friend. They came immediately to our house at West Point, and my father approved their conduct, and received them cordially. Totten was continually promoted until he became Chief of the Engineer Corps. He accompanied General Scott to Mexico, and superintended the siege of Vera Cruz. When the war of the Rebellion came on, he was one of the chief men who, with General Scott, devised the mode and means by which the war was to be conducted. One of the modes, and the most important one, was to seize the Mississippi river, open communication with New Orleans, and cut off Rebel communication. In the beginning of the war the Mississippi was the axis of the operations of the Rebels. They seized, armed, and garrisoned every defensible point on the Mississippi from Columbus, Kentucky, to New Orleans. The first step necessary to the success of the government was to seize this river. It was the plan of General Scott and of General Totten to seize and use the steamboats, build gunboats, and do exactly what was done when Admiral Foote and General Grant captured Fort Donaldson, and in 1863 captured Vicksburg. It was not until this was done that success in the East was possible, and the military critic of the future will recognize this fact as the element necessary to the success of the government. At the close of the war General Totten died, and on the very day of his death was honored by being brevetted Major-General in the army, for in the Engineer Corps there is no higher rank than that of Brigadier. No better, braver, or more patriotic officer served in the American army than General Joseph G. Totten. The reader will now understand that our family at Ludlow Station was an interesting one. My cousin, afterward Mrs. Drake, Captain Mansfield, and the subsequent General Totten, were persons who would have been respected and admired in any cultivated society. They owed something of their geniality and success to my mother. No one ever associated with her without feeling the magnetic power of a superior mind. She was the perceptible influence which guided the course of several young men who became, in time, among the first in the first rank of their country. But I will return to my narrative. We lived at Ludlow Station from October, 1805, to June, 1809, nearly four years. They were years of interest to me, although, except my memory of pioneer life and of my interesting cousins, there was really nothing which made them of special after value to my life. I went to no school, and have no memory of any sort of education, even of my mother. One event in natural events I well remember. In January, 1807, two men were frozen to death on the Hamilton Road. Nothing is more common than remarks about "This season being very hot," or "This winter being very cold;" but, in the course of half a century, all seasons average as in centuries before. The world may be frozen to death, or wasted to death, but in my time the seasons have averaged just the same as in periods long ago. The Scripture tells us that the earth will be burnt with "fervent heat." I believe it, for the fires in the interior of the earth are far superior to the ice storm, coming down from the north, which we all dread.

My father always had a longing for the land of his birth. He had now been six years in the West, and longed to see his kindred, and to walk under the shadows of old Yale, where he graduated. Accordingly, in the summer of 1809, we paid a visit to his friends and relatives in the East. I was too young to pay much attention to the journey; but some of its incidents were remarkable.

In 1807, the first steamboat in this country, and, I believe, in the world, was launched in New York, called, I think, "The North River." Two years after, when we arrived in New York, the third steamboat, called the "Paragon," had been built. Except these three steamboats, there was no other means of steam locomotion in the country. When we arrived at what is now called Jersey City—then a solitary tavern—the question was, how was the river to be crossed? There was no bridge, no ferryboat, as we now understand a ferryboat, but there was a little schooner called a Pirogue. On this we had to carry our horses, carriage, baggage, and ourselves. The wind was high, and there were two frightened people—my mother and myself—but this ridiculous little craft carried us safely across, and we were landed in New York. One of the first things my father did in New York was to take my mother and myself to see the little steamer "Paragon." He knew that the invention of the steamboat was one of the great events in the world's history, and, therefore, he wanted to see a steamboat. The "Paragon" lay aside one of the docks, and looked about the size of a small schooner, but with neither masts nor sails. She was painted yellow, and her machinery and cabin were both below deck. In these days she would be counted one of the tugs now used to tow ships into New York Harbor. It was twenty years after this, when my father lived at West Point, that steamboats began to take the form and magnitude they now have. It was thirty years after I saw the "Paragon" that the ocean steamers began to cross the Atlantic. The introduction of steam as a locomotive power was the most important event in the mechanical progress of the last two thousand years. We had in New York, in 1807, the little beginnings of steam navigation, and now steamships and steamboats are in all, or nearly all, the countries of the world. This is a revolution greater than any previous generation had seen. The crossing of the Jersey ferry in a schooner and the seeing of the " Paragon " were striking events.

The active memories of men are made up of strong impressions. All that we seem to remember of our youth are these vivid impressions of things which startled or surprised us at the time of their occurrence. But, have we really lost any impression? Are they not all like faded pictures of whose colors only the bright ones seem to remain? If our souls survive, will not every event, thought, and impression survive also in the ages to come? We remained in New Haven two or three months, and on our return passed through Philadelphia. There, my father took me to the bookstore of Matthew Carey, an old friend and a noted man in his day. Here, my father gave me my first library, about twenty little volumes. Of these, I remember only two, one was Mease's United States, and the other the "London Cries."

Both had plates and struck my fancy as wonderful books. Before the warm season was past, and while the sun still illuminated the splendid forest scenery, we returned to Ohio.

On going East, my father had given up Ludlow Station, and, on returning to Ohio, rented a house called Bates' place, two miles nearer Cincinnati, and now within the city limits. In after years it was called Mt. Comfort, b it these names are now forgotten. We rented the place of Colonel Isaac Bates, who had been a teamster in Wayne's army. It was a comfortable two-story brick house, with a lawn and garden, and answered our purpose very well. At this time, our family was not so large as at Ludlow Station.

Totten had gone to the army, John Mansfield lived in town, and, I believe, his sister, Mary Mansfield, was the only one living with us. She was married while living with us at Bates' place, and became Mrs. David Wade; her husband was a lawyer and prosecuting attorney in Cincinnati. Mrs. Col. Kennett and Mrs. Dr. White are her daughters. She took considerable care of me, and even now I seem to hear her sweet voice singing "Highland Mary." She died some years after this, when I was in the East. She was one of the first of those—now many—whose name and memory come to me from the spirit land.

We were established at Bates' place in 1809, in the autumn, and remained there three years. It was an eventful period to me, and a remarkable one in the history of the Western country. I was then eight years old, and this is the first period at which I can remember receiving anything that can be called education. In 1810, in the spring, my father gave me a slate and pencil, and taught me the elementary rules of arithmetic. My mother had taught me to read, and the first line I ever read was in Webster's spelling book, and was: "No man may put off the law of God." My particular admiration in the spelling-book was the picture of the man who pretended to be dead when the bear smelled him, and the old man who called the boys down from the apple-tree, and when they laughed at him for throwing grass, pelted them with stones. There was one thing my mother was very particular about and the effect of her care remains to-day, this was spelling. She drilled me in that, and, I believe, I have never misspelled a word through ignorance. I give a little incident in regard to this fact, characteristic of the day. It was in 1811, that I received two quarters' schooling—all that I received prior to 1813. It was in a log school house, nearly opposite the House of Refuge; at the close of the.quarter in July, there was a spelling battle, in which I came off head of the school. We were then formed in a column and marched to a tavern near the present House of Refuge; there, the schoolmaster treated us to cherry bounce; it was very strong and made my head reel, but my mother, I think, never knew anything of this, and, I may add, would assuredly disapproved of it if she had. It was in 1810, that I read the first book I can remember, besides my school books. This was a sort of pamphlet Life of Napoleon Bonaparte; it closed with the battle of Wagram, fought in 1809. I was enamored with this book, and fired with military fervor, which lasted for several years. I have already mentioned the books my father bought for me at Matthew Carey's, and that one of them was called " The London Cries," and, I believe, no book pleased me better than that; it had much better paper, print, and plates, than children's books have now-a-days. Each "cry," for example, as " Hot Buns," had a good wood-cut, and I delighted in it. Another book was " Mease's United States;" this also had wood-cuts, among them one of the " Bridge over the Delaware "—in those days considered a fine affair; one also of the Indians hunting Bison, and one of the Natural Bridge in Virginia. All these struck my fancy, and books of this kind are the right sort for boys.

Before our return to the East, my stock of reading was, however, small. Our life at Bates' place was quiet, but several incidents, new and striking to a boy, occurred. I had my hens, ducks, and quail-traps, and made many observations on nature. My two quarters at the log school house did something towards breaking up the loneliness of my life. I saw several things which can not be seen except in a pioneer region. Looking, from our house, down the Hamilton Road to Cincinnati, I saw a herd of deer, apparently driven up the road by a hunter and dog. They came along very quietly, until a white-topped wagon passed our house, when, they started and fled, jumping the highest fences. The hunter dropped his rifle to his shoulder, and killed a fat buck opposite our house. Another day, I saw a singular sight. This was a vast army of squirrels, gathered, probably from want of food, in a large corn field below the house. They covered the fences in every direction, devoured the corn, and disappeared. At another time in a meadow below, I saw that curious phenomenon, the army worm. There were millions of them, and they moved in a line across the breadth of the field and cut down every blade of grass. The farmers destroyed them, by going a considerable distance ahead, and, with spades and hoes, digging a trench, into which they fell and could not get out. From these incidents, the reader will see how very different the scenes of country life were then, from what they are now. We were really on the frontier, my father and his surveyors, being in the wilderness where is now the most populous portion of Indiana.

My father's business varied little, although the

scenes of house and family had changed much. He was pursuing intently the business he was employed to do. His surveyors were out through Northwestern Ohio and Indiana, while he, himself, was recording the work, and making astronomical observations.

In the midst of this work an event occurred which was memorable then, and hardly less so now. On the night of the 16th of December, 1811, Cousin Mary and I were waked up by a rattling which we supposed to be rats, but which proved to be the handles of a trunk. In a moment we found the room was shaking, and sprang up frightened. Then we heard my father's voice calling us. We rushed down stairs, and, with the whole family, ran into the yard. While we ran out the bricks were falling from the roof of the house, the chimney having been shaken down. There was a light snow on the ground, and a carriage in the yard. My mother and little sister took refuge in the carriage, and my father went back to the house, saying there was more danger of rheumatism than of the house falling. In Cincinnati, the Columbian Inn, at the corner of Main and Columbia streets, was the principal house of entertainment, where some of the first young men and ladies boarded. It is said, that on that night the street in front of the Columbian Inn presented a strong contrast to all the ordinary rules of propriety; in fact, there was more of nature displayed than of fashion. The presence of a great danger breaks down all conventional rules, and perhaps there is nothing better than a great danger to show what an artificial thing is civilized life. A great danger is the preaching of a great sermon. The earthquake of December 16, 1811, was the first of a series of earthquakes, which continued about five months. My father, in order to test the state of things, put a very delicate pendulum inside of one of our front windows, and that pendulum never ceased to vibrate in nearly five months. In the meanwhile there were, in January and February, several violent shocks. It was May, 1812, before these earthquakes really ceased. The center of them was, I think, at Caraccas, South America. A peculiarity attended them which has, perhaps, not followed other earthquakes. They seem to have had not only a center, but an axis, which caused a reaction or agitation at a great distance. The center of the agitation in the Mississippi valley was at, or near, New Madrid, Missouri. There the Mississippi overflowed, the earth was broken up in some places, and small lakes formed, which are there to this day. Some years since I happened to meet a gentleman who, at the time of the earthquake, was on the Mississippi in a keelboat. He described the fearful rushing and high waves of the river.

The marks of that fearful catastrophe remain on the face of the earth. When we remember what great and sudden changes were thus made in a brief time, it surprises us to hear geologists talk of the ages on ages which, in their imagination, it took to produce certain changes.

At our house the earthquake gave rise to a sort of new life. Our family was, of course, much alarmed, and some of the gentlemen in town would ride out and spend the night with us. In this way we saw a good deal of company, and had, in some respects, a pleasant time. Among those who came was Colonel

McKenna, who was, I think, the same man that thirty years ago was united with Judge Hall in preparing an Indian biography, a very valuable work. McKenna had been much among the Indians, and related many tales and anecdotes of them. So, by way of cheering us and amusing our minds, he told us the most awful stories of Indian fights and massacres. There must have been some truth in his narratives, for he showed us his wrist and arm, which had been injured by bullets in an Indian fight. According to him, "Othello" himself had not met with so many hair-breadth escapes, and the romance of history did not contain such a romance of the border war with the Indians. There are, indeed, several books of anecdotes and of pioneer life which are full of adventures with and escapes from the Indians.

In this manner the winter passed. Severe shocks of earthquake occurred frequently. I remember one happening in the morning, when I was at a neighboring log-house. There was corn on the upper floor, and I heard that corn roll from one side of the house to the other. As I have said, these shocks did not cease until May. At that time we were preparing to go to the East, and the government making ready its troops for the march on Canada. Among the troops who went was the then famous Fourth Regiment of infantry, which, at the battle of Tippecanoe, had made the chief part of the army. The last scene I recall at Bates' place, was the Fourth Regiment marching by our house on a bright May morning. All then seemed hopeful and bright; but nothing could have exceeded the sense of shame and disgrace felt in the country when that gallant regiment was, with Hull's army, surrendered to the British.

CHAPTER IV.

Journey to the East—The Wagoners—The Women of Stonington—Capture of the Macedonian—New Haven — Bishop —Dr. Dwight—Noah Webster —Captain Powell—Libraries—My Studies— West Point— No Text-Books—Cheshire Teaching—Governor Foote.

My father had now fulfilled his office as surveyor-general, and was about to return to West Point, as professor of philosophy and astronomy. In the beginning of 1812, Congress had reorganized the military academy, as a preparation for war. The professorship of philosophy and astronomy was given the rank and pay of a lieutenant-colonel, in accordance with the rank my father then held in the engineer corps. We began our journey to West Point in the beginning of June. No declaration of war had then been made, but troops were assembling and marching to the northern frontier. One day we stopped at Dr. Drake's house, on our way east. It was a memorable day in Cincinnati, for on that day occurred the severest tornado I have ever experienced. It blew down a new brick school-house and some smaller buildings. I was looking out of a window when I saw the roof of the Sargent house blown off like a piece of paper. This house stood near the center of the square, north of Fourth street, and east of Broadway, on what is now called McAllester street. It was, as far as I can recollect, the only house standing in that part of the city at that time. We left Dr. Drake's next day, and in traversing the country found large oak trees torn up by the roots, and thrown across the roads. Here I may mention, as a characteristic of the times, our preparations for this journey. There was then no stage or public conveyance west of Carlisle, Pennsylvania. It would have taken a long time, and have been a tedious journey, even had it been possible to go up the river by keel-boats. So my father was compelled to buy his own carriage and horses, take a driver, and go on the wagon-roads. He put in the carriage-box pistols, ax, and ropes, for they might have been needed at any time. We journeyed in the midst of the war excitement, and were ahead of the mails, so that at every village we were questioned about the news. I remember that when we arrived at Chambersburg, Pennsylvania, a small crowd gathered about the tavern to hear the news. I went out and told them about the battle of Tippecanoe, of the march of Hull's army, and our certain conquest of Canada. In fine, I was a political orator, and had I kept on in that line, who can tell to what eminence I might have arrived. In fact our arrival at Chambersburg created a sensation, and we passed along with something of the eclat of a caravan. I remember little else until we crossed the Swatara, a large stream in Eastern Pennsylvania. There had been heavy rains, and the river was high, but I was riding a fine horse, and plunged in the water, to the great consternation of my father, who was in the carriage. However, I, as well as the carriage, crossed the river in safety. I must here state a fact, which will illustrate the changes in the mode of traveling and the condition of the country. At that time the only tolerable roads were the Pennsylvania turnpikes, and we went over one of these from Pittsburg east. This was the great highway of the Philadelphia wagons, which carried all the merchandise from Philadelphia west. These wagons were called the " Connestoga Teams." They had long bodies, covered with sail-cloth, stretched on hoops, and carried two or three tons each. They were drawn by six horses, of the strongest and largest breed. The front pair had bells on their necks, and the wagoners who drove them had great pride in their teams. Reade has described these men in his " Wild Wagoner of the Alleghenies." He was describing that wagoner as far superior and bolder than most of them, yet the scenes he represented did often occur.

> " On many a dangerous mountain track,
>   While oft the tempest burst its wrack,
>   While lightning, like his mad whip lash,
>   Whistled round the team its crooked flash,
>   And horses scared in fiery flight,
>   While near them burst the thunder crash,
>   Then heard the gale his voice of might.
>
>   .   .   .   .   .
>
> " And oft on many a wintry hill,
>   He dashed from out the vale below,
>   And headed his way through drifts of snow,
>   While all his wheels with voices shriek,
>   Shrieked to the frosty air afar."

While these men were very useful in their day, they were at times very disagreeable. Quite naturally they were jealous of carriages, and gentlemen whom they thought assumed to be above them. On two occasions, when we were stopping for the night, they took the lynch-pins from our carriage, and we might have had a severe accident, but for a gentleman who was riding on horseback with us. Another thing in the then mode of traveling was as peculiar as the Connestoga wagons. That was the " tavern," as it was then called, which was found at certain stations, which the traveler was obliged to reach at certain hours, or else his accommodation was very poor. These taverns had special names, such as " The Black Horse," and " The General Wayne," " The Ship," " The Paoli," etc., and were noted throughout the country. Come what might, it was necessary for a traveler, in a private carriage, to reach one of these places at night, for it was hardly safe, much less comfortable, to lodge elsewhere. So even though we rode late into the evening, my father managed to reach one of these taverns at night. I need not say more of this journey. It took us thirty days, traveling in our own carriage, from Cincinnati to New Haven, where we arrived in July, 1812. The war had then begun, and the United States coasts, especially seaports, were lined with British cruisers. My father was then an officer of engineers, and was detained by the government, at New Haven, on military service, and subsequently by severe illness. In order not to interrupt the narrative, I will here state what relates to our residence in New Haven. My father was ordered to New London and Stonington to superintend fortifications. For some inscrutable reason, certainly not a military one, the British had an inclination to attack these places. Had they taken and retained both, it would have been of no military use. Accordingly the British squadron, of which the frigate Macedonian was one, attacked Stonington by bombarding it, and that gave rise to a story, which was one of the historical incidents of that day. On shore, at Stonington, three or four pieces of artillery returned the British fire; as the local militia were extemporized for the occasion, they were not well provided with ammunition, so, after firing awhile, they were out of wadding for the guns. At this point a Stonington woman deliberately took off her petticoats, to make wadding for the guns! It was not long after this that the British cruiser Macedonian was captured by the frigate United States, and in New Haven we had the pleasure of hearing the band of the Macedonian, giving us fine music, as prisoners of war. On my father's return from New London, we moved into a house in New Haven, on the square where I had been born, directly opposite the present railroad depot. It was on the southeast corner of State and Chapel streets, New Haven. The house was probably built more than two hundred years ago. The front door and windows were carved and ornamented as no woodwork is nowadays. The window-panes were diamond-shaped, set in with lead. The present style of architecture tends to more simplicity of ornament, but the taste of the day is toward extravagance in furniture. Of the two, the old style was the best. Few things can be more absurd than to make a house a storeroom for furniture, which adds nothing to real comfort and is a positive extravagance. If the simple Greek architecture were adopted on the one hand, and handsome but simple furniture in the interior, it would be more consistent with common sense than either the customs of our ancestors or ourselves. But the world is given to fashion and is slow to learn. In the autumn of 1812 we moved into our house, on the old Mansfield square, and remained there for nearly

two years. In the meanwhile my father was visited
by several distinguished men, and events happened
which may be interesting to record. In 1812–1813,
politics were much the same as regards human nature
as to-day. The post-office in New Haven became vacant, and as my father was known to be in the confidence of the administration, his influence was sought
by all the applicants. He at last recommended Jones,
and Jones was appointed. During my father's illness,
Abraham Bishop, collector of New Haven, called upon
him. I think he was the very man to whom Jefferson
addressed his celebrated letter on appointments; at
least he was the occasion of it. Jefferson had appointed some Democrats to office; among others,
Bishop. The Federalists complained about removals.
Jefferson replied in a short letter, stating his reason
for removals: "That of Federal officers, few die, and
none resign." In these days it would be unnecessary
to give any reason, for rotation in office has become
an established principle of all political parties. Bishop
was in some respects a remarkable man. He was a
man to suit Jefferson, for he was a free-thinker of the
most liberal school, and so were many of the men
whom Jefferson brought into office. Bishop had fine
talents of a certain order. He was a wit and an orator. My mother considered him the best speaker of
that time. His wit was sharp and fine compared with
the coarse humor now so common. I remember one
of his witticisms which had a good deal of point.
Noah Webster's garden joined that of my grandfather.
Noah Webster was not only the author of the first
spelling-book I studied, but of the great dictionary
which all have learned to reverence; in other words,

Noah Webster was a learned man. Bishop, who had great respect for him, said: " Noah Webster's head is like a vandue master's (auctioneer's) shop—*full of other men's goods.*" Another man who called on my father in his sickness at New Haven has since been world-renowned. This was the celebrated Dr. Dwight, President of Yale College. Few men had more talent or used it better than Timothy Dwight. He was tutor, professor, and president of Yale College for many years, and impressed himself wonderfully upon the students. While president of the College he made the tour of New England, and published his observations in a book of travels. It was full of acute comments on the customs and institutions of our country. In that book he was, I think, the first to remark what De Tocqueville subsequently put in his book, that the townships of New England, or, in other words, its rural municipalities, were the schools in which our American people had learned the true principles of self-government. It was in this school of political self-instruction they had learned to conduct safely and intelligently the government of the republic. While Professor of Divinity in Yale College, Dr. Dwight delivered the course of sermons which he afterward embodied in his system of theology, and which continues, both in Europe and America, to be a standard work in the school of Calvinistic divinity. It is the most complete work of popular theology now extant. I have read a large part of it, and was delighted with it considered only as a literary work. I never heard Dr. Dwight preach, but my mother said he was the best preacher she had ever heard. I recollect well Dr. Dwight's appearance when he sat and talked with my

father. He was a man of medium height, with a full
rotund body, dark hair and eyes, wearing—as was
then the custom—the hair combed back in a queue
behind. He was dressed entirely in black, and had a
very dignified appearance. In fact, Dr. Dwight,
though not of commanding height, was of *commanding* appearance. I should judge from his conversation
with my father that he was—and such was his character—a genial and pleasant man. He and my father
were in politics and theology of opposite opinions, but
were on that account none the less friendly. The republic of letters and of science is the only free republic
—the only one where men are measured by their merits. Another man who called at our house during that
time was the very opposite of Dr. Dwight. Probably
the reader has never heard of him, but he was a character worth mentioning. He was an Englishman and
an auctioneer, called Captain Powell. I have reason
to remember him, as I do, with kindness and respect;
for he lent me books which I could not have obtained
elsewhere, and which ministered both to my information and my love of reading. One of these books was
the "Gentleman's Magazine," which I pored over with
more avidity than I have since done over the most important and interesting works. I said he was the opposite of Dr. Dwight. He was a free and easy liver,
took snuff, and most unfortunately was quite intemperate. The habit of intemperance at last brought
him to the poor-house, but not to that degradation,
either of position or character, which now attends the
inmates of poor-houses. He had been the associate
of gentlemen, and continued to be so when in the
poor-house. Mr. Bishop and other gentlemen used to

supply him with the best of clothes, and he went round visiting as he pleased. It happened that while he was in the poor-house, the descendants of some of the first merchants of New Haven were also there. Captain Powell was asked if he did not feel the want of society. "Oh! no," he replied. "I enjoy there the society of the best families of New Haven." Many years after, my mother and I were, at the time of my father's death, at the Tontine Coffee-house, New Haven. Captain Powell called on my mother. He was well dressed, and took snuff as usual. My mother was about to go out in a carriage, and Captain Powell gracefully handed her in; then he bowed low, and said: "Madam, we must not forget our politeness, though we are in the poor-house." I always thought it one of the finest sayings I ever heard. I think of Captain Powell as Johnson did of some of his London companions, whose names would never have been heard of but for Johnson—as of those who have contributed to the common stock of harmless amusements. To me he furnished more than amusement. He lent me books which excited my literary taste, and helped to form the habit of reading and study which has been the comfort and solace of my life. If you would see this idea expressed as I feel it, but far more truthfully than any modern author has given it, look to this paragraph of Cicero's oration for the poet Archias:

"At haec studia adolescentiam alunt, senectutem oblectant, secundas res ornant, adversis perfugium ac solacium praebent; delectant domi, non impediunt foris, pernoctant nobiscum, peregrinantur, rusticantur." —These studies employ youth, delight old age, adorn prosperity, afford a refuge and a solace in adversity; please at home, do not impede in the forum, go with us through the night—travel with us, and are with us in the country! Such are the pleasures of literature, portrayed by the most eminent of its disciples.

In New Haven, I had some literary advantages, which for a boy were uncommon. My father's cousin, Colonel Lyon, who was cashier of a bank, had a literary and antiquarian taste. He had a large and rare library, and lent me books to read. No one directed my reading, and the books I selected were certainly curious for a boy. I looked over the "*Politicus Mercurius,*" published in Cromwell's time; read some of Rapin's *History of England*, and the "Life and Campaigns of *Frederick the Great.*" I had also access to the New Haven library, and from that procured several books of modern literature. In fact, my tastes then, as they have been ever since, were decidedly of a literary turn. In New Haven, as I believe I have mentioned, I had two quarters' schooling, one in what would now be called a common school, and the other in a select classical school. In the first school I learned nothing, unless it were to draw ships and pictures on a slate. In the second I learned considerable Latin, and became acquainted with the nicest boys in New Haven. One of them was Theodore Wolsey, afterward President of Yale College; another was Alexander Twining, afterward a distinguished engineer; another Henry White, a lawyer, and most excellent man. Thus my two years' residence in New Haven became a very important period of my educational life. My taste for reading was acquired. The books I read were instructive, and I first learned to think. In the spring of 1814, my father had recovered from his severe illness, and his military duties in Connecticut were over. He therefore proceeded to West Point to enter upon his duties as professor of natural and experimental philosophy. I have already said that in 1812 Congress had reconstructed the military academy, and instituted this professorship for my father. Accordingly we went to West Point. But how? In a steamboat, rail car, or stage? In neither; but in a sloop. Family and furniture were all embarked in a sloop at New Haven, and proceeded down the sound and up the Hudson. There were at that time only two or three steamboats on the Hudson, and they were very expensive. Sloops and schooners were the common means of conveyance in those days, and my father chartered a sloop for that purpose. The weather was fine, but, unfortunately for sailing vessels, calm; so that we were three or four days in going from New Haven to West Point, a distance of one hundred and fifty miles. Five hours is now the time of easy transit between those points. I well remember how impatient I was when the sloop barely moved through the water, and I looked upon the palisades, which, like the Giant's Causeway of Ireland, form one of the curiosities of the geological world. They are granite columns, looking as though artificially put up. Young America did not know that there was a time coming when the most vivid imagination of what he wished and what was desirable would come to pass. So he was very impatient, and had a right to be; for he could have walked from New York to West Point in less time than it took that sloop to go there. When we arrived, there was a curious exhibition of red tape and of human nature.

At a military post, quarters must be assigned with exact reference to the officer's rank. There were not a sufficient number of houses at West Point for the professors and officers, so my father was assigned half of a large double house, which he had had twelve years before, but which was now occupied by Surgeon Walsh. The consequence was, that on the arrival of my father, that gentleman was in a violent rage, because he had to give up half the house. War was declared, but there was no help for the affair, and Walsh had too much sense to perpetuate the squabble. In fact, the storm ended in a quiet, peaceful friendship between the families. It seemed like realizing the Irish saying, that the best way to make friends is a knock-down fight; but I should not recommend a quarrel as the best way of forming a permanent friendship. It was in this old yellow house, looking up the Hudson, which he had occupied in 1802, and now again in 1814, that my father taught the first class in philosophy and mechanics which was ever taught at West Point. This class consisted of five young men, who recited in our parlor, because there was at that time no suitable recitation room for them, and whose text-book was Enfield's Philosophy. Here I will say that the first great difficulty encountered at West Point was the lack of proper text-books. In the pursuit of these by the professors at West Point, has been gradually brought out that immense series of text-books which now make so large and profitable a publication business in this country. Except Noah Webster and his spelling-book, the most successful writer of scientific text-books was Professor Charles Davies, of West Point, who began his mathematical series more than forty years ago.

At that time there was not in the United States a single good text-book on algebra, geometry, or descriptive
geometry, much less on mechanics and philosophy. In
one word, the United States, being a new country and
a new nation, had none of those routine methods and
facilities which are in an old country the result of
time, and which have since been developed in the
United States. I may say further, that the English
had really no good text-books, but the models for these
were furnished by the French. The half century which
is just passed has been fertile, not merely in the methods of steam locomotion, but also in all those expedi-
ents of civilization, which are not so great and important in themselves as in the fact that they are evidences
of the ingenuity and fertility of man in devising
schemes for his own accommodation.

Here I will revert to an episode in my own life. While
my father was beginning his professional career at
West Point, I was sent to an Episcopal academy at
Cheshire, Connecticut. The purpose was that I should
learn Latin, preparatory to entering college. My brief
stay at Cheshire can soon be told, and it is of no espec-
ial importance, save in tracing out my own life. My
father introduced me to Squire Beach, who was his
cousin on his mother's side. One of her brothers was
rector of St. Paul's church, New York, and my father's
family were Episcopalians. The principal of the academy at Cheshire was Dr. Bronson, and I boarded at
the house of Mr. Cromwell, another Episcopal clergyman. Dr. Bronson was a good-natured, smiling old
gentleman, who invited me once or twice to make hay
in his yard, but who seemed to care very little whether
the boys learned anything or not. Mr. Cromwell was

somewhat more strict, but the whole affair was rather
official than either useful or real. I learned little, but
Cheshire had three attractions for me, which, if they
did not advance my education or elevate my thoughts,
perhaps did me quite as much good. First, Cheshire
had a town library, and, like most town libraries, was
chiefly composed of novels. In the second place, it
being summer time, Cheshire abounded in blackberries
and whortleberries. There was a little stream in town,
with some good land near it, but away from that the
hills and slopes produced little but rock and sand. It
was a glorious place for blackberries, and gloriously
did we enjoy it! For every new Latin word I learned
I obtained at least a quart of blackberries, but the chief
thing I had was exercise and pleasure. Lastly, Cheshire
had what was called a town green, and it was a fine
place to play in. So Cheshire had other merits for me
than its renowed academy.

The mention of Cheshire brings up a political reminiscence, connected with a very remarkable chapter in
our history. At Cheshire lived the Hon. Samuel A.
Foote, a friend of my father's, to whose family I was
introduced. He had two sons near my own age, one
of whom has been a lawyer in Cleveland and a trustee
of the Ohio Reform School. Samuel A. Foote was
Governor of Connecticut, and senator and representative in Congress for about ten years. While in the
senate, in 1832, Mr. Foote introduced a resolution, ever
after known as "Foote's Resolution." It was before
the senate for two or three months, and was debated
by almost every member of the senate, involving all
the questions of tariff, nullification, and states rights.
The resolution itself was not of much importance, but

it was used as a text on which the talent and eloquence of the nation went forth to the battle of words, introductory to that greater battle, the rebellion. Governor Foote was a man of moderate talents, but of pleasing manners and most excellent character. I remained, as I have already said, but a brief time at Cheshire.

One summer day, my parents drove up to the tavern in their gig, and found me on the town green, chasing a pig. My mother cried out: "How thin you are! You are nothing but skin and bone." No wonder; for their beloved son had been chiefly engaged in playing ball, picking blackberries, and chasing pigs. I was acquiring the vitality and fiber which was to carry me through the next half century. I was about to enter a new career. It was the summer of 1815 when I returned to West Point. I was just fourteen years of age when I received my appointment as cadet. West Point had then none of the fine buildings and ornaments which it has since received. But nature was still the same. There were the grand old mountains, rocks, and the river —the same scenes which had beheld the treason of Arnold; and on the mountain side stood old Fort Put., almost the only ruin in our country which can remind the traveler of the castellated ruins of Europe. There, too, were the lonely graves of the Revolution, unknown to the present generation, but which I knew and found beneath the shade of the rocks and the cedars. There the trees grew green o'er the homes of the dead, who had fought with Washington and Wayne.

"There the soldier rests in his lonely mound,
    Unmarked by the mountain storm thundering around."

Old Fort Put. is the only witness to their burial. Dr. Vandergild, of New York, in his ode to West Point, begins thus:

> "Dreary and lone as the scenes that surround thee,
> Thy battlements rise midst the crags of the wild."

It was then almost a wild, for no steamboats were seen on the river, no fine buildings rose on the plain, and no bright assembly of ladies and gentlemen greeted the evening parade. West Point was then as the Revolution had left it, before the hand of Young America had adorned it as the home of young officers and the resort of fashion.

CHAPTER V.

West Point—Its Organization—Its Professors—Want of Text-Books—Cadet Life—Oral teachings—Scenery and Memorials.

I AM writing upon Broadway, Cincinnati, which was laid out by Colonel Mansfield in 1808. It was part of sixteen acres which belonged to the government, as the site of Fort Washington. The Fort itself was on Third street between Broadway and Ludlow. His intention in laying out a street so broad was to make a great avenue for the city; but the owners above Fourth street would not extend it. The original street was called " Eastern Row," being laid out only sixty feet broad. But, I need not proceed with this history as it is all on record.

In the spring of 1815, I was appointed a cadet at West Point. I was not quite fourteen years of age, but the term did not begin until September. The history of my life while a cadet is the history of the most important era at West Point; in which was begun and established the whole course of instruction and discipline which has forwarded and made it the first scientific institution of the world. For this reason I will describe, as briefly as I can, what took place there. I must begin with my father, who was the first teacher there, and the real author of the scientific instruction begun and continued at that institution. He was, by nature, a student, and, by education, both a scholar and a man of science. His work in establishing the first Observatory at Ludlow Station; his running the Meridian Lines, and establishing the public surveys on scientific principles, I have already described. He returned to West Point simply from the love of teaching, and the pursuit of science. His professorship was that of natural philosophy, mechanics, and astronomy. His first class consisted of five persons, whom he received and taught in his own parlor. He remained at the military academy fifteen years. He was beloved by his pupils. When he retired, the cadets and officers had his portrait painted by Sully, and it now hangs in the library at West Point. It was after he went there that I was sent to Cheshire. Thence, I returned a mere boy, with no particular plan of life, or any particular ideas of anything, except play and amusement. In fact, I had spent nearly all my time in Cheshire in play, and had no special desire for study of any kind. Why should I? It would be a curious and instructive chapter of human life, if each one who had led a busy, or a studious life could relate just how and when motives began to act upon his mind; for, it is motives of some kind which move the mind to any action, or any purpose. I can tell distinctly when motives began to act upon me, and moral stimulus to invigorate my spirit. It will appear as I proceed. Two years at West Point were almost as useless as the one which preceded them; and then came a change, which will be apparent. In the meanwhile, however, I did acquire much. I could not help it. So many lessons had to be recited each day, and I could not fail to learn something. Those were the days of my algebra, geometry, trigonometry,

French, and drawing. I was quick to learn, and of course, learned all these things, in what was thought a creditable manner. Fortunately for me, nine-tenths of the young men had no aptitude for mathematics, while I had. Something occurred in the processes of my mind then, which made me think, in after years, of the true method of teaching and learning. The most difficult and inscrutable thing, to me, was that which is really the simplest and easiest of all mathematical ideas—the elementary proportions of geometry. For a dozen or two theorems, I went on reciting well and accurately, without having the least idea of the relations of angles, and figures, and surfaces; but, after a little while, I got light on those relations, and from that moment, geometry, mechanics, and mechanical philosophy have been the easiest studies I ever pursued. This taught me the fundamental principle of all teaching, learning, and reasoning. All science and all philosophy have certain units, elementary truths, back of which you can not go, and without which you can make no system of science whatever. Hence, the very beginning of all instruction is the original units, and if they are once understood, all else is easy. Hence, we see the wisdom of the great music professor, who kept his pupil nine years practicing on the notes and chords, and then sent him out the best singer in Europe.

The professors of the academy, when I first went there, were my father, professor of philosophy and astronomy; Andrew Ellicot, professor of mathematics, who had been in the service of the government, and was, I think, the man who laid out the City of Washington; Claude Crozet, who had been an engineer in

Napoleon's army, and was one of the few who survived the retreat from Moscow. CLAUDIUS BERARD was professor of French. He was a man of letters and a scholar. CHRISTIAN ZOELLER was professor of drawing. Besides these, there was a commander of the battalion, a fencing master, and two or three assistant professors. My immediate teacher of mathematics was Stephen H. Long, afterward a distinguished civil engineer. The first two years were occupied with mathematics, drawing, skating, fencing, football, and dancing. Up to this time I had no motives for action, except the simple ones of not being degraded in my class, and the better one of pleasing my mother, who was always admonishing me upon the duties of life. Thus passed the first two years at West Point, in which I acquired a tolerable knowledge of mathematics and French. But, now, in 1817, came a change over me, over the institution, and over the very place itself. How this came about is best related by describing the situation of affairs before that change, as compared with their present condition.

During the years 1815 and 1816, of which I have spoken, the institution was conducted on something like a patriarchal system, by Captain Alden Partridge of the engineers, who had practical ideas and paid very little attention to the laws and regulations established for the teaching. He thought that a great military school might be conducted upon the same principles with a college, he being in the light of a president, who should advise and admonish the boys and regulate things generally, without much regard to the army regulations. In one word, the academy was conducted without system, and without much regard to anything save the opinion of Captain Partridge.

Here, I may say, that he afterward (having resigned
from the army) established two military schools, in-
corporated in Vermont, and Connecticut. He was an
able and popular man, but very little fitted for the
army.

To the unsystematic and in some respects illegal
manner of conducting the academy, my father was
strongly opposed, and so in the end were all the officers
and professors. After a decided conflict, a change was
effected in the institution. Captain Partridge was
ordered away and resigned. In his place was appointed COLONEL SYLVANUS THAYER, one of the most
accomplished men in the army, and the very best
fitted for the place. He was a polished gentleman,
and a strict disciplinarian. He voluntarily retired
from the academy a few years after, took charge of
Fort Warren, in Boston harbor, and recently died at
more than eighty years of age. No improvement has
been made in the academy since he left it; I mean in
the course and manner of studies and discipline. A
greater amount of means has been provided, new
buildings erected, West Point beautified, and the
world admitted into hotels; but, in the mode, morals,
and discipline of the institution, no change has
been made. COLONEL THAYER took charge of the
academy on or about the first of January, 1817. This
was rather a memorable date with me, for I was looking at a battery firing—New Year's salute—when one
of the cadets was instantly killed by a cannon, prema-
turely discharged. This was Vincent M. Lowe, whose
name I mention, because what is called the "cadet's
monument" was erected to him while I was there.
After Colonel Thayer took command everything was

changed. Order took the place of disorder. A faculty
was formed with the professors and superintendent,
and they were governed by the law creating the academy, and the regulations of the army. In one word
the academy became a great school of military science,
and from that date competed with the best in the world.
Among other changes made, there was one which had
a particular bearing on me. It was ordered by the war
department, that at each annual examination, five cadets
of each class should be enrolled according to merit, and
their promotion in the army be determined by this order.
When this order was issued, I remember very well, when
sitting at the breakfast table, my mother (who was ambitious for her son) said that I could and must be one
of the "five," who, by the way, were to be honorably
recorded in the army register. I don't think this
mention moved me much, but my father looked up
and said: "Edward, if you will be one of the five, I
will give you the best gold watch I can buy." That
struck my attention, and, to tell the truth, was the
leading motive to my increased activity. A gold watch
is rather a stirring prize to a youth. I had only two
years to make up time in, but I did it, and the watch
I wear is the evidence of my diligence. From that
moment I waked up, and did a good deal of hard work
before my graduation. I have often said, and repeat
here, that our class had harder work than any one
since has had. For this there were some good reasons,
and if this page should be seen by anyone interested
in the history of scientific institutions, it may be well
to note some of the conditions of science in this country
at that time. We were the first class organized and
taught in the mode and on the principles now adopted

at West Point. Here we had all the difficulties of pioneers, and they are not small. First of all was the difficulty of text-books. Nobody now can imagine what that was, for now men of science and great publishing houses are engaged in preparing and publishing text-books. Then there were literally no text-books for students. There were books of science for men of science, but none for students. The French were the earliest and best makers of text-books; but we were not then prepared to study science in the French language. Hence our course of study was a rough one, compared with what is now. I will give you some examples. My father could not find any book for mechanical philosopy but "Gregory's Mechanics." This was a book written for men of science, and, of course, hard for students, but that was our text-book. But there were some subjects on which we had no text-book, good or bad. A French mathematician named "Monge" had devised, or first published, a system of practical geometry, called "Descriptive Geometry." The primary idea of it is the representation of all objects, or geometrical figures, by projection on two planes, perpendicular to one another. It is a very useful thing in some practical problems. This was studied in the French Polytecnique School, and we had to *study* it, and that without any text-books whatever. Our professor of engineering was CLAUDE CROZET, whom I have mentioned was an officer of engineers in Napoleon's last army. He was a graduate of the Polytechnique School, and fortunately had all his drawings and books with him. Here, then, were we to study descriptive geometry, and the problems of engineering connected with it, without the slightest

idea of what we were to do, and without any books on
the subject. But we had what was better. We had
Claude Crozet, a large black-board and chalk, with
the drawings of the Polytechnique Institute. We were
compelled to adopt the old Greek method of oral instruction, and it is the best. I have often thought, since,
that, if it were possible to teach all sciences and languages orally, the education acquired would be better
and higher. The result would be that each student
would *make* for himself the science or language he was
learning. Some years after that I saw this idea realized, when my sister was learning French. Mr. Du-
commun, a French professor at West Point, volunteered to teach her. All the books she had was a
blank-book. Each day she wrote in that the lesson,
beginning with the alphabet, and going through all the
parts of grammar. The end was that she had made
and written in her blank-book the whole French grammar. After that she began at once to read French.
She began with a French story-writer, *Florian*, whose
tales were beautiful. This part, I shared in, for I
read Florian, Madame De Stael, Moliere, and other
French writers with great delight.

But I must return. For the want of good text-
books, our class had a far harder time of study than
any succeeding class. We also had a far harder time
in work and discipline. You will see this when I tell
you what we had and what we had not. You go to
West Point now, and you see a fine drill-room and a
cavalry-house, and soldiers to do the hard work. In
one word, you find West Point quite an elegant retreat
for young gentlemen who are not expected to do much
hard work in this world, and whose health a little rain

might endanger. Now, when we were there, none of those things existed, and our work was adapted to harden, if not refine. We invariably arose at the tap of the drum after reveille, summer or winter, and drilled to breakfast, which was at seven o'clock. In the long days of summer, there was a two hours' drill before breakfast; and, with sleepiness and weariness, without rest or food, it seemed as if human nature could scarcely endure it.* In winter the drill was shorter, but more severe. I have drilled at West Point when the plain was covered with a sheet of ice and the thermometer at *zero.* No warm house covered us, and no fear of weather alarmed us. The afternoon drill was at four o'clock, as now, and that was not unpleasant; for in summer it was good weather, and we had an assembly of lookers-on to admire us. But I can not say that I ever greatly admired drilling, especially the artillery drill, when we had no horses. You go there now, and the young gentlemen manage their artillery admirably, for they have good horses. We were our own horses, and many a day have we drawn the cannon over hill and dale by a leather harness thrown over our shoulders. It was very hard work, and it was unnecessary; but I have no reason to complain, for these four years were years of regimen and discipline, to which after-life furnished no equal. He who comes forth from an education with a strong body, a clear mind, and an unstained conscience, has got from it all that human teaching can give.

---

* I do not mean to say, that the drills are not the same; but that the facilities and conveniences are so much greater, that the cadets have no longer so severe a regimen. The order of the institution has remained the same since 1817.

You can see from what I have said that West Point was to our class almost an unmixed scene of work and study; but we had some amusements. In summer, the latter part of the afternoon, we often played foot-ball, a game I was fond of, as I was a fast runner, and alert in all field games. In winter the Hudson furnished the best skating in the world; and when they could get an hour to spare, much did the cadets enjoy the ice of the Hudson.

Saturday afternoons were always given us, and in summer that was my time for walking, and much did I enjoy the sublime and picturesque scenery of the highlands. I have seen many beautiful and grand scenes, but I never saw one which surpassed that up the river from West Point. I would often run to "Old Fort Put.," and look off from its battlements upon the rock-built mountains and the lake-like river, shut in between Beacon Hill and Crow Nest. One day I was looking from the walls of the old fort, when a storm rose suddenly from the north, and a large sloop, near the Point, was struck before the sails could be taken in. Over she went, and women and children were drowned in the deep water below. It was on old Fort Put. that Dr. Vandergild wrote these beautiful lines, beginning with—

"Lonely and drear as the scenes that surround thee,
Thy battlements rise 'midst the crags of the wild."

West Point is no longer lonely, but as you look upon the ruined walls of the old fort, and again upon those bold and rock-built mountains, there is a scene of wildness and grandeur which reminds you of some mysterious ruins, which the hand of civilization has left untouched.

In wandering through the woods and hills are found the remains of no less than thirteen forts and batteries, which had been built in the revolution. The trees are grown upon most of them, and nearly all will be unknown to the next generation. In the woods were the remains of the huts in which the revolutionary army encamped, and all around were the little raised mounds, which indicate the graves of the dead :

> " There they sleep in lonely tombs, forgetting, forgot,
> Unawak'd by the mountain storm thund'ring around."

These memorials are even now unknown, and soon nothing but these lines will record their existence. Near by, above Washington's valley, rises the beautiful cemetery, which contains the marble monuments of those who come after, and they, too, with their cemetery, will soon pass into the unrecorded and unremembered past. Very probably the picture of my father, which hangs in the library of the academy, will survive all the monuments, and transmit to other generations the calm and abstract expression of him who was the first teacher of West Point and one of the most scientific minds of America.

But I must pass on. One of the amusing things to be found among a large body of young men is the singular and original characters one meets with. I only remember here and there an incident which amused me at the time. I have often mentioned them as they were told to me. One young man, who had been made a butt of by the cadets, it is said, went to old Captain Partridge, then superintendent, and with melancholy face said : " Captain, I have come to resign my resignation, because I have no comfort in my happiness." I believe he was comforted and induced to remain.

Another was Corbin, of Virginia, who came at a later date, and was what is commonly called a "green" young man from the rural districts. It happened to be Christmas time, and for a marvel there was a turkey on his mess-table, and for an equal wonder—it being Christmas—the carver was polite to the stranger. So he said: "Mr. Corbin, what part will you take?" Corbin instantly replied: "Imparticular—*big* piece—anywhar!" He was rather smart, but continued rough, but good natured.

I had a classmate named Rupp, who was not smart. On the contrary, it took him a great deal of labor to get his lessons, and he wanted all his study hours. Corbin, on the other hand, was lazy, and went about visiting. He took a fancy to Rupp, and would go to Rupp's room when the latter was hard at study. At length Rupp asked him to come at some other hour. But no—his good natured friend would drop in, much to his discomfiture. So he told Corbin he must not come in any more in study hours. But all in vain, all in vain. Soon after in comes Corbin, when he was puzzling on a mathematical problem. Poor Rupp could stand it no longer: "Corbin, get out, and if you come in again, I will *kick* you out!" The calm voice of Corbin replied: "Now, Rupp, none of your *hints!*" Ever after we would speak of "Rupp's *hints*" as among the new measures of the day.

Corbin I remember particularly, from being in my company, and in my room, in the old City Hotel of New York, when we were marched down to be reviewed by Governor Clinton. The old City Hotel of

New York was on Broadway, below Wall, and almost the only real hotel in the city. The city was then only one-tenth of what it is now, and the old City Hall was thought the finest building in the country, and so I think it was. St. Paul's Church was then the best in the city, and there it now stands with old graveyard and its monument to Emmitt. Our company was encamped, as it were, in the City Hotel. The band of the battalion, with another company, occupied the great ball room. The next day after our arrival we were reviewed in front of the City Hall. It was one of the hottest days I ever experienced, and we had a long and weary march. When dismissed, I rushed to an ice-cream shop, and I think nothing ever tasted better than ice-cream then did.

In the evening of that day we were marched to the theater, where old Barnes, a famous comic actor, played. I was not much interested in the play and altogether disgusted with the theater. Whatever people may say, the theater, at least in its manner and outward appearance, has much improved since that day. It is true that great tragedians were highly valued then, and that the melodrama and the menagerie plays are more common now, but the general tone of the best theaters has improved.

In the following winter the superintendent allowed our fencing master to give dancing lessons, and on the days or evenings in which we were allowed to go we had a jolly time. The ladies were few, but there were enough to make up a dance, and make it pleasant for us who were allowed to go. I can not recall but two ladies of that number now alive. I will say that our teacher said I was the best walker at the

Point—a quality which I retained until, a few years since, I was thrown out of a buggy and so injured that I have not walked so well since.

The time now drew near in which I was to finish my career at the academy. The annual examination was the dread of all good students; the poor ones, I imagine, were less anxious. I had began real study only when half my time there had passed; but then the last two years had been years of hard work, and now I must prepare for the examination, which at West Point was then very severe—more so than it is now. It was the only time in my life in which I sat up late at night to study, and then only for two or three nights. It was hot weather, and my mother made me strong tea. The examination passed off very well, and I graduated the fourth in my class. I was, I believe, the youngest who has ever graduated. I had not reached my eighteenth birthday, when I was commissioned in the engineer corps, and ordered to Washington City. It was the best appointment the government could give, and it may be questionable whether it was wise to decline it; but I did, and left all military service behind me. Who is it says:

"There's a divinity that shapes our ends,
Rough-hew them how we will!"

In this case the agent of divinity was my mother, who did not want me in the army, and who did want me to come West. Then it was decided I should enter college and study law. This changed the whole course of life, and what came of it I will relate hereafter.

CHAPTER VI.

Go to a Connecticut Academy—Farmington—New England Society— Young People's Party—Timothy Pitkin —Missouri Compromise—Effect in Connecticut—Return to West Point—Classic Studies—Mr. Picton.

I GRADUATED at West Point in June, 1819. I stood fourth in the class, and was commissioned second lieutenant of engineers. My commission was signed by John C. Calhoun, Secretary of War. It was determined in the family council, however, that I should be a lawyer. This required a new departure and a new preparation. I therefore declined my appointment as lieutenant of engineers, and my father offered to pay back to the government all the money spent upon me at West Point. The government, however, would not receive it, there being no law authorizing it to do so. I then proceeded to buy citizens' clothes, which I mention here because of the difference between that day and this in price and fashion. It (the cloth for my suit) was bright blue broadcloth, and cost fourteen dollars a yard; was made close fitting, and ornamented with bright gilt buttons. At the present time the cloth used for gentlemen's suits would not be probably more than half this cost for the best, and is not so well made up. In one word, gentlemen do not dress so well now as then. The gentlemen of the revolutionary school dressed with powdered hair, white top boots, silk breeches, and silver knee-buckles. This had passed away before my time, as a fashion at least, though I saw two or three gentlemen so dressed in Connecticut. It is to be hoped that the manners of gentlemen have not declined so much as their dress. In August, 1815, my father took me to Farmington, Conn., to prepare, under a private tutor, to enter college, preparatory to the study of the law. There were then, and I believe are still, academies and private tutors in New England for the purpose of preparing young men for college. They are the feeders of the New England colleges, and have done much to sustain their high reputation. The winter after this I was wandering with Virgil and puzzling over the intricacies of the Greek grammar or the Epistles of Paul.

As this was to me a new and striking life, I will give a little description of it, chiefly for the sake of the inside view I had of New England society. My tutor, Mr. Hooker, was a descendant of one of the old New England families, and had all the characteristics of the Puritans; was very religious and exact in all his duties. He lived on what had been a farm, but a portion of it had been embraced in the town. Having got forward in the world, he had built a new house. His old house was one of the oldest in the country, large, dark-red, with a long, sharp, projecting roof. This was the residence and schoolroom of the students, and we called it "Old Red." There were about fourteen of us, from nearly as many states. There we lodged, and there we recited, while we took our meals at Mr. Hooker's. His son John afterward married Miss Isabella Beecher, now the noted Mrs. Isabella Hooker.

Mr. Hooker was a deacon in the church—*the church*

I say, emphatically, for it was the only one in the village—a monument remaining to the old and unquestioned orthodoxy of New England. It stood on the little green, its high, sharp spire pointing to heaven. The pastor of that church was Mr. Porter, who preached there for nearly half a century. He was the father of the present Noah Porter, president of Yale College. Mr. Hooker took a large pew for the students, and told us to make notes of the sermon, upon which he questioned us. I was always thankful for this exercise, for I got into such a habit of analyzing discourses that if the speaker had any coherence at all, I could always give the substance of the sermon or address. This is to a newspaper man a useful talent. I have tried to discover what was the religious effect of this continual hearing and analyzing sermons, but could not find any. Such exercises become a habit, and are purely intellectual. A striking figure is sometimes remembered, but any spiritual effect is wanting on young people who have not learned to think seriously. I remember one of Mr. Porter's illustrations of the idea of death, which I think he must have taken from Sir Walter Scott's "Talisman." At any rate, Scott has beautifully described it in that work. It is that of Saladin, who, in the midst of the most splendid fete, surrounded by his chiefs, had the black banner unfolded, on which was inscribed, "Saladin, remember thou must die!" Mr. Porter was more than half a century minister in that parish, a most successful clergyman, honored in his life and in his death. Such was the ministration of the church to me, but I must say that in the service the chief objects of my devotion were the bright and handsome girls around. At that

time, and to a great degree yet in a New England village, out of the great stream of the world, its young
women were the largest part of the inhabitants, and
by far the most interesting. The young men usually
emigrated to the cities or the West, in hopes of making
fortunes. The old people were obliged to remain to
take care of their homesteads, and the young wome a
stayed also.

No place illustrated this better than Farmington,
where there were at least five young women to one young
man. The advent of the students was of course an
interesting event to them. And a young gentleman
in his nineteenth year was not likely to escape wholly
the bright shafts which, however modestly directed,
he was sure to encounter. I soon became acquainted
with these young ladies, and never passed a pleasanter
time than when days of study were relieved by evenings in their society. My father went with me to
Farmington, and introduced me to the Hon. Timothy
Pitkin. This gentleman was then a very distinguished
man. He was one of the leading men of the old Federal party. He was sixteen years a representative from
the State of Connecticut, and had written a very good
book on the civil history and statistics of this country.
He was a plain man, of the old school, living in an
old-fashioned house, near the church. In two or three
weeks after I had been in " Old Red," Mr. Pitkin
called upon me, and said his daughters would be glad
to see me on a certain evening. Of course I accepted;
and on that evening, arrayed in my unrivaled blue
coat, with brass buttons, cravated and prinked, according to the fashion, I presented myself at Mr. Pitkin's.
It was well I had been accustomed to good society,

for never was there a greater demand for moral courage. On entering the parlor, I saw one young man leaning on the mantle-piece, and around the room, for I counted them, were eighteen young ladies! During the evening my comrade and self were reinforced by two or three students, but *five* made the whole number of young men who appeared during the evening. The gentleman who was in the room when I entered it was Mr. Thomas Perkins, of Hartford, who afterward married Miss Mary Beecher, the daughter of Dr. Lyman Beecher. The town of Farmington furnished but one beau during the evening, and I found out afterward that there were but two or three in the place; I mean in that circle of society. This was perhaps an extreme example of what might have been found in all the villages of New England, where, in the same circle of society, there were at least three girls to one young man. You may be sure that when I looked upon that phalanx of eighteen young women, even the assurance of a West Point cadet gave way. But the perfect tact of the hostess saved me from trouble. This was Miss Ann Pitkin, now Mrs. Denio, her husband being Mr. Denio, late Chief Justice of New York. Miss Pitkin evidently saw my embarrassment, which was the greater from my being near-sighted. She promptly came forward, offered me a chair, and, introducing me to the ladies, at once began an animated conversation. In half an hour I felt at home, and was ever after grateful to Miss Pitkin.

I will mention here as one of the characteristics of New England manners, that Mr. and Mrs. Pitkin never once entered the room on this occasion, and the older people never appeared at any of the parties or sleigh-rides given by the young people, or at any gatherings not public. This was contrary to the customs of my father's house, where people of all ages attended the parties, and my mother was the most conspicuous person and the most agreeable of entertainers. I think it both more agreeable and useful to have parties composed of all the members of families; but, perhaps, this custom gave the young women of Connecticut that self-command and independence of character which is characteristic of them. Parties for young people in those days were given cheaply and simply, even the largest parties at New Haven and Hartford were given at a tenth of the cost of one in Cincinnati at the present day, where the object seems to be less hospitality than show. I attended a very large wedding party in Hartford, at Gen. Terry's, the grandfather of the present Gen. Terry, where everything was hospitable and pleasing, rather than expensive. In those days aristocracy had something of reality, but in these times proclaims itself parvenu. I only regret that American society should imitate the vanities and vices of aristocracy rather than its virtues and talents.

But to return to Farmington, the evening passed pleasantly away, and I was launched into Farmington society; as there were only three of us, at the close of the entertainment, to escort the young ladies home, it was fortunate that Farmington was built almost entirely in one street; so one of us took the girls who went down street, one, those who went up street, and a third, those who branched off. Of these young ladies, more than half bore one name, that of Cowles. I was told there were in that township three hundred persons of the name of Cowles. There were on the main street five families of brothers, in all of which I visited, and to whom I was indebted for many pleasant hours.

It was a very interesting period in my life. I was introduced into the ways of society, especially New England society, under the best auspices calculated to make me pleased with this human drama, in which we are engaged, attracted by what is good, and not affected by any of that morbid sensibility which so often does affect those who meet society under disagreeable circumstances.

There also, I received my first political ideas, and they have remained to this day little changed by the passage of time and events. I will relate the political condition of things, then, because part of it is unwritten history, which, if you do not get in this way, you will not get at all.

In the winter of 1819–1820, the reader will see by the public history, began the agitation of what was called the " Missouri Question." Missouri, then a territory, was part of the original Territory of Louisiana, acquired by treaty with France. It was entirely and exclusively national domain. Its settlers had introduced slaves. When it applied, at this time, for admission into the Union, objection was made to slavery ; and it was moved in Congress to exclude and forbid slavery from the new states. Of course, this was supported by the Northern people, who foresaw clearly, that if no restriction was placed upon slavery, every new state was likely to come in with that institution, and slavery become dominant in this country. This was not the beginning of the Abolition agitation; but it was the beginning of the political controversy. The Abolition question had begun with the very beginning of the Constitution. My father, Dr. Rush, and Dr. Franklin, with the whole Society of Friends, had petitioned Congress for abolition thirty years before. You will find that fact and the debates upon it in the records of Congress, and set forth in Benton's Debates in the Senate. Those petitions were, even in the first sessions of Congress, received with disgust, and bitterly opposed by the Southern representatives. But the first political agitation on the subject of slavery arose on the Missouri Question, in 1819–1820. I received my ideas upon it then, and, as they were more and more confirmed in after years, I will anticipate a little to show you how they affected my after political conduct. I was afterward a great admirer and disciple of DANIEL WEBSTER. My ideas of Constitutional Powers were derived from him. We went along together until 1850, when Mr. Webster, as a Whig Conservative, and yet a Northern man, was surrounded with great difficulties. On the 7th of March, 1850, he made a speech in the Senate, in which he undertook to get rid of the question by climatic laws. He said it was unnecessary to restrict slavery in New Mexico, Californian, etc., because, it never could prevail there, on account of climate, soil, etc. In other words, he was unequal to treating the subject on that high, moral, and social ground, upon which alone it could be properly treated. In the slang of the day, he "dodged" the question both morally and politically. From that day, I never walked with Mr. Webster. He was a great man, of whom I shall speak hereafter, but not great in that superior and higher sphere of intellectual liberty in which must be discussed all questions of Christian morals and human freedom. I have anticipated this much, because my first ideas on slavery were received while I was at Farmington. The Missouri Question was then on hand, and it was the popular and exciting theme of the day. I, you see, was visiting in the family of and instructed by a distinguished statesman of the old Federal school. I was in a part of New England where people were of the primitive stock, and who looked upon the Southern people with jealousy, and upon slavery with abhorrence. I was a youth easily impressed with the opinions of my friends ; but, in this instance, they were also the opinions of my mother—it is more than probable that she had more influence than all others. It was then, I have said, the Missouri Question arose, which was simply whether slavery should be excluded not only in Missouri, but from all the territories. The parties in it were then, as they have since been, the North and the South. In the Senate the South prevailed. In the House the North. The result was a compromise, which remained nearly forty years. Missouri was admitted with slavery ; but it was excluded from all the territories north of 36° 30′ of latitude. This compromise was exceedingly unpopular in the North, and hated in New England. It was only carried by the desertion of six members from the North. Three of them happened to be from the State of Connecticut, and nothing could exceed the popular excitement upon that occasion. The three members were burnt in effigy at various places, and popular indignation rose against them ; and my Farmington friends were bitter in their denunciation.

This brings me to one of the unwritten facts of our history, which is, nevertheless, as true as any recorded. The flame of the anti-slavery agitation *then kindled never went out.* The public attention was diverted. Other public events absorbed the public mind. Presidential candidates were discussed ; but, underneath them all, quietly burning in many hearts, was the determination that slavery should be destroyed. The tariff question soon arose, but that was largely a question of money. Then nullification, when South Carolina showed her teeth against the Union. Then, in 1837, came the great discussion on the rights of petition, but I need not recite after events. The careful reader of history will see that the anti-slavery sentiment continued to grow from the Missouri Compromise until the War of the Rebellion. The fires, smothered for a time, never went out, until they burst forth into irrepressible flames. No one, but one present at the time, can tell how bitter was the feeling of New England against Southern slavery. But that time is past, and all its feelings, excitements, and doings have entered into the shades of that history, of which shadows alone will remain.

The time had now come for me to leave Farmington. My sleigh-rides, my parties, my pleasant visits, and, alas! my pleasant friends, were to be left forever. My path lay in different and sometimes far less pleasant scenes. I well remember the bright morning on which I stood on Mr. Pitkin's step, bidding farewell to my kind and gentle friend, Mary Pitkin. Married and moved away, she soon bid farewell to this world, where she seemed, like the morning flower, too frail and too gentle to survive the frost and the storm.

In May, 1820, I returned to my father's home, at West Point, to complete my preparations for Princeton College. I recited Xenophon to my father, and the Greek Testament to our next-door neighbor, the Rev. Mr. Picton. He was the chaplain at West Point, and one of my earliest and best friends. He was a Welchman by birth, but had come to this country quite young; and, before coming to West Point, was minister to the Presbyterian Church at Westfield, New Jersey. There he had been rather obscure, with a salary of only $500 a year. How he came to be appointed at West Point I never knew, for he was not an eloquent preacher, although a very good scholar. In the forenoon of the summer of 1820, I used to go to Mr. Picton's study and recite. I think nothing ever did give me so much trouble in studying as some of St. Paul's Epistles. It is difficult to understand some of his phrases, even in English, and more difficult in Greek. There has been, I think, too much literalness in the translation, and I can easily imagine that good scholars might make a simpler version than we now have. In the afternoon I would read Xenophon to my father, who, I may here say, was one of the best scholars of his day. Toward evening, I would run down to the river, or up to " Old Fort Put.," on whose rock-built battlements I would often stand alone, and gaze with delight on that unequaled scene, where the dark mountain, the deep river, and the blue skies seemed to mingle together on the indefinable horizon of nature. I think it was that summer when Mrs. Minor, of Virginia, came to the Point, where she had a son, with letters, I think, to my father. At any rate, she was at our house. She had a daughter with

her, who, notwithstanding all my partiality for the
Farmington girls, seemed to me more like some starry
vision from enchanted land. She was really beautiful,
and beauty is a power over all hearts. She was lively,
and evidently amiable. All this, perhaps, I should
not have known, but that I was almost the only young
man at the Point disengaged from all duties, and,
therefore by necessity her beau. I took long walks
with her, especially one to "Old Fort Put.," descant-
ing, of course, on the poetic and unrivaled beauties
of that scene. I quoted the Lady of the Lake, and
to the purpose, too :

> "And mountains that like giants stand,
> To sentinel enchanted land.
> High in the East, huge Break-Neck
> Down the river in masses threw
> Crags, knolls, and mounds, confusedly hurled,
> The fragments of an earlier world."

The two or three days Miss Minor was with us,
were to me another glance at paradise—but Paradise
Lost. I never saw her again, although I often heard
of her good work, and believe she is still alive.

In the evenings of that summer, I often dropped in,
as they say, to see our neighbor, Mr. Picton, although
quite naturally, one of my attractions was Miss Mary
Picton. She was a friend of my sisters and a favorite
with my mother. She also was very pretty and very
amiable. At that time—all the beaus that West Point
could furnish, and I was one, were fluttering around
her evening levees. I was not as much pleased with her
as Miss Minor, or with two or three of the Farmington
girls, yet she was undoubtedly one of the most lovely
young women I ever saw. Her praises were in the

mouths of all her friends, and it was with no little sorrow I heard of her early death. She married Edwin Stevens, who recently died one of the wealthiest men in this country. It was a happy marriage, and when we see such lovely women cut off so early, when they could live so happy and so well, we wonder at the inscrutable ways of Providence; but, there will be sometime a rolling up of its veil, when all the acts of Providence will be as clear and as beautiful as the skies when the darkest clouds have rolled away.

I must reture to Mr. Picton. For some reason, I believe because he was not thought an eloquent preacher, Mr. Picton left West Point. He next became a teacher in a Female Seminary, in New York. I afterward went to see him. Several years before that, an old village called "Greenwich" was near, but enentirely disconnected from the city of New York. When I went to visit Mr. Picton, I found he was on Christopher street, and on inquiry found it in the upper part of the city, but the street seemed old and the houses brown and shabby. I wondered at it, and asked Mr. Picton what it meant. Said he, "Do n't you know where you are?" "No," said I. "Why, you are in old Greenwich." Then I found, as characteristic of our country, that in a half dozen years the city of New York had so rapidly grown as to envelope Greenwich.

In a pleasant conversation I had with my old friend, I asked him how he liked being a teacher in a Female Seminary. "Oh," said he, "very well. I lived under civil and under military government, under ecclesiastical and under petticoat government, and, on the whole, I like petticoat government the best." When Mary was married to Mr. Stevens, Mr. Picton went to their residence, on Hoboken Heights, where I again went to see him. It was the only point from which I ever saw, or, I believe, afforded, a perfect panoramic view of the splendid city and harbor of New York. From that point, the scene below is unsurpassed by anything seen by mortal vision. At last my friend passed away in the peaceful decline and peaceful end of a sincere, an upright, and a happy Christian.

CHAPTER VII.

*Princeton—College Life—Professors—Lindsley—Greene
—Miller—Alexander—Hodge—My Classmates—Senator Pearce—Professor Dod ; Richardson—The Philosophy of Ideas; Witherspoon—Chesterfield.*

I AM writing this chapter under the shadow of
Beacon Hill, one of the principal scenes in Cooper's
novel, " The Spy." It is historical ground, and every
mountain and vale around is associated with the still
vivid history of the Revolution. Through the Highlands, the Hudson, as if by force, bursts its way. According to the average of human life, nearly two
generations have gone since I first saw the Hudson.
I lived on its banks for several years, and in the summer of 1820, as I have said, was preparing for Princeton College. I read the Greek Testament with my
friend Mr. Picton, and Xenophon with my father;
and in September was admitted to the junior class at
Nassau Hall. I was more than prepared in mathematics, but deficient in Greek. Mr. Lindsley, professor of languages, said I might make it up by extra
study. This I did. I was conscientious, and took
everything literally, which I have found would, in the
present age of the world, be a great mistake. With
hard work, I had accomplished before January six
books of Homer. When I came to Mr. Lindsley to
be examined, he said : " Pooh ! pooh ! It 's no matter."
The truth is, he had found me to be the best student

in the class—not the hardest worker in the classics, but the best general student. Those six books of Homer were totally unnecessary. Still, the classics were always more or less of a burden to me, simply because I had not begun them early enough. There is no doubt that the study of languages should be begun in childhood. Children learn language not by reason, but by imitation. Hence the study of language by the Hamiltonian method, of reading before studying grammar, is probably the best. But to make it so, the study of languages should be begun in early childhood. As I grew older, abstract reasoning became easy and pleasant, but the study of languages still remained difficult. In saying this, I do n't mean the study of literature, but the study of words and grammar. Literature is gained best by the reading of the best authors. That reading will seldom be done without a taste for it. I had that taste from the day I learned to read, and while in Princeton College enjoyed some happy hours in reading, but those hours were few and far between, because to one, like myself, determined to stand high in his class, the college studies were quite severe. Upon the whole, my two years in Princeton College were years of the hardest work I ever did. In the meantime Mr. Lindsley and I got on capitally together, not only during my time at college, but in after years, when he continued my firm friend.

Philip Lindsley was a man of fine mind, of broad scholarship, of liberal views, and of better acquaintance with the world than is possessed by most college men. He was rather eccentric in manner, and not at all given to the prim ways of presidents and tutors. Perhaps for that reason he was much loved by the students. He was in Princeton College professor of belles-lettres, as well as of languages, and afterward president of Nashville University.

Strange to say, that while my life has been largely spent in the cultivation of letters, yet it was the hardest study I had at Princeton. Reading, I was accustomed to—writing, not at all. Still less was I used to that critical analysis which is necessary to the proper understanding of the finest elements of language— the right use of words and expression of thought. This study was difficult to me, but in after-times was of incalculable value. For my facility in writing I am indebted to Princeton College, and have less regret for time misused there than for that of any other period of my life. I worked hard, and I received the reward of my work. I need not describe college life; it varies little the world over. The morning prayers; the day recitations; the Greek of Homer; the criticism of Longinus; the Odes of Horace; the demonstrations of mathematics; the analysis of chemistry; hydrocyanic acid; electricity; magnetism; the speeches at evening prayers; the Sunday exercise on the Bible; and all the varied and continued employment of a student, made up my daily life in one of the most rigid and disciplined institutions in America. It is true that some of the students managed to get through the course with little labor and less thought, in that superficial and careless manner which makes a collegiate life almost, if not altogether, useless. But to me, my two years of college life involved hard work, and left me with less strength than when I began. Indeed, the winter previous to my graduation I was quite out of health, and recovered in the spring only by my determination to take regular exercise, which saved me, and might save thousands of others, from an untimely grave.

Passing over the incidents of college life, I will mention some of the men I saw there—some of them among the most remarkable of their day. Nassau Hall—legally the College of New Jersey—had been founded, at Princeton, about one hundred years before I went there, by Presbyterians of the straitest sect—men who were memorable in the history of the State and in the history of the Church. As successive classes graduated at Princeton, its alumni made their mark upon the mind of the country, and, in some degree, upon that of the world. James Madison—perhaps the most enlightened of our presidents—graduated at Princeton ; and if the reader will examine the triennial catalogue, he will find that prior to 1840, a large number of senators and statesmen were educated at Princeton. The Southern States had then scarcely any institutions of repute, and sent many of their young men to Nassau Hall. There was also at Princeton a Theological Seminary, founded a few years before I was there, and already distinguished, and which has been since the source of much of the theology as well as polemic controversy in the country. Its professors were men who impressed themselves upon the mind of the church, and that influence still continues. The late Charles Hodge was then tutor, and became afterward professor and doctor of divinity. For half a century, in the Assemblies of the Presbyterian Church and in the columns of the Princeton Review, and in the teaching of students, Dr. Hodge has been a lead-

ing theologian of the Calvinistic school, and of wide
and permanent influence upon the rising clergymen
of the day. Dr. Miller, who had been a writer of
some reputation, was then professor of ecclesiastical
history and church government. I knew little of
him or of his family, except that they were very
handsome people. There are not so many handsome people in the world, that they can pass un-
noticed. I know that Ovid says " Os homini sublime
dedit," but it has not been my fortune to see many
evidences of the sublime, much less of absolute beauty
in the human countenance. I can imagine that man
was once a beautiful animal, but among the innumerable evidences of the fall, may be counted the sin-
convicted, care-worn faces one meets in every class of
life. I used often to meet Dr. Miller and his daughter,
in my daily walk upon the streets. Both father and
daughter were erect, of regular features, and blooming,
ruddy complexions. It was said in college, that one
of the students, himself a handsome young man, had
fallen in love with Miss Miller, and used to say lisp-
ingly: " The heighth of my ambithion is Miss Margaret Miller !" Whether so or not, such ambition was
not to be gratified, for she married my tutor, the well-
known John Breckenridge. The man who at that
time exerted the most religious influence at Princeton,
and since then, also, through his distinguished sons,
was Professor Alexander. The theological professors
used to preach in the college chapel, and I have often
heard Dr. Alexander. A plainer, simpler, or more
unpretending man you can scarcely find. To all appearance—for 1 did not talk with him—he was the
very man to represent in this age the plainness and

simplicity of the apostles. I was not struck with his preaching, for he had no brilliancy and no artificial rhetoric. He entered the pulpit, plain in garb and manner, and taking his text, talked on without form and without uttering anything but the simple truth. I think he was not, with the students, a popular preacher, but the weight of his character, the simplicity of his manner, and the naked truth of his doctrines produced then, as such qualities ever will, a profound influence upon the institution with which he was connected and the generation in which he lived. I believe he was quite a learned man, and is said to have read a great deal, and was acquainted with all modern books. Some one said to him : " Dr. Alexander, how do you manage to read so many books ?" He replied : " I do *not read* them *through*. I have learned to read only what is valuable. I look at the index, turn the pages rapidly, and by a glance at the paragraphs, can tell whether I want them." I have done the same thing, and thought it a good suggestion. In reading some novels lately, I found I could finish one in an afternoon or evening, and yet get all that was interesting in the book. Why should one be compelled to read the crudities of a novelist or the criticisms of a historian ; or why should one be obliged to wade through a mass of facts and thoughts he already knows, to get at a few things he does not know ? The impress of Dr. Alexander upon the country has, I think, been greater than that of some renowned statesmen.

Dr. ASHBEL GREEN was then president of the college, and a very able one he was, though never very popular ; but he was better than that, very success-

ful.   The president of a college does not need to be a
very eloquent or very learned man.   He needs to be
dignified, impressive, and *executive.*   He is, in fact, the
executive officer.   Dr. Green was, in all these particulars, admirably adapted to his place.   He had been a
chaplain in the Revolutionary army, I think, under
Washington.   He had good address, and was a fine
elocutionist.   The actors, it was said, came sometimes
to study his manner.   At the time I was in college
he had evidently less power and less ambition than
he once had.   Yet his Bacchalaureate addresses were
very fine.   He was a good classical writer, and one
of his discourses was the best of its kind I ever
heard.   It was on "False Honor."   It was strong
in satire, truth, and eloquence.   Dr. Green resigned
when I graduated, although he lived many years afterward and became quite an old man.   One of his
sons was professor of chemistry in the college; another was an eminent lawyer of New Jersey; and the
other day I was introduced to his grandson, an eminent lawyer of New York.

Of my classmates I need say but little.   One of
them was ALBERT DOD, afterward professor of mathematics in the college, a man of genius and of worth.
Another was JAMES MCCORMICK, my room-mate, a distinguished lawyer of Harrisburg, now dead.   Another was JAMES ALFRED PEARCE, of Maryland, long
a representative and senator in congress from his
state, and one of the best that state ever had.   A
fourth was RICHARDSON, attorney general of Maryland.   Of many I have known nothing since.

At length the time came for me to graduate.   At
Princeton they divide the distinguished graduates into

what are called " Honors," sometimes several having
the same "Honor." The first " Honor " was given to
me, Mr. Pearce, and Mr. Mearns, of Pennsylvania,
who afterward became a clergyman. I believe the
idea was that Mearns was best in the classics, Mr.
Pearce in belles-lettres, and myself in science. It became my lot to speak the Latin salutatory, as it is
called. You may depend I was puzzled, for this was
not my forte, and I scarcely knew what to do.

It was not uncommon—on the contrary quite common—for the students to get their commencement
orations written by others, and pay for them; but
that did not suit me. So I went home and went to
work. I wrote a good oration in English, and then
translated it into Latin, and finally my father, than
whom I never knew a better scholar, wrote the ex-
ordium and peroration, and you may depend they had
the *ore rotundo*. When I came to speak it I was in
fear and trembling. But I had one comfort, that if I
happened to make a mistake or stumble not a soul in
the audience would know what it was about. In
looking back upon it, I think that to write a Latin
oration, commit it to memory, and speak it without a
blunder to a great audience of learned men and bright
women, is, in relation to his capacity, equal to one of
the labors of Hercules. I got through quite credita-
bly, and returned home with my honors fresh upon
me. I left Princeton without much regret or affec-
tion. But I have since learned to regard it more
highly, for I have learned that it was one of the first
institutions in the country where pure and undefiled
religion—the religion of the cross—was taught without any mixture with the false philosophies or the

corruptions of the world. There I received, perhaps not the first, but the strongest of my religious impressions. They have never left me, nor has the conviction that those doctrines which are commonly understood as Calvinistic, are the real doctrines of the cross, as interpreted by St. Paul, and now preached in the Evangelical churches. I have heard them preached in the Episcopal pulpits, as they have never been preached by Presbyterian ministers, and I will say here that, notwithstanding the outcry about sectarianism, I never heard Presbyterianism, as such, preached at Princeton College. The doctrines of Alexander, Miller, Green, and Lindsley, were those of the Evangelical Church, preached in earnestness of spirit and simplicity of style.

I returned home by stage to New Brunswick, and by steamboat to New York. So, you will understand, that at that time there was not a mile of railroad in the United States, nor was there any railroad of importance in the next ten years. It seems but yesterday since the first train of cars began to run, and now there are in this country 80,000 miles of railroad, half of all upon the earth. Such has been, and is, the extraordinary range and whirling progress of this, our country.

I remained at home the next ten months, and went to Litchfield in 1823, in the month of June. Those ten months at home was one of the happiest, and to myself most profitable, periods of my life; and yet, you will see that, practically, as people so often speak, it was of no use. It was this: It had been decided that I was to be a lawyer, and, as I was to spend some months at home, I marked out for myself a course of reading which I supposed was to be introductive to the law. I read Hume's "England," Vattel's "Laws of Nations," Rutherford's "Institutes," and intermixed it all with Madame de Stael's "Germany," and other French works. Of course I read Mrs. Radcliff's and Jane Porter's novels. I liked Hume and Vattel, but I reveled in the "Scottish Chiefs," "The Romance of the Forest," "The Mysteries of Udolpho," and those wonderful sensations which creep upon you as you walk at midnight through the long corridors, hear the rattling of chains, and see the sheeted ghosts pass before you? I never despised such things, for sure I am that they are more entertaining, and, I believe, more useful, than modern philosophy, for they lead the mind from the dull cares of this earth to the dreams of joy, without debasing the intellect and without poisoning the soul.

I said these studies and readings were not *practically* useful, and they were not, for in the practical affairs of life nothing is useful but what pertains to the business of the hour. When I think of these studies I think of Chesterfield's remark to Mr. Harris, on his entering parliament.

Harris was an elegant writer on grammar and philosophy. He had written "Hermes," one of the most analytical and instructive works on the theory of grammar. Finally he was elected to parliament. When there he was introduced to Chesterfield, who said to him: "Mr. Harris, you have written books? You have written on grammar and philosophy." "Yes, my Lord." "Well, sir, what the devil has grammar and philosophy to do with the British Parliament?"[1] "Sure

[1] Adams' Correspondence.

enough ; and what have they to do with the American Congress?" Chesterfield drew at once the distinction between mere men of business and men who are merely men of letters and of science. I said my reading in 1823 was not practically useful, and yet it was useful in the highest sense. It gave me a wide field of interesting thoughts, and strengthened my mind for other pursuits.

Connected with the men and teachings of every college—especially of the old colleges—are its *traditions*. From class to class, and generation to generation, come down certain stories of men and ideas and customs, which illustrate the tones and ideas of those days. I will mention one or two, because they are connected at least by contrast with some ideas prevalent in the present time. In the beginning of the Revolution, Dr, Witherspoon was president of the college. He was a great patriot, entered congress, and signed the Declaration of Independence. He was a Scotchman by birth, and a man of strong common sense, as well as sound principles. At that time the Berkleian theory of ideas was fashionable, which assumed that all external existences were ideal, and all objects were ideal. It was so much more dominant than materialism is now, that almost all the professors and students adopted it. It is said, that Dr. Witherspoon, finding it impossible to reason upon this subject logically with people whose minds were on fire with the ideal theory, entered the class-room one morning, and, in the course of his remarks, said : " Young gentlemen, if you think there is nothing but ideas in the world, just go out on the campus and butt your heads against the college walls ! You will at least get an *idea* of matter." On another occasion, it is said, the students were at supper—then, as now, at long tables, with a tutor presiding at each. There was one student of the senior class who did not believe in the theory of ideas. They had hot mush and milk for supper, when all at once this student uttered a dreadful cry. Everybody started up to know what was the matter. The student said : " Mr. Tutor, I ask your pardon. I have just swallowed a red-hot idea !"

I do not say that such traditions as these are literally true ; but I do say that they prove that different fashions of mind, as well as body and manners, prevail in different generations. While philosophy has neither limits nor foundations, and there are none, unless the philosophy of Christianity be accepted, it must ever be the creature of imagination, of theory, of wild and exaggerated—however beautiful—dreams. The philosophy which assumes that all is ideal, is certainly as acceptable and as probable as that which assumes that all is matter. The philosophy which assumes that there is a God, and He governs this universe by His will, whether it be by natural or supernatural laws, is certainly as probable as that matter made itself, and then holds itself together. The fashion of this world passeth away.

CHAPTER VIII.

*Again at West Point—Reading, History, and Interna-
tional Law—A Party—Distinguished Visitors—De
Witt Clinton — Dr. Mitchell — Eliza Leslie — Mrs.
Emma Willard—Percival the Poet—Female Educa-
tion—Sally Pierce—Nathaniel Carter—Colonel Stone
—Percival at Midnight.*

I write to-day from the summit of the geological
island of which Mount Auburn is the center. Looking to the north at the Widows' Home, you see in the
distance apparently a range of hills, while immediately beyond the Home is a valley. Beginning on
the Miami, at the mouth of Duck creek, and pursuing
its little vale, you will arrive at Mill creek, and thence
by its valley on the Ohio again. On the space within
are Walnut Hills, Mount Auburn, and Clifton, embracing one of the most beautiful suburban districts
to be found in the United States. West of it, on Mill
creek, is that Ludlow Station, which was my earliest
remembered home. Nowhere have I seen more beautiful views and richer landscapes than those which
surround Cincinnati. In the midst of them we are
now placed. Sixty-five years ago, I was a boy solitary, reading the life of Napoleon, who was then at
the height of his glory, and trying to amuse myself
with quail traps (set where Spring Grove Cemetery
is), and raising white ducks in Mill creek. That
scene seems real, but shadowed with a dim mist.

which takes away the sharpness of the outlines, but leaves a solid reality behind.

I must now return to Princeton, and ask you to go with me in what may be called a little episode to my Princeton life. I left Princeton in the autumn, and it had been determined that I should be a lawyer. It was thought best that I should commence my studies at Litchfield, where I was to go the next summer. My parents were doubtless willing to see a little more of me than they had recently done, and besides there was a practical advantage in being able to read works of general history and jurisprudence, which few young men can spare the time to do. So my plan was soon marked out, and I never regretted it. It was a part of education which few can get, but which none can be thoroughly educated without. I determined to take the forenoon of each day to read history, the laws of nations, and general jurisprudence, leaving the latter part of the day to society and amusement. Notwithstanding I was wholly unrestricted as to what I should or should not do, yet I pursued this plan strictly and most profitably. About eight months of time was passed in this kind of study. During that time, Hume's History, Robertson's Introduction, Vattel's Law of Nations, Rutherford's Institutes, Beccaria, and other works, which were historical and legal, I read with the greatest interest, and in regard to my intellectual advancement, with great advantage. This course, as was all that I ever after pursued, I chose myself, and I can not at this day see that I could have chosen any better. The simple fact is that after a school or college has given a young person what may be called the tools of education—

that is, the elementary studies—all the rest must be of their own making. People talk of "self-education;" but all education which is practically useful for either mind or business, must be self-directed. It is in vain to force any young person to pursuits for which they have no taste and to ends for which they have no ambition. The law, or medicine, or merchandise may be pursued profitably without any scholastic education, except mere details of business. Hence, as the love of money and the necessity for means of sustenance are almost universal, three-fourths of those engaged in those professions have no regular or complete education. Hence, also, when persons of this kind are very successful in their business, the newspapers say they were "self-educated." As an evidence of industry or sagacity, this is well enough. But there is no man among them, who, for the happiness and influence of his life would not have been better off if he had been better educated. It is not true that the educated, cultivated men are not "self-educated" also. When the young man leaves college, henceforward his education is his own—self-directed and self-made. Here it is that we see the development of natural tastes, whether it be to self-cultivation or the mere pursuit of business. Although the great body of college graduates enter what are called the learned professions, not more than one-fourth have the taste or the ambition to pursue science, learning, or literature beyond the mere wants of their professions. Those who do find their reward, if not in place or wealth, at least in the advancement of their minds, or in the happiness of a self-cultivated life.

While I was thus pursuing my literary and legal studies, I was also gaining a knowledge of society, and that of the best kind the country could afford. My father, as the principal professor at West Point, received letters of introduction brought by cadets from all parts of the country. Their parents or friends also came to the Point quite often to see the young men. New York was near, and the distinguished men there also frequently visited this place. Many public characters came there, and most of them found their way at some time to our house. My mother was a fine talker, and hospitable, so many of these persons used to call at our house and talk with her, and occasionally she gave an evening party. Thus I came to see and know something of many men and women who came to be distinguished in the country, and some of whom were in themselves very interesting people. I was afterward, between 1822 and 1825, often at home, seeing and enjoying much of this kind of society. Without referring to a particular date or occasion, I will here briefly describe some of these persons. Many of them are almost forgotten now, but they were marked persons at that time.

First among these was Dr. SAMUEL L. MITCHELL, whom I saw one evening in a party at our house, and who was really a remarkable man, though, for some peculiarities, often laughed at. He was, at one time, United States Senator from New York, but that was the least of his distinctions. He was chiefly known as a naturalist (being a pioneer, in this country, of that department of learning), and was in fact a learned man. He was very fond of natural history, and taught the

public mind many things which now seem very simple.   There was quite a controversy in the newspapers because Mitchell said, in some statement, that a
whale was not a fish.   The public took it for granted
that anything which swam in water was a fish.   A
whale is no more a fish than a bird.   The whale
belongs to the class of mammalia.   It was on account
of some of his natural-history peculiarities, and other
what are called "notions," that the wags, often very
ignorant of such things, made fun of him.   He insisted upon calling the United States "Fredonia," because "Columbia" was wrong.   Columbus did not
discover the United States, and "States" did not
mean anything; but Fredonia would signify the land
of freedom.   Some wit, in reference to these peculiarities, wrote a bagatelle, in which was this:

"Of all the birds and fishes rarest,
Fredonian Mitchell is the queerest.

Dr. Mitchell was a large, portly man, full of conversation; and, as I remember, on that evening very
complimentary to the ladies.

Another man, whom the world will not forget so
soon was DE WITT CLINTON.   He was occasionally at
West Point; and no man of that period is, or ought
to be, better remembered.   For twenty years De Witt
Clinton was the bright particular star on the horizon of New York politics, whose light also extended
to other and remote parts of this country.   Clinton
had the honor of doing one great thing, and that is
what nine-tenths even of the greatest statesmen can
not say.   In England and this country men have risen
to the highest places, and have been regarded as great
statesmen, without having accomplished even one

great original work. They have risen by force of talent, or opportunity, or achievements in war; but not by having suggested or done a single really great thing. Of all our presidents, an examination will show that three only, WASHINGTON, JEFFERSON, and LINCOLN, actually did, in and of themselves personally, an original work. De Witt Clinton had as much talent as either of them, and more cultivation. He was much better educated than Washington or Lincoln, and was quite as good a writer as Jefferson. As a literary production, his oration at the anniversary of Union College, N. Y., is equal to anything produced by our public men, unless it is some of the addresses of John Quincy Adams.

De Witt Clinton was in person remarkably handsome and dignified. He was portly, with a ruddy complexion and high forehead. His address was polite and pleasant, without inviting to any familiarity. He appeared to a mere bystander rather stiff; but not enough so to be haughty and uncourteous. In fact his dignified manner, as compared with the frank, bluff address of many public men, was used against him by the petty politicians of the day. The one great thing, which I said Clinton did, was the Erie Canal. That was carried through by his talent and popularity.

He always had a band of choice friends around him, but the current of the public mind, and especially of the party which afterward became dominant under the lead of Van Buren, was against him. They represented the enterprise as a "big ditch," to float mud-scows. It was the turning point in regard to the present enterprise and improvement of this country. If the construction of the Erie canal had been delayed for several years, the physical improvement of the whole county would have been delayed as much. A canal, however great and however important it is at this day, was not, in itself, of so great magnitude; but it was the *initial* step in those vast improvements which the country has since made. At the head of this great enterprise, and at the head of all the statesmen who have since promoted the improvement of the country, stood De Witt Clinton, and I may add, he was the head of the really American statesmen. The only man who could compete with him on the same level of ideas and sentiments was Henry Clay. Three years after this I had an opportunity of seeing those statesmen together. Ohio adopted the policy of Clinton, and made her own great canal. In July, 1825, the first ground for the Ohio canal was broken, near Middletown, by Governor Morrow and De Witt Clinton. A few days after Mr. Clay was detained at Lebanon by the sickness of his child, and Mr. Clinton also arrived. My friend, Dr. Drake, and I traveling with him, were there also. A dinner was given to the distinguished strangers by the people of Lebanon, when' I saw three men, really great in their day. I was not much struck by anything said or done, but I remember the different impressions made upon me and Dr. Drake by these very different men. Dr. Drake, himself an impulsive Western man, preferred Mr. Clay, especially for his ready address, his off-hand manner, his dash, and force. Mr. Clinton, he thought heavy, on account of his slow and dignified address. There was, in fact, however, little comparison to be made between the two men. After allowing for all the impulse, and eloquence, and pleasant address of

Mr. Clay, he fell far short of the high culture, the well-armed and vigorous mind of De Witt Clinton. A finished education and the culture of letters may not make a great man, but the *want* of them will leave the finest intellect in the world defective and deficient. In three years, Mr. Clinton, in apparently the vigor of life, had passed from the stage of human action. He was not a mere comet, suddenly flashing, dazzling, and disappearing; nor was he a fixed star, but rather a planet, which, for some unknown reason, left our system before its career was finished.

I turn now to another person, who was the very opposite of Clinton. This was ELIZA LESLIE, a woman with but common education, and occupying no public station. Miss Leslie was, nevertheless, a very interesting person. She was often at our house, and I would sit and listen, with pleased interest, to the conversation between her and my mother. Both were the best of talkers, and their strong minds never wanted a subject to discuss. Miss Leslie's mind was not very broad, and her chief topics were those relating to society, manners, customs, ways of doing, dress, and character. In these she took great interest, and she was mistress of the subject. She moved in the best society of Philadelphia, and had strong social tastes. She wrote a series of stories, of which, " Mrs. Washington Potts " was the principal, and which, at the time, were very popular. I thought they had merit. Her talk and her stories were exactly alike, showing great knowledge of society, and flowing on, in a clear and animated style. Eliza Leslie is now best known as the author of a " Cook-Book," which I imagine must have been very successful, as it has kept the stage for many years. Toward the close of her life, she undertook to write the life of John Fitch, the supposed steamboat inventor, but the book was never published. There was a curious piece of history about this. Neither Fitch nor Fulton was the originator of steamboats. David Rumsey, a native of Virginia, was the first who launched a steamboat, and that was on the waters of the Potomac, about the year 1787. Mr. James, of Chillicothe, told me he was acquainted with this fact. Some five or six years after that John Fitch put a steamboat on the Delaware, at Philadelphia, and succeeded, and my father saw his boat moving. But neither Rumsey nor Fitch succeeded in the practical part of making such a boat as would be profitable. This honor was reserved for Robert Fulton. So, Fitch, being neither the original, nor the successful one, in this undertaking, could not be lauded as the author of the steamboat. Perhaps, for this reason, she gave up the undertaking. She was of rather a remarkable family. Charles Leslie, the great painter, was her brother; General Leslie, who recently died in New York, was another, and one of her sisters married one of the Careys, so long distinguished as book publishers.

I will now introduce you to another lady, whom the world has not forgotten, who lives in the memory of thousands of women, and who, perhaps, will be remembered as long as any woman of her time. This was Mrs. EMMA WILLARD. History may preserve royal names, and the poetry of Mrs. Hemans may live, but none of them could have impressed their powers and minds on so many thousands as the founder of Troy Seminary; the educator of thousands of women, and the author of those inimitable stanzas :

> " Rocked in the cradle of the deep."

Emma Hart, which was her maiden name, was born in Berlin, Connecticut. She married Doctor Willard, of Vermont, who was a man of strong sense, and though with none of the flashing spirit of his wife, seems not to have impeded but rather aided and encouraged her in her plans for female education, for it was in her married life in Vermont that she began to form these plans for a higher and better culture for women. Subsequently she removed to Albany, New York, laid her plans before the legislature and the people, and succeeded in getting aid from the people of Troy, so that in a short time she established that great seminary for girls, which continued half a century, and was the model on which similar institutions have been built. But in saying this, I must also do justice to another person whom I know, and who preceded Mrs. Willard in what is called a female school proper. This was Miss Sally Pierce, of Litchfield, Connecticut. It must not be supposed that Mrs. Willard was the first person to set up a female school, any more than we are to suppose our grandmothers were without education. Somehow, and in some way, they got an education suitable to ladies in their generation. Where the celebrated Mrs. Goodrich got her education I do not know, but certain it is that she and others, like the Edwards and Dwights, would shine in any circle of ladies at this day. At that time, however, the education aimed at was not to advance the mind in higher cultures so much as to shine in society. In New England of that day no useful art in housekeeping was likely to be neglected; but, between these useful arts, and that of shining address, there seems to have been little or none of that solid intellectual education which is given now. The idea of highest female education seems to have been that of address and refinement. It may be illustrated by an anecdote told of the eccentric Judge Brecken-ridge, of Pittsburg. It is said that, attending court in one of the mountain counties of Pennsylvania, he noticed a handsome, well-formed girl, who proved to be the daughter of the landlord, who took his horse, watered him, and in returning jumped over a five-barred gate. He was so struck by the girl that he determined, other things being inquired into, to make her his wife. But to do this it was neccessary to have her educated, that the native diamond might be polished into form and brilliancy. So he took her to a lady in Philadelphia, renowned for her fashionable education of girls. He stated his object, and the lady said: "What will you have her taught?" "Madame, 'Dress and address.'" "Sir, it shall be done." And it was done. The lady became an elegant and accomplished woman. That was undoubtedly the common idea of the day, when anything was meant beyond the common elements of education. There were, however, long before Mrs. Willard's time, schools in which young women were educated to perform well all the useful, practical duties of life. One of these was, as I have said, that of Miss Sally Pierce, of Litchfield, Connecticut, which was in the full tide of success when I entered the law school in 1823. It had then, I think, been in existence for more than twenty years. I mention this because eminent as were the services of Mrs.

Willard in this course of education, it would be wrong to suppose that she alone inaugurated the system of more advanced female education. Mrs. Willard was an intimate friend of my mother, and a teacher of her daughter. Hence she was often at our home, and I saw much of her. She was a woman of genius, handsome, dignified, and commanding in presence, of most genial and pleasant manners, quick and ready in conversation, and, in one word, attractive in society, and amiable in conduct. I said she was a woman of genius, and that is a very rare quality. She wrote on various subjects, and wrote well. Besides essays on female education, and the hymn "Rocked in the Cradle of the Deep," she wrote a medical disquisition on the cholera, which she sent to me. It contained the most novel and ingenious ideas, but passed for little with the medical fraternity.

Among other traits of her character, she was fond of humor, and was a good teller of anecdotes. I will relate two or three little stories which I heard from her. "There was an old clergyman living near her place, quite remarkable for eccentric ideas and sayings. Among other things he was very *literal* in his way of applying ideas. On one occasion, immediately after the election of Jefferson, he being a Federalist, and a detester of Jefferson, was, as in duty bound, praying for the president, when he said: 'And now, Lord, bless thy servant Jefferson, for, Lord, thou knowest *he needs it.*' Among other curious ways, he was in the habit of asking a blessing on each particular thing on the table. At breakfast there was some bear meat (bears being then common in Vermont, and he abhorring it), when he prayed: 'Lord bless the coffee, bless the bread and butter, but as to this *bear meat*, Lord, I do n't know what to say!'"

There was another story told by Mrs. Willard, the force of which, as told by her, can not be put on paper, but you will see the point. There had been an affray among some men in which one was hurt. A trial took place, in which the object was to find out who hurt the man, and Salstonstall was supposed to be the wrong-doer. One of the witnesses was up, who was supposed to know. "Well, what was Salstonstall doing?" "Oh, he was slashing around." "Well, what is that?" "He was just knocking about him here and there." "What did he do to this man?" "Why, he *enticed* him." "*Enticed* him, how?" "Oh, he enticed him with a crow-bar—so!" And Mrs. Willard enacted the crowbar scene.

Mrs. Willard died in ripe years, surrounded by her friends, in the faith of a Christian, and the conscious-ness of a well-acted life.

Another person we at that time saw something of, was NATHANIEL CARTER, author of "Letters from Eu-rope," and editor of the *New York Statesman.* His letters from Europe were at that time very interest-ing; for few Americans then knew much about Europe, and Mr. Carter was a close observer, and a literary man, with a pleasant style, putting things in an at-tractive form. His paper, the *Statesman*, was well ed-ited, and Clintonian in politics, showing, as many other things did, how the high qualities and command-ing character of De Witt Clinton drew literary men around him.

Mr. Carter was in ill-health, and died comparatively young; one of those who, by dying in their prime, with

a life unfilled and with much promise, are a real loss
to their generation.

Another person occasionally at the "Point," was
COL. WILLIAM L. STONE, editor of the *New York Commercial Advertiser.* He was the author of the "Life of
Brandt," the celebrated Indian chief, Thayendinega.
He is the first man who seems to have got an idea of
the modern art of making a profitable newspaper. If
you take up a newspaper of the old school, two generations since, you will find that nothing could be
more dry or inane. The ship news, the historical facts
of the day, and some political abuse, with the advertisements, made up nearly all of it. It was seldom
that society, science, or literature had any representation. Of course, there were exceptions to this. Here
and there a man got into a newspaper, who had some
idea that society would be interested in itself, and
would like to see the movements of the great world
around. But these were the exceptions. The great
body of newspapers were dry enough. I said Col.
Stone began to have an idea of the modern newspaper,
because of an incident which happened while I was
there. While Stone was visiting the "Point," for a
day or two, an Irish woman, for some trouble, threw
herself off the high rocks near Kosciusko's monument, and, of course, was killed instantly. It was a
striking incident, but Stone immediately dressed it up,
with a tale of romance, and extraordinary misfortunes,
and it appeared in his paper as an extraordinary
drama. When my mother saw it, who saw in the
affair only the simple fact of a half-crazed woman
killing herself, she looked upon Col. Stone as a fabu-
lous story-teller. But in this Stone only exhibited one

of the signs of the coming newspaper; when crimes and accidents should be reported not only in the fullness of detail, but in exaggerated imagery. This is one of the arts of a newspaper; but, happily, the newspaper has now a better side than that. It is now a fair representative of the good as well as the evil of society. Society loves to look upon itself, and thinks, to use a classic sentiment, that nothing is foreign to itself which is common to human nature.

It was, I think, about this time, that JAMES G. PERCIVAL (the poet) held, for a short period, the post of professor of chemistry. He was occasionally a visitor at our house, and I saw something, though not much, of this singular man. Singular he was, in his genius, learning, character, and manners. Not much of this would be visible in ordinary company; and there, he seemed nothing extraordinary, except a very evident retiring, shrinking manner, the outward semblance of that unfortunate trait of character which marred much of his life. This was a remarkable diffidence. It is said that his friends, to help him, had instituted a course of lectures at Charleston (S. C.), which were likely to be profitable, and the room was crowded when Percival, from mere bashfulness, ran away, and the lectures were not delivered. He sought society very little, and seemed to learn very little of it. Yet, Percival was a learned man, and America has produced few so eminent in knowledge as he. Being essentially a student, his studies and acquirements extended to various branches, especially languages and natural history. Once, at our house, he told us that he knew twelve languages, and, I think, spoke ten of them. Latin, Greek, and Sanscrit

as well as French, Spanish, German, and Italian, were
familiar to him. In addition to that, he knew the
languages of the North of Europe, and what few persons do the Slavonic tongues. He made some translations of Slavonic poetry. I saw, in a biographical
history, this statement, that Percival had made some
translations of Slavonic poetry with all the spirit and
reality of the original, and that this could not be, for
he could not have been so very familiar with the original; but I think he was, for he seized upon all
languages, and all poetry, as if he had been born
to them. In natural sciences, chemistry, geology, and
kindred subjects, he was at home. He was a short
time professor of chemistry at West Point, and died,
I think, while geologist of Wisconsin. Percival was
a man of real genius, but seemed almost a stranger in
society. He was never married, and it was said, as it
frequently is in such cases, that he had an early dis-
appointment in love, of which nothing now can be
known. I do n't think he had any horror of young
ladies, for he was a visitor at our house, when my
sister was young and thought beautiful. I remember one evening, in the early part of summer, the
month of roses, Percival was at our house and exhibited the true character of a poet, something to the an-
noyance of poor human nature. The evening had
passed in conversation, when, at ten o'clock, my father, as he invariably did, retired. Soon after, my
mother, quite unusual for her, stepped out, too. Percival, my sister, and myself, were left in the parlor.
The lights were dim, but the moon cast its silver rays
through the window, which probably suggested an
idea to the poet. He began to describe a visit to Ni-

agara by moonlight; the beauty which shone from
rocks and waters; and, finally, what certainly must
have been a beautiful phenomenon—a rainbow under
the Falls of Niagara! All this was in the highest degree poetic and interesting; but, alas! never did I
have such a time to keep awake. The spirit was
willing, but the flesh was weak. This is a very good
illustration of Solomon's saying, there is *a time* for all
things; and never let poet or orator throw away their
eloquence upon sleepy people. I cast away all poetry,
and said to myself, Oh, for one hour of

> " Tired nature's sweet restorer—balmy sleep."

I did not know a great deal of Dr. Percival, but
what I have said here is exactly correct. He, like Mrs.
Willard was born in the little town of Berlin (Conn.),
from which have come others of that high, spiritual
cast, who seem to have shed the light of genius over
this dull, plodding world.

On inquiring for the poems of Percival, I found
them out of print. This is due, no doubt, to the
fact that he wrote no long, elaborate poems. But
there are, among his fugitive pieces, some which de-
serve immortality; and there will come a time when
the gatherer of literary remains will place them higher
than many of those which are now talked about.

I have now finished the account of, so far as I can
remember it, one of the most profitable and interesting periods of my life. I only regret that in this half
century which followed, there were only two periods
in which I saw so much of genius, so much of that intellectual life, which seems to shine upon and beautify
the materialism of the world. The social history of

both England and America shows that there are times and circles of life in which there is a sort of shining forth of light, which seems almost to set fire to the mind of the day, and be felt in after history. Of this, I shall show you more hereafter.

CHAPTER IX.

*Litchfield—Law School—Noted Men—Judge Reeve—
Judge Gould—Anecdotes—Uriah Tracey—John Pier-
point — The Wolcotts — The Demings — Col. Tall-
madge — Talk with Governor Wolcott — Connecticut
Politics — The Seymours — Dr. Sheldon — Mode of
Life—Dr. Beecher.*

It was about the middle of June, 1823, that my
father and I drove up to Grove Catlin's tavern, on the
"Green," of Litchfield, Connecticut. It was one of
the most beautiful days of the year, and just before
sunset. The scene was most striking. Litchfield is
on a hill, about one thousand feet above the sea, and
having fine scenery on every side. On the west rises
"Mount Tom," a dark, frowning peak; in the south-
west, "Bantam Lake," on whose shores I have often
walked and ridden. In the north and east other
ridges rolled away in the distance, and so, from Litchfield Hill, there is a varied and delightful prospect.
One of the first objects which struck my eyes was interesting and picturesque. This was a long procession
of school girls, coming down North street, walking
under the lofty elms, and moving to the music of a
flute and flageolet. The girls were gayly dressed and
evidently enjoying their evening parade, in this most
balmy season of the year. It was the school of Miss
Sally Pierce, whom I have mentioned before, as one
of the earliest and best of the pioneers in American

female education. That scene has never faded from
my memory. The beauty of nature, the loveliness of
the season, the sudden appearance of this school of
girls, all united to strike and charm the mind of a
young man, who, however varied his experience, had
never beheld a scene like that. In the evening my
father and myself walked up to the home of Judge
Gould, who was to be my future preceptor. The
judge was a handsome man, a very able lawyer, with
a keen and superior mind, subtle, discriminating, and
yet clear as crystal. His treatise on "Pleading,"
which was one of the law titles upon which he lectured to our class, is the ablest law book there is extant. My father was acquainted with him, and it was
soon announced that I should enter as a law student,
and, as it turned out, my residence in Litchfield continued the next two years, and I was admitted to the
bar by the county court of Litchfield, in June, 1825.
The next morning my father introduced me to Governor Wolcott, and my room and board were arranged
for at Mrs. Lord's, whose house was just across the
street from Dr. Lyman Beecher's, then pastor of the
Litchfield Congregational Church. As my residence
at Litchfield was one of the most important periods
of my life, and, as I was there introduced into a society, of which this country has had none superior, I
will state something of the growth and character of
Litchfield before I was there. Litchfield was settled
nearly a hundred years after the first settlement of
New Haven, and chiefly by immigrants from Hartford.
The Wolcott family early came there, and they and
their connections were among the most distinguished
people in the state. Three successive Wolcotts were

governors of the state, the second being one of the
signers of the Declaration of Independence, and the
third the successor of Hamilton, as secretary of the
treasury, in the administration of Washington. This
was the one then living in Litchfield. Then there were
the Tallmadges, the Seymours, the Buells, with Tracy
and others, who had made Litchfield noted for talent
and social aristocracy long before I came there. Many
striking anecdotes were told of the men and women
of the former days, which still lingered in tradition.
Two or three are worth preserving, because they at-
test to a wit far superior to what we have now.

URIAH TRACY, who lived at Litchfield, was a very
superior man, and noted for wit. He was United
States Senator, from Connecticut, in the time of Washington and Adams, and to him are attributed, whether
true or not, some of the sharpest sayings of that day.
It is said that he was standing on the steps of the
Capitol, which you know looks down Pennsylvania
avenue, when a drove of mules was coming up. Randolph, who was standing by him, said : " There, Tracy,
are some of your *constituents*." " Yes, sir ;" said
Tracy, " they are going to Virginia, to keep school."
At another time Tracy was standing by the British
Ambassador, in one of those receptions which Huntington has so well depicted, in what he calls the " Court
of Washington," in the midst of which Mrs. Goodrich
appears as one of the characters. This lady was, I
think, of the Wolcott family, and distinguished for
beauty, grace, and manners. The ambassador was
much struck by the appearance of Mrs. Goodrich,
and exclaimed : " By George, Tracy, Mrs. Goodrich
would be di tinguished in the Court of England !"

" Yes, sir;" said Tracy, bowing, " she *is* distinguished even on Litchfield Hill!" Tracy was right, for, to be admired in the society of Litchfield, at that time, would have required talents and graces sufficient to secure distinction in any court of the world. But, all this is gone, and nothing can illustrate the evanescent state of our society more than the changes which it has undergone in many of the old places in the old states. However excellent or able may be the people who live in Litchfield now, there is no such social glory, no such marked superiority there, as that which distinguished the noted people of Litchfield in the generation just passing away, when I came upon the stage. The change in people, manners, and conditions is quite as great as the change in the dress of gentlemen. When I was a law student, a few old gentlemen still retained the dress of the Revolution. It was a powdered queue, white-topped boots, silk stockings, and breeches with buckles. I can remember to have seen David Daggett, chief justice, and a half dozen others, walking in the streets with this dignified dress. It is in vain to say that the present dress is at all equal to it—in what ought to be one of the objects of good dress—to give an idea of dignity and respect. The man who is now inside of a plain black dress, with unpretending boots, may be as good a man, as able a man, as he in white-topped boots and breeches, but he is not respected as much, for he no longer assumes as much. In ceasing to claim the superiority due to high social position, he has lost a part of his own self-respect. He has become only one of a multitude instead of being one above a multitude.

But I must hasten on. Perhaps you will like to

know how the day passed with a law student, in a school and place which has furnished many a great man to this nation. My room, at Mrs. Lord's, was in the northwest corner of a large house, and, from its windows, I looked, on one side, over at Dr. Beecher's house, and, from another, west, to "Mount Tom." From the rooms of my fellow-students, on the south side, might be seen Bantam Lake, and the distant ridges and blue skies in the south. It was a pleasant house, and a good landlady, and to Mrs. Lord I was indebted for many an act of kindness. She was the widow of Sheriff Lord, the mother of Mrs. Pierpoint, wife of the celebrated poet and minister. Pierpoint was a noted Unitarian; but Mrs. Lord was a member of Dr. Beecher's church. The Pierpoints came from what was called "South Farms," a part of Litchfield township, on the road to New Haven. The father of John Pierpoint was a deacon in the orthodox Congregational church; but the poet, for some reason, wandered off and became a noted Unitarian, having at one time a congregation in Boston. Whatever else may have been his qualifications, he was a real poet, and also a wit. I have always thought that some parts of his "Airs of Palestine" were among the best specimens of American poetry. It is unfortunate that so many fine pieces of poetry are likely to be lost, because they are forgotten, and are only preserved in collections, which themselves are likely to be ephemeral. But I will return to my day in the law school. We breakfasted from seven to eight in the morning, and at nine o'clock went to the lecture-room to hear and take notes of Judge Gould's lecture. The founder of the Litchfield Law School was JUDGE TAPPING REEVE, and, if tradition is correct, few better men have ever lived, and scarcely any one was then better known to the bar. He was the author of a Treatise on Domestic Relations, which the lawyers admired, but said was not law, on account, I believe, of its leaning too much to women's rights, a fault which would not be found with it in this day. At the time I arrived in Litchfield, Judge Reeve had given up the law school to Judge Gould, who had been his partner, and he soon after died. He was a man rather noted for eccentricities. After the death of his first wife, he married his housekeeper—a most respectable woman, however, distinguished for piety and benevolence. He was quite absent-minded, and one day he was seen walking up North street, with a bridle in his hand, but without his horse, which had quietly slipped out and walked off. The judge calmly fastened the bridle to a post, and walked into the house, oblivious of any horse. It was under the teaching of Judge Reeve that such men as John C. Calhoun and John M. Clayton, of Delaware, were law students. The school was now under the sole care of Judge Gould. At nine o'clock we students walked to the lecture-room, with our note-books under our arms. We had desks, with pen and ink, to record the important principles and authorities. The practice of Judge Gould was to read the principle from his own manuscript twice distinctly, pausing between, and repeating in the same manner the leading cases. Then we had time to note down the principle and cases. The remarks and illustrations we did not note. After the lecture we had access to a law library to consult authorities. The lecture and references took about two hours. Those of us who were in earnest,

of whom I was one, immediately returned home, and
copied out into our lecture-books all the principles and
cases. My lecture-books made five volumes. The lectures, the references, and the copying took me, on an
average, from nine o'clock until three or four o'clock,
with the intermission of near an hour for dinner. I
did not then, as I do not now, study or write in the
evening. Of course there were some exceptions. I
regard night work, in which nine-tenths of students
indulge, as injurious to the health and even to the
mind. Still, as man is an omnivorous animal, so he
may be as capable of choosing all times as he is of all
meats.

From five to six hours a day employed in this manner was my regular work at Litchfield, and very
seldom was a day missed. At four o'clock in the
afternoon I was generally at leisure, and that was
usually employed in walking or riding—sometimes in
visiting. At Mrs. Lord's were six of us; two from
Georgia; one each from New York, Pennsylvania,
and Massachusetts, and myself. We often rode in the
afternoons, and the vicinity of Litchfield affords the
most beautiful rides I have ever seen. A rolling country, on high ground, with here and there a mountain
top or a little lake, and rapid, pure streams of water,
nature presented most various and lovely pictures of
beauty. We prolonged our rides in summer time,
having taken an early tea, into the starlit shades of
night. In the long days of summer, no candles were
lit in the farm-houses of Connecticut. When the deep
twilight came, every family had gone to rest as completely as the chickens to their roosts; but, when the
dawn of day came, they were up; and when we lazy

students were at breakfast, they had done hours of
work. Such were the Connecticut farmers of that day.

It was commonly my practice to walk in the afternoons of summer, and the opportunities for pleasant
walking were, like those of riding, very good and
tempting. Litchfield, like many New England towns,
was built chiefly on two main streets, one going north
and south, and the other east and west, and the whole
on a hill or ridge, with Bantam river running on the
east and another stream on the west. North and South
street was more than a mile in length, shaded nearly
its whole length by those lofty and broad-spreading
elms for which some of the towns in Connecticut were
noted. In the warm days of summer, and in those
beautiful and cloudless sunsets, like the day in which
I had first seen it, most of the young people would
be on the streets, and among them those of the students who, like myself, were lovers of beauty and of
scenery. Owing to my introduction to society, which is
always a great benefit to young men of any sense, I
was soon acquainted with the best families, and my
afternoon walks, as well as my evening visits, often led
me among those distinguished in beauty, grace, and
position. One of my temptations to an afternoon walk
was to meet the girls, who, like ourselves, were often
seen taking their daily walk. Among these, were the
Wolcotts, the Demings, the Tallmadges, the Landons,
and Miss Peck, who afterward became my wife. The
Demings were always my warm friends, and to them I
am indebted for many a kindness, at a time when I
was ill and weak, and the bystanders hardly expected
me to live. Of the Wolcotts, there were four, and I
think now, as I did then, that I never beheld more

beautiful women than were Hannah and Mary Ann Wolcott. Many a time have I met them on North street when it was a pleasure to look upon them, with the clearest complexions of white and red, the brightest eyes, with tall and upright forms, and graceful walk. These ladies would have attracted admiration in any place of the world. The two other Wolcotts were also very handsome. Elizabeth married my intimate friend, John P. Jackson, of Newark, and Laura married another friend, Mr. Rankin. Their children are numerous, and likely to maintain, in various ways, the fine character of their ancestors. Of that circle of twelve or fifteen girls at Litchfield, with whom I was specially acquainted, all but two were married to non-residents and moved to other states. Two went to New York, three to New Jersey, one to Pennsylvania, two to Vermont, one to Ohio, one to West New York, one died unmarried, and two are living unmarried. These simple facts show what a moving and in some respects unstable country is ours. The young men of the East migrate to the West, and the young women marry those who also migrate, and there are few parts of our country where there are families whose ancestors were there one hundred years before. In New Haven are still some Mansfields whose ancestors were born two hundred years before. But a far greater number have emigrated, and still our American population are moving on, restless, while there is any hope of gratifying ambition or acquiring wealth. Connecticut has ever been a great hive, from which the young have swarmed out; making their homes in the vales of Ohio, on the mountain tops and on the ocean waves.

My afternoon walks led also in a different direction,

into a society where there was less to admire and more
to learn. At the lower end of South street, in a large but
plain house, lived Oliver Wolcott, who had been a member of Washington's cabinet, and a man of great weight
in the country. He was not the father, but the uncle of
the Misses Wolcott, who were the daughters of his
brother. The first Oliver Wolcott known to history, was
governor of Connecticut, one hundred and twenty years
ago. The second was also governor, and was a member
of the Revolutionary Congress and signed the Declaration of Independence. The third Oliver Wolcott, of
whom I speak, was in early life a merchant, then became
comptroller of the treasury in the early part of Was-
ington's administration; then, on the resignation of
Hamilton, he was appointed secretary of the treasury,
and served until Adams was elected. He was now in
retirement, living in his ancestral home, and quietly
waiting the turn of events. Doubtless, he had other
anticipations, but he made no public efforts, and lived
in that quiet simplicity, which characterize a true Republican. He had two sons who died young, and with
them has perished in the direct line, the Oliver Wolcott political distinction. My father had introduced
me to Governor Wolcott, and occasionally I called
upon him and had most interesting conversations on
the past and future of our country. Several times,
when my duties were over, and the pleasant summer
afternoons invited a walk, I went down to Governor
Wolcott's and talked with him alone on the condition
of the country. From him I got some ideas which
have remained with me ever since. He was a strong
tariff man, and so was my father, and most of the
public men of that day. They saw that, owing to im-

mense importations of foreign goods, a large part of which might just as well have been made in this country, the country was drained of its specie, industries kept back, and commercial affairs liable to sudden and ruinous fluctuations. They, therefore, concluded that to lay a high tariff on foreign fabrics would encourage American industry, and so far diminish importations, and give stability to trade. This view was earnestly taken by Governor Wolcott, and has continued with little exception to be the policy of the country ever since. Since the war of the Rebellion, the necessity for a large revenue has imposed the necessity for a high tariff, and will continue to do so for many years. In the meantime, also, American manufactures of almost all kinds have risen up, and become so successful that the question of the tariff is not likely to again agitate politics. In the next thirty years, however, it did enter largely into political discussions. Happily for the country, the views of Wolcott and of nearly all the old statesmen prevailed, and the country has been saved from seeing its labor and industrial institutions prostrate at the feet of European capital.

Governor Wolcott had old-fashioned ideas about many things. He did not believe in the necessity of having men of genius or brilliancy to carry on the government. You know that young men are inordinately attracted by those very qualities. The brilliant orator or writer, the man of great schemes, and the professor of new ideas, are the sort of people who win the admiration of young men. At this time—the summer of 1824—there were several men of this sort looming up as candidates for the presidency. There were Adams, Clay, Calhoun, and De Witt Clinton—

all men of brilliant qualities. It was probably with these in his mind—in fact, we were talking of them— that Governor Wolcott said to me, in substance: "You do n't want a man of genius for president. You want a plain, practical man. There is old Sitgreaves, of Pennsylvania, will make as good a president as any other." Now, Sitgreaves was a member of congress, full of statistics and political economy. I have thought since that the American people had realized Wolcott's idea of getting a man without genius, but had often failed in getting one equal to Sitgreaves. Just look in the calm light of history upon the administrations of Polk, Pierce, and Buchanan! Of genius, no human being would accuse them. Of anything like a broad and sagacious statesmanship, just a little. Clinton, Calhoun, Webster, Clay—all rejected; and Polk, Pierce, and Buchanan accepted! What a record for a great and enlightened nation to make!

Governor Wolcott was elected governor as the candidate of the Democratic party, which had never at any time been able to elect a candidate. The manner of it was curious, and as it involves a chapter of political history which will probably never be written, I will notice it here. Connecticut had always been governed by the old Federal party, which contained unquestionably four-fifths of the good and great men of the state. In the times of Jefferson and Madison, the Democratic party, to which my father belonged, was a small minority, which probably never would have come into power but for certain laws peculiar to that state. Connecticut had, in fact, coming down from Puritan times, a sort of state church. It con-

sisted in this, that a tax was levied for the support
of religion, and paid to the churches. I believe only
to the Congregational; for that was for a long time
the only church in the state. But in the meantime
the Episcopal Church, largely founded by my great-
uncle, Richard Mansfield, had grown up to be a large
body. Then came in the Methodists and Baptists,
and with them all, some able men who were Deists.
Then came complaints against the dominant influence
of the Congregationalists and the imposition of a tax
for religious purposes. This question came to be agitated. Then the Democrats took advantage of it, and
uniting with these discontented elements formed what
was called the "Toleration" party. Wolcott, whose
family were Federalists, and who had been a member
of the Federal administration of Washington, was the
candidate of this Toleration party, and was thus
elected governor. By this combination Connecticut
became for many years a Democratic state, and was
by no means improved in either the quality or caliber
of its public men. There was some reaction in after
years, when such men as Huntington and Buckingham came into the United States Senate. But, as a
whole, the political changes in Connecticut have been
for the worse, as I fear they have in the whole country. It is a sad and ominous thing for a great country, when it can be truly said:

"The post of honor is a private station."

Let me now turn to some other characters. On the
North street was the residence of COLONEL BENJAMIN
TALLMADGE. He was one of the gentlemen of the old
school, with the long queue, white-topped boots, and

breeches. He had been an officer in the guard over Andre at the time he was ordered to execution. After the war he had retired to Litchfield, and was one of the most marked as well as dignified men who appeared in that aristocratic town. When the Western Reserve of Ohio was set off to Connecticut and sold for the school fund, he became a large owner of lands there, and a township was named after him. One of his daughters married into the distinguished Delafield family of New York, and was herself a noted lady.

At the upper end of North street, and near where I boarded, was the unpretending and home-like house of Dr. Daniel Sheldon. He was my physician in an attack of sickness, and one whom I always regarded with great respect. When he had just graduated from a medical college, he had an attack on the lungs, and was supposed to be fast going into consumption, and was saved by what may be called heroic treatment. He went to Litchfield to practice medicine, which involved much riding on horseback, and he began taking opium, until he took incredible quantities. Nevertheless it cured him; and he recovered from the habit of taking opium as resolutely and bravely as he had began it. He survived all danger of early death, and lived to be eighty-four years of age, quietly and peacefully declining, until he passed from this life as gently as the setting star. One of his sons was secretary of legation in France, and one was a very successful merchant in New York. I was indebted to him for a comforting assurance, when we students were charged with being uncommonly "fast." There were more than fifty law students boarding in Litch-

field, many of them of wealthy families, and many
of them from the South. Of course, there must be
some amusement, and often the midnight air resounded
with the songs of midnight rioters, and sometimes
stories were circulated to the students' disadvantage.
After hearing some remarks on the "fast" students,
I met Dr. Sheldon walking, and said to him:

"Doctor, they say we are the worst students ever
were in Litchfield." "Pooh! pooh!" said the doctor,
"they are not half as bad as they were in my day."
So I was comforted with the idea that we were not
casting shame on those venerable Puritans, who had
condescended to become our ancestors. Be this as it may,
I greatly enjoyed those evening sleigh rides, and those
country suppers, when we would ride off to Goshen, or
Herwinton, or other village, and order our turkey and
oysters, served up with pickles and cake, and then set
Black Cæsar to play jigs on a cracked fiddle. But the
grand occasions was something beyond this, when we
got sleighs with fine horses, and buffalo robes, and
foot-stoves, and invited the belles of Litchfield, who
never hesitated to go, and sat off to the distant village
to have a supper and dance. I seldom danced, and
some of the girls did not, but there were always some
who did, and we had jolly times. So passed my days
in Litchfield, doing a great deal of good work in study,
enjoying much of good society, and passing its hours
in innocent amusements.

Perhaps, before I close, I ought to notice two or
three other families, not so much on their account, as
by way of illustrating how Connecticut, in that generation, became the great hive of the teachers and
leaders of the country. I do not exaggerate when I say

that at that time, when the country had not one-third
of its present population, Connecticut, in proportion to
its own population (which was then 300,000), sent out
three-fold as many as any other state of those who became eminent in wealth, literature, law, or politics.
If any one shall deny this, it can be proved by the recorded history of the country. One of the peculiar
characteristics of Litchfield was, in popular phrase,
that they "stuck to their men," and that is a good
characteristic of any country. Litchfield elected two
representatives to the legislature, and for nearly a century two or three names made up four-fifths of all the
representatives. This certainly is one of the reasons
which gave Connecticut the soubriquet of "the land
of steady habits." One of the common names in the
township was that of Buell. I was well acquainted
with Dr. Buell, who lived on South street, and one of
whose daughters married a law student, a Mr. Franklin, of Pennsylvania, and was the mother of General
Franklin, in the army of the Potomac. Another noted
man in Litchfield was JULIUS DEMING. This gentleman was a merchant and eminently successful. No
man in the county was more honored and respected
for integrity of character than this Litchfield merchant.
He became very wealthy. His sons were wealthy, and
his only surviving daughter has inherited the family
mansion, and lives unmarried, preserving still the dignity and character of the family.

Another family there was that of the SEYMOURS, and
there is scarcely another family more distinguished
than theirs. Moses Seymour, the immediate ancestor,
was an officer of the Revolution, and settled in Litchfield. One of the sons emigrated to Vermont, and

became a United States Senator from Vermont. Another emigrated to New York, was a land commissioner, and mixed much in politics. His son, Horatio Seymour, was governor of New York, and the democratic candidate for the presidency in 1868, against Grant. The main stock of the family remained in Litchfield, and were not without honors there. One of the sons was sheriff of Litchfield county, and ORIGEN SEYMOUR, who was at the law school in my time, became Judge of the Supreme Court of Connecticut, and is yet on the political stage.

Since I have given an account of the Litchfield law school, in its beginning and its prime, I may as well continue to the end. It was near by. Judge Gould becoming infirm in health, J. W. Huntington, Esq., who was a relative of the Wolcotts, became his coadjutor until Gould died. Huntington, who soon after became judge and United States Senator, had other affairs on hand, and soon gave up the school. Practically the school died with Judge Gould. It was a private enterprise, and when such really great men in law as Judge Reeve and Judge Gould ceased to live there were none both able and willing to conduct it. The mantles of such eminent lawyers could fall on few, and those few did not prefer this line of life.

I might mention other families in Litchfield, for there was scarcely any family whose sons and daughters might not be found on the fields of the West and South, building up this great Republic. At this time, Dr. LYMAN BEECHER was pastor of the Congregational Church in Litchfield. His house was just across the street from Mrs. Lord's, where I boarded, and, as my window was on that side of the house, I used often to see him and hear his violin, of which he was very fond, sending forth merry tones. It is said, that he would return from a funeral and send forth the quickest airs from his fiddle. He was of the most cheerful temperament, as I, who knew him for thirty years, can well testify. Few clergymen—probably none—have been more noted, more able, and I may add more useful than Dr. Beecher. He was then in his prime. It was in Litchfield, the year after I left there, that he delivered his celebrated lectures on temperance. It was a good place to begin work, for Litchfield had several able and distinguished men, who died or lost their influence by intemperance. Dr. Beecher was called the "great gun of Calvinism," and it seemed to me the very irony of fate to see him tried ten years after by the Presbytery of Cincinnati for heresy in Calvinistic Theology. In the meanwhile, he had been called to one of the principal churches of Boston to combat Unitarianism. Whether he had much to do in repressing it, I know not. But it is certain Unitarianism has grown very slowly since that time. At the time I was in Litchfield, the Congregational Church on the little green embraced two-thirds of the people of the village, and more than that in the surrounding country. Dr. Beecher was so far superior to all other preachers of that section, that all the students who went to church at all went to his church. I was always a regular attendant, not losing, I think, more than two or three Sundays while I was there. Dr. Beecher was remarkable for great irregularity in what may be called the quality of his sermons. There was none inferior, but there were times when he was dull. A friend said to me once that he had heard much of

Dr. Beecher, and went to hear him, but he never heard a duller sermon. I can realize that might have been, but Dr. Beecher was at times exceedingly eloquent. His spells of eloquence seemed to come on by fits. One very hot day in summer, and in the afternoon, I was in church and Dr. Beecher was going on in a sensible, but rather prosy, half sermon, when all at once he seemed to recollect that we had just heard of the death of Lord Byron. He was an admirer of Byron's poetry, as all who admire genius must be. He raised his spectacles, and began with an account of Byron, his genius, wonderful gifts, and then went on to his want of virtue, and his want of true religion, and finally described a lost soul, and the spirit of Byron going off, wandering in the blackness of darkness forever! It struck me as with an electric shock, and left an imperishable memory.

CHAPTER X.

Return to Cincinnati—Voyage Down the Ohio—Judge Baldwin—Judge Torrence—My Case—Nicholas Long- worth—Martin Baum—Peyton Symmes—Dr. Wilson —Father Burke—Churches in Cincinnati—Bishop Fenwick—Aydelotte—Johnson—Jacob Burnet, his Use- ful Life—David K. Este—Nathaniel Wright—Gazley — William Lytle—Robert Lytle.

THE time had now arrived when I was to begin my professional life, if such I was to have. In May, 1825, I started, in company with my father, for Ohio, where, as it was intended, and it turned out in fact, I was to remain. We went by the route through New York, *via* Buffalo. At that time a large part of the New York and Erie Canal was completed. It seemed to my inexperienced mind that nothing could be more pleasant than a calm, unruffled voyage, without dan- ger or noise, and with time to read and observe the scenery, in a nice, well-fitted canal-packet. So, we took passage in such a packet for Albany to Utica, ninety-five miles. Never was a youthful vision so speedily and so utterly dispelled! The quiet and beautiful canal-boat proved to be the dullest, the most tedious, the most wearisome of all earthly convey- ances. Arrived at Utica, we were too glad to take an old-fashioned stage-coach, and complete our journey to Buffalo. At that time the beautiful towns and villages of Western New York had just risen, fresh with the newness of white houses and green fields, while here and there a calm and smiling lake, with its glassy surface, contrasted with the sky above and the green earth around. It was a lovely scene, and the more so to me, as I had just come from the rocks and mountains of the highlands.

Arrived at Buffalo, in the latter part of May, we were met by one of those lake storms which are characteristic of that region. The wind blew fiercely, the rain poured down, and it rapidly grew colder; and in what should have been the warm and blooming spring, we were sitting at the hotel, half shivering round the fire. That day we took the stage, on the lake shore, for Erie. The road led through the then famous Cattaraugua Swamp, almost impassable, even in summer. Then the corduroy bridges and mudholes presented a dismal prospect. The driver, to avoid them, often drove into the edge of the lake, where the water was shallow. *Now* the traveler is borne rapidly along by the Lake Shore Railroad, which annually carries its millions to the far-off shores of Lake Superior, where already cities are springing up and new states are formed.

At length we arrived at Erie, and thence passed through Pittsburg and down the Ohio. At Pittsburg my father took me to call on HENRY BALDWIN, an old pupil of his in New Haven. Mr. Baldwin was a distinguished lawyer, but then very much engaged with iron manufacture. He took me to see one of the great rolling-mills for which Pittsburg was even then famous. I have been through Pittsburg many times, and never without seeing the flames and smoke which were continually pouring out of its great iron works.

Mr. Baldwin afterward became a member of congress and judge of the Supreme Court of the United States. His brother, Abraham, was senator from Georgia. Both were pupils and fast friends of my father. It was Abraham Baldwin who introduced him to the notice of Mr. Jefferson, and got him his first appointment as captain of engineers and teacher. You will remember he was the first teacher, in 1802, at West Point. Both these gentlemen were fair examples of those young, active, and ambitious men whom the little State of Connecticut was sending to take the lead in the West and South. There were hundreds of them, whose names you will find recorded among the leaders of their country.

The voyage down the Ohio in 1825, and in a fast steamboat, presented a vivid contrast to that of 1805, in a pine-board ark. Between 1805 and 1812 had come into use for locomotion that mighty power, steam, now used to move tens of thousands of machines, supplying the labor of millions of men. The first steamboat was launched on the Ohio in 1811, and in 1825 there were hundreds on all the waters of the Ohio and Mississippi. All the modes of locomotion were changed, and in this same year (1825) the first railroad was put in operation between Liverpool and Manchester. Commerce received new life, and the face of the world has since been rapidly changed.

I arrived in Cincinnati in June, and found it hot enough. My first acquaintance were my relatives, Dr. and Mrs. Drake. As they were in the midst of society, and my father was well remembered by all the old citizens, it did not take long for me—who, I found, was regarded as a promising young man—to become known to the best people of Cincinnati. So far as my memory extends, I will mention some of them. Among the first I saw were GENERAL and Mrs. JAMES FINDLEY, who were warm friends of my father and mother. He was the brother of William Findley, governor of Pennsylvania, and of John Findley, member of congress. James Findley was receiver of public moneys at Cincinnati, in 1805, when my father first arrived, and the families became intimate. He was now out of office, but in good circumstances, living on Broadway. In that or the following year he was elected to congress, from the Cincinnati district. In a few years he died, and his wife soon followed. He was an amiable, kindly man of good sense and courteous manners. Another family, and connected with the Findleys, was that of JUDGE TORRENCE, then president judge of the common pleas. He had married Mary Findley, a niece of General Findley's. He was a bluff, honest, good-natured man, with not much law, but a great deal of good principle. He was very kind to me, and I have remembered him with gratitude. It was under him that I came to the bar—for a very brief time. The only case I really tried, was that of a man who, standing on the shore near Mill street, had shot somebody in a boat upon the river. The facts were plain; but I hit upon what I thought a happy expedient to clear him. The State of Virginia, in ceding to the United States the Northwestern Territory, had ceded it only from low-watermark on this shore; so that, in point of fact Virginia and Kentucky hold jurisdiction over the main channel of the Ohio. The man was shot in a boat upon the Ohio. Then I rose; made to the court what I

flattered myself was an invincible constitutional argument—that a crime being committed upon the river
was out of the jurisdiction of Ohio. Then I was met
by one of those rebuffs which young lawyers are.apt
to meet with. The common-sense of Judge Torrence
overcame the theory of the law. Judge Torrence
said, that although the crime might have been out
of the jurisdiction of Ohio, yet it had been the uniform
custom of Kentucky and Ohio to exercise *concurrent*
jurisdiction over the river; and thus my constitutional
castle in the air tumbled to the ground. Judge Torrence left several sons, who have been conspicuous
among the citizens of Cincinnati, and one among them
has been mayor of Cincinnati and member of the state
senate. Present at this trial was COLONEL NATHANIEL
PENDLETON, who encouraged me in my effort, and was
always friendly to me. His first wife was a daughter of
Jesse Hunt, one of the early settlers of Cincinnati.
She was well known in her day, and admired for her
piety, benevolence, appearance, and character. Col.
Pendleton was a leading member of the bar at that day,
a popular man, and about that time a member of the
state senate. In 1840, he was the candidate of the
Whigs for Congress, in the great Harrison campaign,
and was elected. Two of his sons have been conspicuous in the public and social history of the times,
holding important offices in both state and church.

Another man whose name has been spoken as often
as that of any other man in Cincinnati, was NICHOLAS
LONGWORTH. He was a lawyer, who had come to Cincinnati at an early day, from Newark, New Jersey.
He soon became well known, and continued so until
his death, for some remarkable qualities. He was

very shrewd, sagacious, quick-witted; with great common-sense and acquisitiveness. He had little dignity or learning, but had a quiet good humor, and a
readiness at repartee, which made him popular. In
the latter part of his life, and since his death, he was
chiefly known as acquiring and holding a great estate.
A part of this he acquired by good fortune, a part by
his practice of law; but far the larger part by sagacious investments in real estate, which constantly rose
in value with the growth of the city. He was a friend
of artists. He assisted Powers, I believe, and I know
he did Mrs. Spencer, a noted painter, whom I found on
the Muskingum river, near Marietta. He was also a
noted horticulturist, especially in strawberries and
vines. It is said that in the Mexican War he offered
to raise a regiment on one condition. What was the
condition? Simply, that he might pick out the men!
The offer was not accepted, for however much Cincinnati may have been benefited, the government certainly would not have been. He was said to have assisted the poor liberally, and his house was always
a hospitable one, which Mrs. Longworth and her
daughters made a most cheerful and pleasant place
of resort for young men. At the time I speak
of, Longworth lived on Front street, near the present
Kilgour place. He soon after moved to " Rose Cot-
tage," on Congress (near Pearl) street, opposite to,
and not far from the stone house, on the corner of
Lawrence, built by Daniel Symmes. In a year or two
after, he bought of the United States Bank the square
on the east side of Pike street between Third and
Fourth streets. The fine, large house on it, and which
still remains one of the best and finest in the city, was

built by Martin Baum. In all these residences the Longworth family were hospitable, cheerful, and entertaining.

MARTIN BAUM, whom I mentioned, deserves to be remembered by all who have prospered in Cincinnati, for she had few citizens who contributed more to her service. He was, I think, a German—one of the very first who came to Cincinnati. He was dark and swarthy in complexion, but of pleasant countenance. He was a merchant, of active mind and public spirit. He was one of those who after the war with Great Britain—from 1815 to 1820—embarked in great public enterprises, which were immediately beneficial to the town, but quite disastrous to themselves. All the leading men engaged in them, however remote their professional business from commercial pursuits.

Among those engaged with Baum and others, in getting up banks and manufacturing companies, were General Harrison, Judge Burnet, Dr. Daniel Drake, General Findley, Oliver M. Spencer, and nearly all the best-known citizens. Baum was, I believe, a stockholder in the Miami Exporting Company Bank, the Cincinnati Manufacturing Company, the Sugar Refinery, and similar enterprises. They all ultimately failed, and are scarcely remembered now; and yet they did an almost incalculable benefit to Cincinnati; for they employed many people, circulated a great deal of money, and set in motion a social machinery which determined the fate of Cincinnati, and brought it from a village up to a city. Of course, these public-spirited citizens all lost a part, if not the whole, of their property; but nearly all of them having held real estate, made up by its rise for what they lost in speculation. Baum was obliged to give his fine square and home to the United States Bank in payment of debts, but managed to save, from the despised and weed-covered Deercreek valley, enough for a handsome estate. When the merchants do honor to their profession, they will scarcely find one more worthy of fame than Martin Baum.

Another German, a Prussian officer, and who died that year, was MAJOR ZEIGLER. He, as well as Judge Burnet, was, like Baum, of very dark complexion. He used to speak of Burnet and Baum, as his "two black brothers." I scarcely knew him; but he was one spoken of in society, and who seemed to leave a pleasant memory behind him.

I mentioned the stone house at the corner of Lawrence and Congress streets. This was built by Daniel Symmes, a brother of Judge John Cleves Symmes, the patentee of the Miami country. About the time I came out, in 1825, this house came into the possession of PEYTON SYMMES, his son. No picture of the social life of Cincinnati, from 1815 to 1840, would be complete without Peyton Symmes. He was seen in almost every gathering—at the corner of every street, and at odd times in newspaper offices, and sometimes in the theater, of which he was very fond. If not a man of genius, he had the eccentricities of one, and these eccentricities were entirely out of what may be called the common line of eccentricity. He was unworldly and unselfish, and yet not very generous or benevolent. He was really a literary man of a good deal of talent; but thought the dotting of an "i," or the crossing of a "t," was a matter of supreme importance. He was great on "hyphens" and "italics."

Accordingly, when an article was to be printed, he was the terror of the type-setters. He would publish a paragraph, or a couple of stanzas, and go to the printing-office half dozen times to see that the "hyphens" and the "commas" were exactly right. In this he was wiser than many writers; for, undoubtedly, the correctness of printing an article is like good dress to a lady, and does much to set off natural beauty. With the same zeal with which he pursued dots and commas he pursued "puns." He was the great punster of the town; and there was scarcely anything he could not make a pun upon. Sometimes people were annoyed by his pun-making; but, in general, they liked it, and were glad to have something to laugh at. Another practice he had was pencil portrait taking. He had real genius for that; but his pencil portraits, while they were generally very accurate, often inclined to caricatures. Symmes would sometimes be found at a party, standing in a corner, with a large white card, pencil in hand, taking the portrait of some stranger. He would have dozens of these portraits in his pockets. When the Duke of Saxe-Weimer was in Cincinnati he was much amused with this eccentricity. When an American gentleman met the Duke on the Rhine, he asked about several persons in Cincinnati. He described Longworth and asked about him, and about "the man who took pictures with a pencil on cards." With a love for literature and a love of ease, and no habit of industry, Symmes, who had early advantages of property and business, closed his life with little of either. He was one of those who please and interest living society, but who leave no impressions for posterity. The water is stirred for a moment and closes forever.

Among the noted, and certainly the most important members of society, are the clergy, and I will here describe the clergy of Cincinnati in 1825, as far as my memory can call them up. The first church in Cincinnati was the First Presbyterian Church, which was built on the corner of Main and Fourth streets, where it stands now. It was still the most important church in the city, although several others had been built. The pastor of the church was the Rev. JOSHUA L. WILSON, and after making due allowance for generals, lawyers, and merchants, there was no man in the Cincinnati of that day more noted, more respected, or more remarkable. Personally, I knew little of him, but his name and acts in society were known to everybody. He was a man amiable in character, just in life, of great authority, and scarcely less pugnacity. With strong opinions and strong character, he thought what was worth preaching was worth fighting for. So, though no Ishmaelite, his hand was uplifted against the Ishmaelites when they came in his way. About the 1st of June, 1812, two volunteer companies of Cincinnati were about to join the army of Hull, marching for Canada. They, with a large congregation, assembled in the First Presbyterian Church to hear a parting sermon from Dr. Wilson. My father and myself were among the number. The doctor took his text from Jeremiah: "Cursed be he that dealeth deceitfully, and cursed be he that keepeth back his sword from blood." Whether the sermon corresponded with the warlike character of the text, I was too young to notice. But there is no doubt of

the doctor's zeal in a war for the country or a war for
the church. Wilson took the Bible in the simplicity
of faith and its terms literally. It is said he never
would have a portrait or picture in his house, because
it was an image. He was a strict Calvinist, and
thought he should earnestly contend for the faith
which was once delivered unto the saints. Accordingly, when the controversy of 1836–'37 came on, he
was clad in battle array, or, in the language of the
Scots, entered on the foray. One of the first acts of
the war was to call the men who differed with Wilson,
Breckinridge, and others of the old warriors, a "New
School," although those who heard Beman, Beecher,
Fisher, and others preach, could never tell in what the
doctrines of the "New School" differed from those
of the others. However, the controversy had not at
this time began, and Dr. Wilson, as pastor of the First
Presbyterian Church, was pursuing the peaceful tenor
of his way. He was a beloved pastor in his own congregation, respected by the people, and many years
after died much lamented.

The Second Presbyterian Church had now come
into existence, and was, I believe, worshiping on Race
street, in an old building, which was said to be the
same occupied originally by the first church.

At this time there was only one Roman Catholic
church in the city, and that was near where St. Xa-
vier Church now is, on Sycamore street. The preacher
at that time was Bishop Fenwick, the first Roman
Catholic bishop in Ohio. I remember one bright
Sunday in summer to have strolled into that church
to hear what the bishop would say. I forget what
was the text or the subject; but I remember to have

been very much struck with his illustration of the doctrine of good works. He represented a man as going up to the gates of heaven, and St. Peter weighed his good deeds on one scale and his evil deeds on another. The good a little predominated, and into heaven he was received. Bishop Fenwick was much respected in his own church._ The first Catholic church in Ohio—St. Joseph's, in Perry county—was consecrated by the then Rev. Edward Fenwick in 1818. He was a native of Maryland, and a member of the order of St. Dominic.

At the same time there was only one Lutheran church in Cincinnati. This stood on the north side of Third street, just east of Broadway, on the original site of Fort Washington. For a long time this was a small but earnest congregation, which a few years after removed to Sixth street. It was several years before the German immigration became large, and then the Lutheran churches increased in number and magnitude.

I do not know much of the Methodist and Baptist preachers of that day, but some men among them were quite remarkable. Among them was "FATHER BURKE," who occasionally preached in the next few years, but was now postmaster. He was a Southern man, and had many of the prejudices of the South. He seemed to have lost his voice, and always spoke low and in guttural tones. He was always chewing tobacco, and being a postmaster, was always a Democrat. He was a strong Methodist, and seemed an amiable man. Speaking of him brings up the memory of some other people connected with the post-office. When we left Cincinnati in 1812, the post-

master was COLONEL WILLIAM RUFFIN.   His office was
on Front street, near Lawrence.   You may judge from
this fact that there was very little of Cincinnati west
of Main street in 1812.   Just before we started for the
East, we were at the house of Dr. Drake, on Sycamore street, just below Fourth street.   It was then I
witnessed the great tornado, and one of the things I
remember was that there were no houses above Fourth
street and east of Sycamore, except the "Sargent
House," in the center of the square bounded by Fourth
and Broadway.   Looking southeast, we could see as
far as Front and Lawrence, with only here and there
a house intervening.   The bottom below Third and
above Front was even then wet and swampy, and in
winter was frozen over, and furnished skating for the
boys.   But we must return to the post-office.   The
daughter of Colonel Ruffin married MAJOR WILLIAM
OLIVER, who, when Harrison was elected president,
also became postmaster.   When quite young, Oliver
had been a volunteer soldier at the siege of Fort
Meigs, and performed good service.   In after times he
was one of the original proprietors of Toledo, and his
daughter, Mrs. Hall, is still a proprietor there.   Oliver
was an amiable and intelligent gentleman, and to the
hospitalities of Major and Mrs. Oliver, I was after-
wards indebted for many a pleasant hour.

Returning to the clergy.   There appeared upon the
stage in 1825 one whom I thought quite a remarkable
man.   This was JOHN P. DURBIN (now Dr. Durbin),
high in the confidence of the Methodist Church.   Mr.
Durbin was this year appointed professor in the Augusta (Kentucky) College.   It was after this, however, that he preached in Cincinnati.   I heard him

several times, and always found him eloquent .and
earnest. He was one of the very few men whom I
thought orators. He was not striking in either imagery or argument, and yet he carried his audience
immediately along with him by the fervor of his
thought and the grace of his manner. He would
begin with a very low voice, and gradually ascend
and warm with his subject. Why he did not continue
a popular preacher I do not know. He was advanced
high in the church, but put to other work.

There were, I think, already (in 1825) two Episcopal churches, Christ's and St. Paul's. Christ's (now
on Fourth street) was the original Episcopal Church
in Cincinnati, and it was for several years the only
one. My family having been Episcopalians, this was
the Church I attached myself to. At this time the
pulpit was vacant, and I was one of the original meeting which called the Rev. B. P. AYDELOTTE. He ministered to the church for many years, and it has grown
up to be one of the largest and most efficient churches.
Dr. Aydelotte, in after years, became president of
Woodward College, and has since been an author and
philanthropist—in all situations adorning, by his life
and worth, the profession to which he belongs.

Of St. Paul's, which either began at this time or
soon after, the Rev. SAMUEL JOHNSTON was pastor,
who was highly esteemed by the congregation, and
whose name has been held in grateful remembrance.
Such was the general state of the church and clergy
in 1825. The city had more churches in proportion
to its population than it has now ; but I do n't think
the standard of religion was any higher. It is true
the immigration from Europe of many free-thinkers,

the multiplication of amusements, the worldly spirit, and the fashionable life and luxury which are so apparent on the surface of society, gives an impression that the church has not grown much in numbers and strength; but a closer examination will show that the church never was so strong, so earnest, or so effective in its work, as it is to-day.

Let us now look at the bar. Lawyers will always be, as a profession, men of mark and influence in society, because they are, in the average, the best educated class, and because they have most to do with business, and because the law commands respect. At this time there could not have been more than forty lawyers at the bar, and three or four of them had really retired from practice. In this small body were several men of mark and influence—men of mind, and weight, and character—some of whom had influence on the nation. I will mention two or three. At the head of the bar, undoubtedly, though now retired from practice, was JACOB BURNET. This gentleman was the son of Dr. Burnet. of Newark, New Jersey, a distinguished man in the Revolution. Jacob studied law, and about 1797 came out to Cincinnati, where he subsequently married Miss Rebecca Wallace, daughter of the former pastor of the Presbyterian Church, and ever after continued to reside in Cincinnati. Burnet at first boarded at the tavern on Front street, kept by Griffin Yeatman. Public houses for travelers then, and for thirty years after, had only two names, "taverns" and houses of "private entertainment." The former were plain, honest taverns, and the latter more like private houses. "Hotels," "restaurants," "saloons," and a whole class of modern hostelries, were

unknown, and so were also the enormous prices and
notorious shams of public houses in this day. Good
board, lodging, and reasonable comforts could be had
then, and for thirty years after, for one-third the prices
of the present day. What have we gained with our
enormous prices and imitation of European shams?
Luxury, intemperance, extravagance, peculation,
fashion, and ambition, which, in people without fixed
principles, lead to unbounded desires and unconscion-
able means for their gratification. There was intemperance then, and much of it in the highest classes
of society, and beyond doubt we have in that respect
improved. But there were no low grog-shops at
every corner, tempting and seducing workingmen, and
thus impairing the very strength of society. Burnet
boarded at Yeatman Tavern, on Front street, a short
distance from Fort Washington, associating with the
officers and gentlemen of the then village of Cincinnati, which he well described.

Here I want to say a word for " Old Griff," as he
was called fifty years afterward. His tavern was
well liked by his customers, and I know of no
one who was for half a century so popular in
Cincinnati. Years after the time I speak of he
left tavern-keeping, and was elected recorder of the
county, an office which now has immense business,
but was then of small dimensions. " Old Griff "
did his business well, and with his plain, blunt honest-
ness, satisfying everybody. Often I have carried deeds
to the office and found him sitting in the same old
chair, writing in the record book, looking up with a
smile, and spitting out tobacco, of which he was a
great chewer. The host of the Front Street Tavern,

though not a great man, was a better one, who thought nothing human beyond his care. Such a character was the puzzle and opprobrium of politicians, who would nominate somebody else for recorder, but were invariably defeated. "Old Griff" kept his chair in the recorder's office until death laid him in the grave. At his tavern, Burnet, as I have said, for some time boarded, and was intimate with the officers of the Garrison, in Fort Washington. With one of them he became a life-long friend, and at length did much to make him President of the United States. This was WILLIAM HENRY HARRISON, then a lieutennant in the Fort, who having escaped the danger of intemperance, then abounding among the officers, and the dangers of disease, of field, and flood, was, in 1840, elected President of the Republic. No man did so much for his election as Jacob Burnet, whose intimacy with him began in Fort Washington. Burnet had come out as a lawyer, and in that profession he began and grew with the city, in whose name, and fame, and interests he was at all times no small part. In that day, to practice law at Cincinnati required the lawyer to ride the circuit. And what was the circuit? No less than the whole Northwestern Territory, now comprising five states and ten millions of people. In the circuit which Burnet rode, were Marietta, Detroit, and Vincennes. He would tell of hair-breadth escapes by field and flood. Here there were almost impassable swamps, and there unfordable streams. One night they were belated in making a certain point, and their horses stopped suddenly and would not go. They got off and had to camp there. Next morning they found the horses had stopped just at the edge of a precipice

which overhung Wolfe Creek. At other times they
would stop in an Indian village* and be caressed by
greasy squaws, and joked with by swarthy warriors.
Such was a part of the Cincinnati lawyers' practice in
the close of the last century. Burnet says that when
he came to the bar, there were nine lawyers, who, all
but one, became intemperate. The officers of Fort
Washington were hard drinkers, and this led the citizens to be intemperate. In a few years, Burnet was
the sole survivor of the early Cincinnati bar. When I
came back, Burnet had retired from active business,
but was still the most influential private citizen.

He had taken great interest in the early improvements of the city, of which I have spoken, and yet at
this time, when retired, he was spoken of as without
public spirit, and rather illiberal. The very reverse was
the fact, and to illustrate how much was done by the
early citizens of Cincinnati to aid its progress, I will
mention what he once told me in a conversation upon
public improvements. He said that he had paid for
public enterprise full $80,000, and lost nearly the
whole of it. He was a stockholder in the Cincinnati
Manufacturing Company, the Sugar Refinery, the Iron
Foundry, at the corner of Lawrence street, the Miami Exporting Company Bank, and perhaps some
others. The stock in these companies was a total loss,
except the bank, whose assets subsequently paid something. The upshot of all this was that he became
largely indebted to the United States Bank, and for
that debt, sold the square on which the Burnet House
and Shillito's store now stands, for $25,000. This was

---

* Burnet's Notes on the Northwest Territory.

in 1825, and the price was about one-fortieth part
of what the ground alone is now worth. Burnet, however, held a large amount of city lots, in what was
then almost out of the city, and to-day is the very
heart of it, where the Second Presbyterian Church now
stands, and extending through to Sixth street market.
It need not be supposed, therefore, that Burnet, Baum,
and other enterprising citizens of that day died poor.
On the contrary, some of them left large estates, and
nearly all had a competency. Judge Burnet lived
nearly thirty years after the financial storm had passed
by. He had ceased the practice of the law, but in the
meanwhile entered upon public life. A few years after,
he was elected judge of the Supreme Court of Ohio,
where, as in everywhere else, he was distinguished for
great acuteness of intellect and solid integrity. Yet,
Burnet was by nature and by habit of mind, a lawyer
—that is, not merely a man acquainted with law, but
a man who always has a side, and who thinks, whether
by a virtue of a fee, or of his own opinion, that his
side ought to prevail, unless he changes for cause. It
was related of Burnet, in his early practice, that he
defended a man for stealing an ax, and by his ability
had him acquitted. Just then, as Burnet looked round
for his client, the man had slipped out without paying
the fee. Upon this, Burnet said: " Well, I really
think that man was guilty after all."

Burnet, on the bench of the Supreme Court, manifested a good deal of the same acuteness, and the same
one-sidedness. He gave dissenting opinions, which
manifested more of his own opinion than of law. No
man ever questioned his integrity, but no man ever
knew him swerve from his own side. After the Whig

party was formed, Burnet was elected to the United States Senate. When asked about his politics Burnet would smile and say, "I am a Federalist, sir." But no man was a stronger Whig, and few men a stronger partisan. It was impossible for him not to have been a partisan. In the Senate of the United States, as in all the remainder of his life, he belonged to the great Whig party, and was fully up to the level of its great leaders, Clay and Webster. He was intimate with them, with Harrison, Crittenden, and others of the brilliant circle of public men who have not been equaled since, and whom to think of makes me almost doubt whether this age of leveling has not also leveled genius and dignity. Judge Burnet was present in the senate when Daniel Webster delivered his great speech in reply to Colonel Hayne. Much as I have read and admired that speech, I got a higher idea of it from his descrip- tion of the manner and effect of it. He described it as most impressively delivered, and as listened to with wrapt attention. Well it might be, for it was not only a most perfect piece of oratory in itself, more forcible and argumentative, but very much like some of Cicero's. But it was also *the* argument, the reply, which annihi- lates the argument for nullification and secession. It was a demonstration that such proceedings must ulti- mately result in war. If Webster could have known or foreseen the effects of that speech on the minds of the young men in the country, he would have thought the presidency a little thing compared with this crown of his reward in forming the public mind of the nation. With so cool a temperament and so acute an intellect, Judge Burnet was a witness, who may be trusted for the truth of history. The most important part Burnet took in politics was that of a delegate to the Whig convention at Harrisburg, in 1839. He was there the leading representative from Ohio, in favor of General Harrison. He had been, as I have said, intimate with Harrison, when the latter was a lieutenant in Fort Washington, and he was a man who never gave up his side. So when Harrison was brought out for the presidency he became a strong advocate of the General, and the hero of Tippecanoe never had an abler or more active adherent than Burnet. I was told by a delegate from New York, who was in favor of Scott, that no man in the convention did as much for Harrison as Burnet. The result is now history, Harrison, ninth President of the United States, and Burnet, his advocate, now lie in that silent grave where presidents and judges, heroes and their followers, are alike leveled with the dust.

Two or three other members of the bar may be mentioned on account of their subsequent career. One of these was, DAVID K. ESTE, who came to Cincinnati about 1813. He, like Burnet and Longworth, was a Jerseyman, and, like them, very successful. He was a graduate of Nassau Hall (Princeton), and, at the time of his death, the oldest living graduate. He died in his ninety-first year, and one of several members of the Cincinnati Bar who have shown remarkable longevity. He was a good lawyer, but chiefly distinguished for courtesy of manners, propriety of conduct, and success in business. Like Burnet, he was one of those cool and careful temperaments, who are incapable of being excited beyond a certain point, and who never commit themselves out of the way. He was several years president judge of the common

pleas, and acquired the respect and esteem of the bar.
With that he also acquired a large fortune, made by
investing the surplus avails of his practice in real
estate, which rose rapidly in value. Here I may add,
that while we see many people who have accumulated
large property by trade, I will venture to say that the
Jerseymen, who came to Cincinnati, and who all stuck
to real estate, got more property in the aggregate than
all the leading merchants of the city. Este died at
ninety-one, and his longevity brings to my mind some
things he related of Dr. Rush, of Philadelphia. His
brother persuaded him to attend medical lectures one
winter. He was much interested, and told me the last
remarks of the celebrated professor. In his last lecture,
Dr. Rush said: "Young gentlemen, I have taught you
the resources of the profession, I have told you of the
necessity of temperance, of air, of exercise, and diet,
but one thing I have not told you. The exercise of the
mind is as necessary as that of the body. Let no day
pass without reading or reflecting upon some subject
for an hour or two. Young gentlemen, your health is
in your own hands." Judge Este was always careful
of his health, and often quoted Dr. Rush as authority.
He was an Episcopalian in the church, a gentleman in
society, and a Republican in politics. After a worthy
life, he died respected by all classes.

Another lawyer of that day, who died recently in his
ninetieth year, was JAMES W. GAZLEY. He came to
Cincinnati at an early day, and practiced law, but was
rather given to politics. In 1819–1820, he was elected
to congress from the Cincinnati district, against General Harrison. It was rather surprising at the time,
since one would have thought that such a man as Har-

rison would have been elected at once. The election was affected, however, by circumstances arising out of the great financial difficulties which were then in mid-crisis. Some question arose about aristocracy, and Gazlay represented the plebeian interests and was elected to congress. He was not re-elected, and after that did little at the bar. In the latter part of his life he retired to the country, and was much engaged in writing. He was a patriotic man, lived respectably, and died old.

NATHANIEL WRIGHT was another of the old lawyers, who died recently at eighty-eight years of age. He was a native of New Hampshire, and began life, as many lawyers have done, as a school-teacher. He came to Cincinnati several years after Este, married a niece of Judge Burnet, and soon got into good practice. He was one of the founders of the Second Presbyterian Church, of which he was an elder until death. Mr. Wright was a good lawyer, but was never in public life.

Another noted lawyer at the bar was BELLAMY STORER. He was a New England man, I believe from Maine. He had a remarkably quick and sprightly mind, also a certain species of humorous wit. In 1825, when the "Crisis and Emporium" was published by Samuel J. Browne, Storer was said to be one of the "twenty-five" editors of that paper. I suppose, in fact, the young lawyers, who were Adams men, wrote for the "Crisis," of which, Browne, who lisped a little, used to say, he was "the thole editor and proprietor." He may have been, and yet the twenty-five young men wrote for it. Storer was, I think, one of the first three judges elected to the Superior Court, of which he was an able judge and ornament until near his death. He was once member of congress, and became one of the principal members of Christ's Church. " Horace in Cincinnati" described his then life as "youthful, gay, and wild," but he ended it, at the age of eighty, as one who had been a judge in the land, a legislator, and an elder of the church.

I must hasten on. " *Horace in Cincinnati*," whose account of the bar in 1821 was very just, says, in his 16th Ode:

> With person of gigantic size,
> With thund'ring voice, and piercing eyes,
> When great *Stentorius* deigns to rise,
>   Adjacent crowds assemble,
> To hear a sage the laws expound,
> In language strong, by reasoning sound,
> Till, though yet not guilty found,
>   The culprits fear and tremble.

This is the picture of "Joe Benham," as he was called. He was not a "sage," but he was an orator, and few men were more impressive in power and manner. I walked into the court-house one afternoon, when a boy was on trial for stealing some trifling article. Except the jury, there were not a dozen people in the house ; but a more eloquent and pathetic appeal than Benham made for that boy, I have scarcely ever heard. Benham died in rather early life. He was the father of Mrs. George D. Prentice, of Louisville, and will probably be remembered by his descendants.

Mr. Corry, father of the present William M. Corry, was then at the bar, and, I believe, mayor of Cincinnati. Of him, *Horace* says:

"Slow to obey what 'er to call,
 And yet a faithful friend to all;
 In person rather stout and tall,
  In habits quite domestic.
Devaux in elegance is found
To run the same unvaried round;
Ne'er grov'ling lowly on the ground,
 Nor sailing off majestic."

In 1825, there were also at the bar two sons of General William Lytle, who had been an early pioneer, and was a gentleman of standing and wealth. WILLIAM LYTLE, the eldest son, was spoken of in the highest terms both for talents and character. He was consumptive, and died young. ROBERT T. LYTLE was for several years a marked man in Cincinnati. His father was a warm personal friend of General Jackson, whom he was thought to resemble in many things. Robert was a young man of decided talent, and popular appearance and manners. So about 1832, when Jackson was at the height of his power, Robert Lytle was elected to congress, and became a protegé of the General. When the war on the United States Bank began, Lytle, of course, sided with Jackson; but that did not at all suit his constituents, especially merchants and manufacturers, who depended largely on the bank for money. So, in the election of 1834 there was a revolution in the politics of Hamilton county, and he was defeated, as I have related, by Bellamy Storer. Mr. Lytle lived a few years longer, but died at an early age, and left behind him the memory of a brilliant, generous, and popular man.

I have said enough to show the character of the bar of Cincinnati in 1825. It will be seen that in no larger number than forty, it certainly had as large a proportion of gifted and remarkable men as perhaps ever adorned a similar body, and yet I have left out some (one in particular, to be mentioned hereafter) who were fully equal in talent and standing to the others. It is noticeable that there were among them some examples of uncommon longevity. Burnet, Gazley, Este, Wright, and Storer averaged eighty-five years of age, and two of them reached ninety years. In the year 1825 there was a little society of not a dozen young lawyers assembled for mutual instruction, and at the end of half a century, four of them were living, and of the forty lawyers at the bar then, eight were living. This shows that the pursuit of intellectual professions is by no means unfavorable to health; but, on the contrary, the regular exercise of the mind, and a uniform life of business, aids, rather than obstructs, a life of health and happiness. In connection with this, we may note the remarkable fact, stated by Judge Burnet, that of the nine lawyers of the bar in 1795, all but one perished sots. It is not, therefore, labor, or intellectual excitement, or even business cares, which shorten life, but the irregularities, and exhaustions, and excesses of indulgence and intemperance. The bar of this day has very little intemperance comparatively, for all things are relatives. This is one evidence that society is not going backward, and that we may expect better things for the future.

Having described all that I know of ministers and lawyers, let me proceed to notice doctors and editors, and here we shall find a much less harmonious scene, but some characters who had quite as much influence on society.

CHAPTER XI.

Dr. Daniel Drake, his genius and character—Dr. Go-
forth—Cincinnati in 1805—Medical Practice; Drake
founds the Ohio Medical College; is turned out by his
Colleagues; " Horace in Cincinnati;" Drake's Mon-
ody on the Death of his Wife—Moses Dawson—
Charles Hammond, Editor and Lawyer—States Rights
in Ohio—Literary Institutions—Hiram Powers—Poets
— W. D. Gallagher.

In 1825, and for many years after, DANIEL DRAKE
was much the most distinguished physician of Cincinnati. He was a man of genius, of strong intellect,
of warm temperament, zealous and ambitious. For
forty years he was engaged in nearly all public affairs
—the founder of some, and the friend of all good institutions—a life-long teacher in his profession, and
a writer of no small eminence. In his little book
called the " PICTURE OF CINCINNATI," he did more for
this city than probably any one man had then done,
and should be held in grateful remembrance by those
who profited by his labors. He was a native of New
Jersey, born in 1785. His father—a plain farmer—
moved to Kentucky, near Maysville, and subsequently
to Cincinnati. The young Daniel seems for some
cause to have been destined to the medical profession
at an early day. He came to Cincinnati while he was
quite a youth, studied, and afterward became a partner, with the then noted DR. WILLIAM GOFORTH. Of

this gentleman, Drake, in some of his discourses, has given an interesting account. Goforth was one of the earliest and best of the medical practitioners. He was a gentleman of the old school. With a gold-headed cane, a wig, and stately step, Goforth went forth. Of the kind of practice in those days we can get an idea by hearing that the learned doctor would be called out in the night to visit a patient, four miles off, on Mill creek ; ride in the dark, sometimes leading his horse ; and then get twenty-five cents in specie, besides a bite for his horse. The doctor, it was said, was a very kindly man, but quite oblivious of the necessity of collecting or keeping money. Of course, he did not succeed very well, and some years after went to New Orleans. I have a characteristic letter from him to my father, in which, after relating his experiences, he concludes with " New Orleans is hell upon earth." This was probably a correct, however brief, picture of it at that time. It was bad for Goforth, for he got the liver-complaint, and returned to Cincinnati to die.

At the time Drake studied with Goforth, the town of Cincinnati was a dirty, and, what some persons will scarcely believe, even a marshy place. I have already said, that the bottom, below East Third street to the river, was a marsh, the river bank being higher than the land back. This marsh was frozen over in winter, and made a skating-place for boys. So also Fifth street, where the government buildings are now erecting, was an alder swamp. Drake relates that, when studying medicine, he resorted to the bowers of Deer creek. This dirty little run had high banks, overgrown with trees, shrubs, and flowers. There

Drake, with his books, and while listening to the song of birds, the croaking of frogs, and the rustling of the wind, studied the science which has made Hippocrates and Galen, Boerhave and Rush, famous. He was very fond of natural scenery, and in the latter part of his life wrote " Reminiscential Letters," which are full of the most beautiful descriptions, thoughts, and sentiments.

Drake began his practice young ; went into partnership with Goforth, which partnership did not flourish very well. It was soon dissolved, and Drake had managed to get enough to take him to Philadelphia, there to hear the lectures of the celebrated Dr. Rush and his colleagues. Improved and stimulated by intercourse with great minds, he returned to Cincinnati, to begin a career which, in this country, is unique in the variety of its incidents, the magnitude of its labors, and the usefulness of its work. The country was new ; the town was young ; society miscellaneous ; and every public institution had to be founded, and the social character to be formed. There was no man better fitted for this than he, and no man did more of it. In the course of this varied career, he was at times involved in bitter controversies, but time smoothed them over, and he lived to forgive, if not forget, his enemies. He was a founder of good things, an author, teacher, and physician. In 1818–1819, he went before the legislature, and presented personally his views on medical education, and procured the charter of the Medical College of Ohio, and of the Commercial Hospital of Cincinnati, both of which remain monuments to his memory. He had been the *first medical student* in Cincinnati, and on the organization of the college became the *first medical professor.* It was this which led him into a great controversy. He fell into the error which the University of Virginia, and several institutions of the West, have fallen into—that of importing professors from abroad, either from Europe or the East. All of these institutions found out their error, and some of them by severe suffering. Drake's medical college suffered. He got his professors from the East; and the medical college opened, in 1821, with the announcement of Daniel Drake, Jesse Smith, Benjamin L. Bohrer, and Elijah Slack as professors. The three last had been imported. Bohrer was an intriguer, who immediately began a cabal to supplant Dr. Drake. There was a great defect in the charter, which made the professors also the trustees; so that, in fact, the majority of the faculty could turn out the others, and elect whom they pleased. Bohrer left of his own accord, but had alienated the other professors from Drake. This occasioned a singular and very ludicrous scene. The three professors met in solemn council, Drake presiding, when Smith moved the expulsion of Drake, and Slack seconded it; whereupon Drake put the motion, and the founder of the Medical College of Ohio was expelled from the institution he had created, by the colleagues whom he had made! The society of Cincinnati was not so large then as not to sympathize with a medical quarrel. The town was soon filled with partisans, and the medical war went on for nearly twenty years. Two years after "Horace in Cincinnati" wrote "Ode 24th," on the Æsculapian war. He says:

> " The warfare was begun
> Long ere we shook with laughter,
>   To see Pilgarlic run,
> And Dr. Pompous after.
>
> " And t' other day we find
> (Here none can think me bouncing)
>   Professor Pill designed
> To give " one Ben " a trouncing.
>   Though famous as a Turk,
> The last seem'd not to mind him,
>   But promptly drew a dirk,
> And popt it in behind him."

This is an actual fact. *Dr. Pill* is supposed to have been Dr. Morehead, an Irish doctor, who was afterward quite a popular physician. " *One Ben* " was Drake's brother Benjamin, who encountered Morehead in the manner described. The incident is trifling, but it illustrates the manners of the day, when Cincinnati was yet a small town, and, of course, partaking in all the feuds and bickerings of its leading men. Twenty years scarcely allayed these quarrels, in which nearly all the then citizens of Cincinnati were engaged.

In 1825, when I arrived in Cincinnati, Drake, whose wife was my cousin, had apparently got through with those quarrels—although they broke out subsequently. He was a bankrupt, financially ; had been expelled, in the way described, from the institution he had founded ; and was now turning round to see what the world would be to him. He was poor, and nearly all Cincinnati were also. Even Burnet had been compelled to sell his house and square for what turned out to be a song ; and Baum, just after building his fine residence on Pike street, had sold that and the whole square to the Bank of the United States. The wealth-iest citizens were those who suffered most. Drake had not been wealthy, but he had gone into the speculations of the day, and become one of the unfortunate victims of the United States Bank. In this condition, and in the spirit of that economy which few now realize, he went into a log cabin, at the foot of the hills, above Liberty street, which he aptly called "Mount Poverty." But he had the practice of his profession, and was altogether too able and brilliant a man to be neglected. In the year 1825 he was making arrangements with Transylvania University, at Lexington, Kentucky, to become a professor there—which he was for several years. In the summer of 1825 he lost his wife, for whose loss he mourned as few ever do. Annually he made a pilgrimage to her tomb, and commemorated her death with an anniversary hymn, for the composition of which he had much aptness. I quote the last three stanzas of that for 1831—in reference to something he did for the then graveyard:

> "Thou lonely widowed bird of night,
>   As on this sacred stone,
> Thou may'st in wandering chance to light,
>   Pour forth thy saddest moan.

> "Ye giddy throng, who laugh and stray
>   Where notes of sorrow sound,
> And mock the funeral vesper lay,
>   Tread not this holy ground.

> "For here my sainted Harriet lies;
>   I saw her hallowed form
> Laid deep below, no more to rise,
>   Before the judgment morn."

The reference to the "giddy throng who laugh and stray" round graveyards was very apt in reference to that of Cincinnati. The principal graveyard at that time—the one set apart to Presbyterians and Episcopalians—was what is now called "Washington Square," between Twelfth and Fourteenth, Race and Elm streets. At this time it was quite full of graves and grown over with weeds, and frequented by idlers of all descriptions. Here the body of Mrs. Drake was deposited, and the doctor immediately set to work to clear and improve the grounds. He got some small subscriptions, cleared off the ground, and planted trees, so that in a short time the grounds assumed a decent and pleasant aspect. It was perhaps well that the home of the dead was soon converted into a park for the living. In the beautiful cemetery of Spring Grove, at least one generation of the dead may rest in peace. More than that can hardly be expected, when we reflect that in twenty years two successive graveyards of the pioneers have been broken up and built upon!

After the death of his wife, Drake removed to Lexington, Ky., but the next year returned to Cincinnati, where, until his death, he was known as teacher, journalist, and author, eminent at home and distinguished abroad. In these characters we shall see him again, and especially in social movements, where he was not only conspicuous, but very useful in his influence.

About this period there were several respectable physicians in Cincinnati, although not distinguished as literary or scientific men. Among them was Dr. Ramsey. He was of Scotch descent, one of the old school gentlemen, stiff, starched, and stately, with his *queue* and high-topped boots, visiting his patients on horseback or in his gig. Then there were Pierson, Jesse Smith, Cramner, Morehead, and others. We can see from this that the medical, as well as the legal faculty, at that time was of a high order of talents and attainments.

Now, if you please, we will turn to a very different order of men, and one which, in all the changes of time, has an immense influence. I mean the newspaper writers. The term "editor" is constantly used in a false sense. The editor of a book or journal or newspaper is the one who makes it up, prepares it, and ushers it before the public. He is not necessarily the writer at all; but, in the economy as well as necessities of nearly all newspapers, the editor is the chief writer, and hence the confusion of terms. At this time, and I mean from 1825 to 1828, Cincinnati had two remarkable newspaper writers. These were MOSES DAWSON and CHARLES HAMMOND. The former (Dawson) was an Irishman, who then published and edited the *Cincinnati Advertiser*, which, in the new formation of parties, become the Jackson, and subsequently the leading Democratic paper of this region. Dawson was a rough, ungainly man, but quite a vigorous writer. He wrote, I think, a life of General Harrison, and as the leader of the rough and uneducated class of the community, although respectable himself, was quite a conspicuous person. I was naturally averse to such people, and so never became much acquainted with him. Some time after this, CHARLES HAMMOND became editor of the CINCINNATI GAZETTE. Hammond, of course, came right into conflict with Moses Dawson, for Hammond was a firm Federalist of the old school, had edited a paper in

Belmont county, Ohio, was an able lawyer, and compromised nothing of his opinions for anybody. Such a man on one side and an Irish Democrat on the other would of course, and actually did, make a literary and political pugilism worthy of Donnybrook. Newspaper conflicts have never been confined to polite usages or tender language. So Dawson and Hammond kept up a running fight which was more worthy of Ireland than of America. There was, however, no equality in the contestants. Hammond was not only an able lawyer, and familiar with the political history of the day, but was one of the sharpest and most vigorous writers. While Hammond was firing rifles, whose balls invariably hit the mark, Dawson would reply with a blunderbuss, heavily charged, but making more noise than execution.

Both these men were jovial companions, and would often meet in a " coffee-house," as the saloons of this day were then called. It was told me, by one who was present, that they would meet at a noted coffee-house on Front street, where they would banter each other over their toddy. Dawson would say: " I'll beat you, Charley," and Hammond would say: " I'll give it to you in the morning." If anyone objects to this undignified proceeding, they will please to remember that it was a counterpart to the convivial scenes of London, when Fox and Pitt frequented the club-rooms. But Hammond had a higher and a nobler office than Dawson or any other editor of the West could then perform. It is singular that no one has prepared a memoir or sketch of this remarkable man. He was born, I think, in Western Virginia, near the Pennsylvania line, at any rate near the border; he set-

tled in Belmont county, Ohio; practiced law, and was
known as an able lawyer, in the day when Doddridge,
of West Virginia, was yet on the stage, and John C.
Wright and Tappen practicing at the same bar. He
had great fondness for politics, and edited the leading
paper of that section. He was a firm Federalist and
opposed the Democratic party at all times. Yet he
was found at one time supporting the leading heresy
of that party, "State Rights." Of this, however, he
quickly repented and made amends by a long, vigorous defense of the true constitutional doctrine. The
occasion of his error was the attempt of the State of
Ohio to tax the United States Bank, branches of
which were established in Cincinnati and Chillicothe.
The state taxed them $50,000 each. The bank re-
fused to pay, and the auditor of state collected the
tax by force. Upon these proceedings, the Circuit
Court of the United States ordered the money to be
refunded, which was done, and a case was made—that
of *Osborne against the Bank of the United States*—which
was ultimately decided in favor of the bank, by the
Supreme Court of the United States. The entire
principle was discussed and finally decided in the case
of *McCollough versus the State of Maryland.* In that
case, the supreme court decided that the charter of the
bank was constitutional, being one of the means appro-
priate to the objects of government; that the bank
had a right to establish offices of discount and deposit
within any state, and that no state had a right to
tax this, or any constitutional means employed by the
Government of the Union for constitutional objects.
This settled that question, but it seems strange now,
and will seem more so in future history, that the State

of Ohio, in 1820 and 1821, deliberately affirmed the States Rights heresy embodied in the Virginia Resolutions of 1798, and protested against the right of the supreme court to adjudicate questions concerning the states. It was a series of decisions in the supreme court which bound the American Union and educated the coming generation into just ideas of nationality. Nevertheless, it took forty years of discussion, of nullification, of secession, and of civil war to terminate this political controversy and settle the American Government upon, we hope, durable foundations. In the proceedings against the bank, it was understood Mr. Hammond was the adviser. Being, however, a consistent believer in law and government, he yielded at once to the decision of the court, and never again advocated the doctrine advanced in the Virginia or the Ohio Resolutions. In fact, the whole affair was an episode in Ohio history, produced, no doubt, by the great and extraordinary financial embarrassments which took place between 1819 and 1823. This controversy began in 1820 and ended in 1824. About this time, Mr. Hammond removed to Cincinnati, where he practiced law, and in a short time, probably 1826, became editor of the *Cincinnati Gazette.* "*Liberty Hall*" was a weekly paper, originally conducted by the Rev. John W. Browne. It was for many years the title of the present *Weekly Gazette*, which was established in an early day. The *Gazette* was a semi-weekly at the time Mr. Hammond took it, and resembled in size and appearance the second-class country papers of the present day. It had been edited by Isaac Burnet, mayor of the city, and a brother of Judge Burnet. Hammond soon made himself felt, although the amount of editorial matter he furnished seems surprisingly small when compared with the ponderous articles of this day. There was a lesson in them, however, which might now be heeded with advantage. He made up in quality what he wanted in quantity. I know of no writer who could express an idea so clearly and so briefly. He wrote the pure old English —the vernacular tongue, unmixed with French or Latin phrases or idioms, and unperverted with any scholastic logic. His language was like himself—plain, sensible, and unaffected. His force, however, lay not so much in this as in his truth, honesty, and courage, those moral qualities which made him distinguished at that day, and would distinguish him now.

In 1828, while editor of the *Gazette*, he edited " TRUTH'S ADVOCATE," a monthly, which, for about a year, was published by the friends of Adams and Clay against the claims of GENERAL JACKSON. Several historical and some very able articles appeared in it. Jackson's illegal marriage (for it was illegal, although morally right), his duels, his arbitrary conduct, his despotic character, were all shown up in strong colors, and the account was, with little exception, true. Yet, I could not see that it made any impression upon the people, who looked upon Jackson as a patriotic man, who had fought the battle of New Orleans and beat the British. The popular sentiment was expressed by Counselor Sampson, of New York, in some speech before a jury, in which an old soldier was a party. " This war-worn soldier," said he, " who bled upon the field of New Orleans—that death-bed of British Glory ! " The popular feeling against the British continued many years after the war, and Jackson was a sort of popular synonym for the Anti-British feeling. In truth, Jackson had more than this form of patriotism. He was in every sense patriotic, and the country owes a debt of gratitude to him, for his stern opposition to the nullification scheme, and to all those anti-national ideas, which afterward resulted in secession and civil war. His determined course postponed the time of the outbreak and strengthened the feeling of Union, which afterward sustained the government. That his administration contained much evil, as well as some good, no future historian will deny. His election brought on a fierce and bitter controversy, which continued for thirty years, and which terminated only in the greater controversy upon the question of slavery.

At that time, HENRY CLAY was the great political leader in the West, to whose fortune, both Ohio and Kentucky steadily adhered. Hammond was the personal and political friend of Clay, often practicing in the same courts. So he made war on Jackson, and was unrelenting in his attacks. Although he failed to defeat Jackson, he laid the foundation for the overthrow of his successor, Van Buren. Mr. Hammond, although exercising a wide influence on politics and public men, was always a private citizen. He seemed not ambitious, but on one or two occasions, he rejected office for other considerations. He was asked to accept the place of supreme judge, but conscientiously refused it, because he knew himself to be in some measure intemperate. The rejection was more honorable to him than any office could have been. His opposition to slavery and its influence on the government was firm, consistent, and powerful. Probably no public writer did more than he to form a just and reasonable anti-slavery sentiment. In fine, as a writer of great ability, and a man of large acquirements and singular integrity, Hammond was scarcely equaled by any man of his time. We shall hear more of him as I proceed.

In addition to the pulpit, the bar, and the press, all ably manned, there was, at this time, some germs of a literary society. JOHN P. FOOTE, a native of Connecticut, had been for several years a book publisher, and took a great interest in literary matters. He, in connection with some young men, of whom Benjamin Drake, John H. James, and Lewis Noble were, I believe, a part, had established a literary paper, which continued for three or four years. In the year 1822, appeared the odes of " Horace in Cincinnati," which, at the time, caused quite a sensation ; for they were, in most cases, descriptive of well-known persons and scenes. They were republished in a little volume, without the author's consent, and were, as he said in a note, on subjects so local and transitory as to be of little general interest. Nevertheless, many of his descriptions were very accurate. The author was not known at their publication, but was soon after found to be THOMAS PIERCE, educated, I think, a Quaker, and in business a hardware merchant. He died many years since, and, except in some library, " Horace in Cincinnati " died with him.

At this time also there were the wrecks of several literary schools. I have already mentioned that Wilson and Drake were the originators of the " Lancasterian School." Lancaster was an English educational reformer who was just then in vogue, with a new fashion in education—for education has its fashions, as all other things. His system was that of mutual instruction among the pupils. Drake obtained the charter of the Lancasterian Seminary, as he did those of the Medical College of Ohio and the Commercial Hospital of Cincinnati. The Lancasterian School was in operation several years, when it gave place to Cincinnati College. This institution was chartered in 1819, and was part of a system of institutions Drake had devised. He was in high spirits at this time, and wrote to one of his friends, that many thousands of dollars had been subscribed to the seminary; that the medical college and hospital would soon be in operation; that there was a school of arts proposed; and that Cincinnati would soon be, what Lexington had been called, the Athens of the West. It was precisely, however, the literary part which failed. After a brief trial of the Lancasterian Seminary, Cincinnati College was substituted in its place, and for three or four years had classes, under the presidency of the Rev. Elijah Slack. Several young men who afterward rose to some distinction, were in this college; but unendowed and dependent only on local support, the college soon ceased its regular classes, and its charter was kept alive only by a primary school. In subsequent years, it was again revived, only to die out in the same manner. The trustees had, however, established a law school, and recently two lectureships —one of Christian philosophy, and the other of Christian jurisprudence. In this way the institution is successful, and will, perhaps, in this form, do the work which the pioneers of education intended.

At the time I returned to Cincinnati all these institutions were comparatively wrecks, and it remained for the coming generation to reveal and recreate the means of education in the metropolis of the Ohio Valley. Drake, Burnet, Lytle, Spencer, Foote, Wilson, and other pioneers in that liberal enterprise, have long since passed away, and few of this generation remember their worth; yet it was, in proportion to their day and means, greater than anything done since. Over their graves there is not a single monument which gives to the passing stranger an idea of their work, and the future city of Cincinnati, great in arts and population, will know little of its founders or or its benefactors.

Some time after this—anticipating a little—I first heard of HIRAM POWERS. I was passing down Main street, when I noticed some posts at the corner—perhaps Third street—which had been put, I believe, for lanterns. But, whatever the purpose, I noticed carved heads upon them. These heads were so far superior to any of the common wood carving that I was surprised, and asked who did them. I was told Hiram Powers. He was then, I think, in the employment of Luman Watson, who was for a long time a clockmaker in the city. He was soon noticed for his remarkable facility in that line, and, I may add, in many things which required ingenuity. In fact, Powers was a genius, one out of only half a dozen I ever knew. Soon after that—probably about 1830—he was employed by Dorfeule, who kept a museum near the corner of Main and Pearl streets, to make what was for several years called the " Infernal Regions." I believe he was first engaged to make wax figures. In a construction of the " Infernal Regions " he came as near what might be imagined the reality as one could come. He had the fires burning—Rhadamanthus, the Judge—darkness enveloping the whole, and an invisible, to the visitor, electrical battery, which nearly knocked down the unfortunate visitor who happened to touch the railing around. This was a popular affair, and remained in vogue several years, when Dorfieule gave up the museum and retired. Powers was with him for a considerable time before he engaged in sculpture. How he succeeded in that the world knows. I have never seen a memoir of him, although a very interesting one might be made. Some encyclopœdia notices have been made, but fell far short of giving a true view of his life and genius.

About this time (from 1828 to 1835) there were two poets in Cincinnati, who, I presume, are now entirely forgotten. They are mentioned in Everest's "Poets of Connecticut," for they were both natives of that state. One was Hugh Peters, a young lawyer, and much esteemed. He was a man of talent and rising at the bar. He began writing for the *New England Review* when in college, but wrote several pieces in Cincinnati. He was the author of "My Native Land," a patriotic and pleasing poem. One verse seems to have been prophetic:

> "And I have left thee, home, alone,
>   A pilgrim from thy shore;
> The wind goes by with hollow moan,
> I hear it sigh a warning tone,
>   'You see your home no more.'
> I'm cast upon the world's wide sea,
>   Torn like an ocean weed;
> I'm cast away, far, far from thee;
> I feel a thing I can not be,
>   A bruised and broken reed."

He was found drowned in the Ohio, in June, I think, 1832. It was supposed he had got up, as he had done the night previous, in an unconscious state, harassed by care or trouble, and gone into the river.

The other name was that of Edward A. McLaughlin. He was a printer, but led a wild and adventurous life, being in Cincinnati some ten or fifteen years. In 1841, he published the " Lovers of the Deep," in four cantos. It was founded on an incident connected with the wreck of the unfortunate steamer Pulaski.

Anticipating time, I may say that about the same period, William D. Gallagher began his career as poet, editor, and writer. He is the best known of all the Western poets, and deservedly so. Some of his productions are very superior, and ought to live in any collection of American poetry. It has been, perhaps, unfortunate for his literary fame that his life has been so various and so employed in business, that he has not been able to woo the muses as assiduously as those ladies require. At least, I can imagine that he had ' the traits and talent to have excelled in poetry.

CHAPTER XII.

Society in Cincinnati — Parties — Theaters — Actors —
Prevalent Diseases—Taking the Census—Mechanics—
Strange Imposition—General Ross.

MY introduction to the society of Cincinnati was
easy and general. My father went with me, and nobody was better known than he. It was just then
that his friend and agent, Martin Baum, had built the
fine house on Pike street, I have already mentioned.
Baum never gave but one party in that house, and I
was there. It was in the summer of 1825, and was
given in the afternoon. We went at four o'clock, and
came away before dark. It was, I believe, only a reception for gentlemen, who had a pleasant time with
the usual refreshments. Several years after that, I
was present in the same house at one of the largest parties I ever attended in Cincinnati, given by Mr. Longworth. Parties are not a test of society, unless compared
at very distant periods of time. A fashionable party is
always the same, unless in the differences only, which
difference of means causes. There will be greater or
less numbers, greater or less display of dress or ornaments, according to the means of the giver, or the
state of the markets, or the fashion of the times. The
lapse of half a century has caused little difference in
the elements of a fashionable party. The cynic and
the philosopher are very apt to denounce it; but actual observation of society shows that even this has

its uses. A fashionable party is almost always given to pay social debts, to celebrate an occasion, or to honor a stranger. If a person has the means to do it, these are commendable ends. So it is said, by many, that they are bores, rather than means of enjoyment. That is just as the guest takes it. A sensible man or woman can enjoy a large party very much. It is a place where you can seek what mode of passing the time you please, and talk upon what you please. It is said that John Quincy Adams, even when president, would be found at a large party in Washington, sitting in the corner playing chess. No doubt, in another corner of the room might be found the belle of the season, surrounded with beaux and rattling away with light and airy manner; and in another some noted lady, adorned in the splendor of dress and diamonds, talking with a foreign ambassador. Such a party is, therefore, not a place to be wholly denounced. At the time I spoke of, there were not, in Cincinnati, the means to make a party as rich and ornamental as there are now. "Modern Improvement" had not reached us. Even oysters were not seen at a party until 1827. Nor could the beautiful array of "cut flowers" be exhibited then, as they are now. Nature produced as much, but there was little attention paid to merely artificial products, and fashion had not made these displays necessary. In fact, Cincinnati parties in 1825–1826 were purely social, not for the mere purpose of display, which is too often the case now. They had an excess of good things to eat and drink; but with them a large share of good humor and good conversation. There was no distinction of old and young, fashionable or unfashionable, married or unmarried;

but while the party, like a family, was mixed in different proportions, it was always composed of the well-to-do, the respectable, and the intellectual. The distinctive marks of pioneer hospitality had not yet wholly departed. The frank manners, the warm reception, the *bon ami*, and the recognition of the pioneer favorites had not gone. I remember one party, which was a fair type of parties in general at this time. It was at the house of Col. C., on Third street, near Main street, where many good families then lived, and I attended several parties on Third street. Col. C. had a large square house, the best rooms of which were on the second floor, and the whole suite were thrown open for the reception and supper rooms. Col. C. had been rather profuse in his invitations. I think there were more than two hundred persons present, and the house crowded. In the front room the ladies and gentlemen were engaged in conversation, as usual, the ladies making no attempt at magnificent dresses, and the gentlemen paying no more attention to young than to old ladies, but mingling in general conversation, and all making themselves agreeable. There was no regular set supper-table. But, as was customary at that day, there were in the back rooms tables for gentlemen, covered with the most solid dishes of meat and game, while the waiters carried to the ladies the best of cakes and confections, with whatever else they desired. With them remained the young gentlemen, who had then even more gallantry than they have now in commending themselves to the graces of the ladies. But with the old, sedate, and unfashionable gentlemen the back room was the charm. There stood the tables, with ham and beef, and venison, turkey, and quails, with bottles of brandy and wine, and there were cards for those who wanted to kill time. Nevertheless, in those rooms were many a charming woman and many an intellectual man. I met at that time, I think, for the first time, NATHAN WARE, a gentleman from Georgia, a brother of Senator Ware, and at one time a partner of Calhoun. He was a man of great intelligence and inquiring mind. I mention him here because of an interesting conversation I had with him, about this, on the subject of a bridge over the Ohio, one winter evening, at his room, on the lower part of Broadway. He took out some maps which he had drawn of a bridge to be erected. The plan was to put it from the foot of Broadway to the mouth of Licking, having one outlet to Covington and the other to Newport. It was to be built on piers, with a draw. The idea was rather better than that of the great railroad bridge, made by the Pennsylvania Railroad Company, which was built on piers, but is confined to the Newport side. Dr. Drake, in his "Pictures of Cincinnati," published in 1815, says: "Some enthusiastic persons already speak of a bridge across the Ohio, but the period at which this great project can be executed is certainly remote." Not so very remote, for it was little more than thirty years afterward when the beautiful suspension bridge was thrown over to Covington.

In the same winter, I think, I attended the wedding of Miss Graham and Dr. Ridgely, at a two-story frame house, on Third street, which now looks like one of the antiquities, but which saw, in those days, some of the brightest scenes of the town. Mr. Graham, the father, was a paper manufacturer, whose mill was at the foot of John street. His two daughters and son were among the first people I was acquainted with. At that wedding, I think, were a number of the young ladies who then entered into society. Some of them I will barely mention. One of them was Mary Longworth, the eldest daughter of Nicholas Longworth, and at that time quite a belle, handsome and interesting. She soon after married Dr. Stettinius, of the District of Columbia, and in a few years died. Another was Mary Ann Burnet, who married Mr. Vachel Worthington, and also soon died. Another lady, of whom I saw little, but who is sung by "Horace in Cincinnati," was Elizabeth A. Lytle. Her father, General Lytle, was a noted man in the early history of Cincinnati, and her brother, Robert, was a few years after elected to Congress. Her brother, William, whom I have just before mentioned, was thought to be one of the most promising young men, but died early. Elizabeth Lytle, soon after I came out, was married to Charles Macalester, a merchant, who removed to Philadelphia. Both were persons in high estimation, much esteemed by those who knew them. Just previous to my arrival she had been one of the belles of Cincinnati. Horace, in Cincinnati, addressed her an ode, which though not remarkable for poetry, shows in what esteem she was held:

> " If virgin purity of mind,
> With nature's loveliness combined,
>   In life's unclouded morning;
> If in her fair and comely face
> Shine here, politeness, ease, and grace
>   Her character adorning;
>
> " If blest with kind parental care,
> To guard her steps from vice's snare,

And if religion summon
To taste her joys, a maid like this,
You must, dear friend, possess of bliss
A portion more than common.

" Unskill'd in coquetry's vain wiles,
Devoid of art and Syren-smiles,
And free from envy's leaven,
Still with untiring ardor run
The virtuous course you have begun,
Beneath the smiles of heaven."

From the society of ladies I must turn, in order to give a true picture of the town in its coarser amusements. Cincinnati seems to have had then, as well as since, no small taste for gambling. The police reports now show that the city is infested with gamblers. These are of a low and coarse sort; but when I came out, and for several years, there were many gentlemen of the bar, merchants, and others, who habitually gambled. Just before then the marshal and his officers had been seized with a sudden spasm of virtue, and arrested nearly an hundred of lawyers, merchants, bankers, and "gentlemen," who (without regard to their gentility) were indicted for gambling—much to their astonishment, and the astonishment of the town. Of this proceeding, " Horace " says:

" Our citizens had long,
Unfearing fortune's evils,
With cards, and wine and song,
Enjoyed their midnight revels.
They grew more free and bold,
Nor thought to be molested;
At length a tale was told,
And every man arrested."

The joke of the town was that the sheriff and the

prosecuting attorney were among the number arrested. " Horace," who was a Quaker, enjoyed it, and his 28th Ode is full of irony.

> " Blush, jurymen, with shame,
> For wantonly commanding
> Some hundred men of fame,
> Renown, and lofty standing,
> To quit their fov'rite sport,
> Renounce their gambling errors,
> And stand before the court,
> In all its mighty terrors."

Facts like these show—what my observation has done—that the grosser vices have diminished in the higher and more educated classes of society, and descended to the lower. It is well known that gambling was at one time fashionable in England, and at the time I speak of it was almost fashionable in Cincinnati. There were wealthy gentlemen, and the most eminent members of the bar, who were known to be gamblers. After a time, this was denounced, and the reputation of gambling was a bad one. Then it ceased to be openly practiced by respectable men. At least it was hid, and in this, as in other cases, vice paid to virtue the tribute of hypocrisy.

At this time there was in Cincinnati a theater, on Columbia (since called Second) street, between Main and Sycamore. In the winter of 1825–1826, I was a frequent attendant, and found much amusement, without anything to regret. It was undoubtedly—if I may judge from what I hear—of a better character than many of the theaters. There, I once heard Booth the elder, in Richard the Third, in which he was celebrated. But tragedy I never admired, and my delight was in the comedy of the then noted Aleck Drake, who with his wife—a superior woman—was famous in the western country. I had seen "Old Barnes," as he was called, in New York, and many years after, Burton. Aleck Drake, totally unlike either, was, in the spirit of comedy, equal to them. He was superior to Barnes, but not equal to Burton, in gentlemanly bearing. In the power to make fun, without coarseness, Drake was unrivaled. His wife was superior to him—not so much on the stage as in mind and character. I once saw a little incident showing what an energetic, spirited woman she was.

A fire broke out on Main street, and at that time there were no fire-engines, and the only mode of carrying water was by fire-buckets, filled at the river, and handed from hand. So a line was formed from the fire to the river. In that line, among the men, was Mrs. Aleck Drake, handing buckets vigorously. She was a person of mind and character, and always a great favorite with the public. I saw her once in the character of "Meg Merriles," which she looked and acted as thoroughly as Meg herself must have done in her wild freaks among the Gypsies, and in her character as prophetess announcing:

"And Bertram's right and Bertram's might
Shall meet on Ellengowan Height."

Drake died while she was yet in her prime, and she married Captain Cutter, the poet. He was author of the "Song of Steam," a noted piece in its day. Cutter was very intemperate, and great efforts were made by his friends to save him, but in vain. The marriage was an unhappy one. They were separated, and in a few years both were dead.

My attendance at the Columbia-street Theater was the last of.my acquaintance with the acted drama. Except very rarely I have not entered a theater. If I may judge by what others say, the Cincinnati theater has degenerated since those days. " Stars" seem to be quite numerous, but the character of the theater itself declined. First comes melo-drama; then the spectacle, which, under the name of a play, is often more than half a menagerie, by introducing animals on the stage. Recently the opera has been introduced, which is, no doubt, a great improvement on the age of melo-drama and menagerie; yet it does not seem, from newspaper accounts, that the theater has risen to any great dignity, either in character or representation. When we reflect how universal were theatrical entertainments in Rome, and are now in France, we must admit that there is something in them well adapted to the taste and amusement of mankind; but the question remains whether this kind of amusement is not abused to evil consequence, and whether we can imagine the early Christians to have frequented theaters. Garrick and Mrs. Siddons were, no doubt, well worth anybody's while to see; but we suspect neither Garrick nor Mrs. Siddons were seen acting in such theaters and accompanied with such circumstances as we have now.

In the summer of 1826, while boarding on Broadway, I had a severe bilious fever. This fact reminds me of the change which has come in the character and fatality of diseases in Cincinnati. From 1825 to 1828 the bilious fever and its kindred diseases were prevalent, and, indeed, alarming. The whole character of disease was different from what it is now. The low types of fever which we see did not exist at all, except as the sequel of inflammatory disorders. When a bilious or other active fever had exhausted its power, the patient immediately began to sink, and he could be kept up only by brandy and other stimulants. These active, inflammatory fevers we seldom see now, but, on the other hand, what is called the "typhoid fever." The introduction of "typhoid" as a general disease was since the introduction of cholera in 1832. Many physicians thought that, from some unknown cause, the cholera, or that which produced cholera, had changed the character of diseases. Be that as it may, it is certain that Cincinnati, in 1825, 1826, and 1827, was the victim of bilious fever, almost to the extent of an epidemic. Within my own knowledge, many of the best known citizens had the fever, and some died. Among those who died was a German engineer, who boarded at the Broadway Hotel, and was much distinguished in his line. Another was my cousin, Mrs. Dr. Drake. A large part of the fever cases occurred in the south-east part of the town, between Third street and the river. The cause seemed to me very evident: all the bottom part in that quarter had been often overflowed, and in early days had been little else than a marsh; many of the lots had been filled and built upon without regard to their former condition. I think there must have been malarial poison in this part of the city for several years. However, the bilious fever pervaded the whole town, chiefly in the bottoms. Being well acquainted with physicians and familiar with statistics, I am compelled to believe there has been a great change in the character of diseases. The diseases now are of a lower type. It is well known that at the close of last century and the beginning of this, bleeding was a common resort and remedy by the ablest physicians. It is equally well known that it is not so now. Somebody will say that is owing to a change in medical theories. In part, no doubt, but not altogether so. It is to be presumed that most physicians are honest in their attempts to heal the patient, and that is the interest of the profession. When, eighty years since, the most eminent physicians resorted to bleeding as an efficient remedy, it is to be presumed that they thought it a good remedy for the inflammatory diseases then prevalent. When, since the introduction of the cholera (1832– 1850), they seldom bleed, but resort to tonic, as well as external remedies, it is to be presumed that 'they do it with an equally honest conviction that this is the most successful. In other words, the change is due rather to the results of practical observation at the bedside than to merely medical theories. There is, and always will be, two schools of medical philosophy in regard to the treatment of diseases. One affirms it best to kill it by destroying its germ by the anti-phlo- gistic system. The other declares it best to strengthen the constitution to meet and conquer it. My mother, who was very intelligent, and herself had the yellow fever in 1794, was of the firm opinion that it was bet- ter to strengthen the system by tonics than to weaken it by any anti-phlogistics. Such is my opinion, and it seems to be the popular opinion of physicians of the present day.

Here we come to another change, or reported change in the character of diseases. This is the much greater number of (at least reported) nervous and heart diseases. That in name and appearance these have largely increased, is beyond question. They are attributed by nearly all writers on medical and social science to changes in society. It is said that society is more active, more excited, more luxurious, and to use the common phase, more high-strung, and, therefore, the brain is overworked, and the nerves over-stimulated. There is, no doubt, some truth in this theory, but it is greatly exaggerated. It is questionable whether, in fact, heart diseases have greatly increased. There are more reported, but are there more in fact? A century ago heart diseases were not understood and defined accurately. Deaths from this cause were called " sudden deaths," or, " apoplexy," or some accident. Now they are understood and properly named like other diseases. So an " overworked brain " is an exaggerated cause of disease. I have seen hundreds, I may say thousands of students and professional men, and never met with an overworked brain yet. That such a thing exists, I have no doubt, but it is much more rare than is commonly supposed. Indolence, to the extent of a neglected mind and body, is a much more common disease than an overworked brain. The celebrated Dr. CADOGAN (an English physician), came much nearer the causes of gout, dyspepsia, and chronic diseases than they do now-a-days. He said that the causes of them are intemperence, indolence, and vexation. By vexation, he meant, I suppose, what I mean by " worry," a constant bother and anxiety about a thousand things, upon which there ought not to be any anxiety, but about which thousands of minds are constantly vexed. Here we come to what I believe to be the real cause of increased nervous and heart diseases. There have been two great causes actively at work within a few years to stimulate and excite the minds of intelligent people. The first is the immensely increased and diffused " news," or events, or gossip of the world instantly made known and made almost ubiquitous round the earth. It is impossible that this should not excite some minds beyond the point of a healthy action. We need not analyze this effect beyond the very evident increase of certain classes of crimes, by the constant repetition of similar events continually committed. Then the vastly increased power of locomotion has caused innumerable casualties, and often crimes, that were unknown before. High living, constant excitement, perpetual going and coming are the real causes of the nervous diseases, insanities, and suicides which are prevalent at this day.

A year or two after the time I have referred to there occurred a social event, which was, at once, strange and amusing. The story, as it came to me, and was current in town, and, no doubt, in the main correct, was this. GENERAL LYTLE, one of the oldest and best known citizens, was coming down the Ohio in a steamboat, when a passenger, a civil and intelligent person, introduced himself to Lytle as General Ross, principal chief of the Cherokees. Now, it was known that Ross was chief of the Cherokees, and that he was an educated person, having been at the school in Cornwall, Connecticut, when I was studying law at the neighboring town of Litchfield. Ross showed General Lytle letters from several persons of distinction, and had one, I believe, to Lytle himself. He, therefore, took the Cherokee chief to be what he repre-

sented himself, treated him civilly, and invited him to
his home. I did not see the chief, but heard for two
or three days of his driving around the city and being
treated as a distinguished person. One evening a
great party was given at Judge Este's, on Ninth street
near Main. Whether the party was given to General
Ross, I do not know; but, he was invited and expected. I was invited, but did not go. Next morning I met two or three gentlemen, on the street, who
were talking and laughing over a great joke. It
turned out that General Ross was not at the party,
and was only a smart, but common mulatto. I was
boarding with a gentleman who had a witty and im-
pudent mulatto servant, and felt sure that he knew
something about it. So I· said to him: "Charley, I
hear General Ross was not at Judge Este's party."
Giggling from ear to ear, he said, "No, sir; he was
tired." "Tired! Where did he go?" "He—he—he!
He said he was tired of the white folks; and went to
a nigger ball!" Such was the end of polite attentions
to General Ross, of the Cherokees. Such impositions
often happen when people are anxious to notice distinguished strangers. In this case the imposition was
harmless and amusing, but I saw one that made no
little shame and mortification. When I graduated at
Princeton, our class, as was customary, gave a commencement ball. At that ball was present, by invitation, the then noted Baron Hoffman. He drove up in
a fine carriage and four horses, making all the show
he could. It was about the last of his appearance as
a distinguished stranger on the American boards. He
had come out from Germany as Baron Hoffman, related to some of the most distinguished of German

nobility, and brought the most ample credentials—
letters from well-known persons—receipts and certifi-
cates of business, and, withal, was a polite, intelligent
man. His bearing was said to be impressive, and, as
a titled gentleman of high standing, made favorable
impression on the ladies. He began rather modestly,
but made his way in society; was well received; managed to borrow a good deal of money, and moved in
the very best society, in days when there was a real
aristocracy. He was engaged to marry, it was confidently said, Miss L., one of the very *elite* of New
York. It was about this time that he made his appearance at our ball, and in a few days we heard the
finale of this well-played farce—very near a tragedy.
There were no swift steamers and telegraph in those
days, but, at length, letters were received from Germany showing that this fellow was the valet of the real
Baron Hoffman, and had stolen letters and money
from his master.

Then came a flood of writs and suits from his deluded creditors, and, under the barbarous laws of im-
prisonment for debt, this pseudo Baron Hoffman was
thrown into jail. True to his character, he determined that the end of the play should be as complete
as the beginning. One morning he was found nearly
faint, with his uncovered arm dripping blood, with a
razor near. He was sadly announcing his determination to leave this cruel world, when it was discovered
that he had opened a vein, but taken care *not* to cut
an artery. He was bound up, and his creditors finding nothing but bones to pick, soon dismissed him;
and Baron Hoffman disappeared from the American
stage. This kind of imposition is common, even now,

and will be, so long as many people prefer empty titles to good character.

In the summer of 1826, Mr. Benjamin Drake and myself undertook to make a little book, descriptive of Cincinnati, as an inducement to immigration. That turned out to be " Cincinnati in 1826." In order to do this cheaply and correctly, we took the census and statistics of the city ourselves. It was a laborious task; but we were young, and the weather pleasant. We divided the work by Main street, I taking the east side. At that time, there were very few inhabitants beyond Race street, so that the division was nearly equal. Taking the census and taking statistics is and must ever be instructive and amusing. Such work takes you into the very homes of the people, and into the very heart of the work-shops. One thing struck me with surprise, to which the present state of society presents an unhappy contrast. I went into hundreds of houses, at all hours of the day, often at meal times, and saw all conditions of people. In all this visitation into the recesses of society, I never met a single pauper family, nor one really impoverished. The great body of people were mechanics, with plenty to do, generally owning their own houses, and, in fact, a well-to-do people. It is such a population which makes the worth and strength of the city, when it grows to great size, filled with all sorts of people. There will be found many improvements, much wealth and show; but beside all the art and elegance, stands gaunt poverty, events which make humanity shudder, and distress which no human power can relieve. In the midst of it all, it is only the great middle class, which preserves the social system from decay and ruin. Cincinnati in 1826, was composed almost wholly of this class, and it was pleasant to see them, in their plain but independent houses, enjoying the fruit of their labor. The contrast between then and now is in every aspect great. Cincinnati in 1826 had 16,200 people. Cincinnati in 1870, had just 200,000 more. Cincinnati in 1826 had neither gaslights, nor public waterworks, nor public schools (although there were schools), for, it was not until 1824, that there was a state law authorizing taxation for schools, and, it was not until 1830, that the law was carried into effect in Cincinnati. The waterworks had been previously established by Col. Samuel Davis, afterward mayor, but were held by a private company, who, several years after, sold them to the city. None of the great institutions for charity, which are now the pride, as well as the beneficence of the city, were then erected, except the Cincinnati Commercial Hospital, which was founded by Dr. Drake. It is true the town was then small, but the condition of the people was widely different. In proportion to the population, there was not one in need of these charities where there are ten to-day. When I look back upon the Cincinnati of 1826, and then upon Cincinnati in 1876, I find it difficult to say that being big, rich, and showy, has made society better or happier.

CHAPTER XIII.

The Presidency—Candidates in 1824—John Quincy Adams—Clay's Vote for Adams—Speech at Mack's Tavern—Henry Clay and his Character.

In 1828, there were six candidates for the presidency in the canvass, and four in the election. In the summer of this year Adams, Clinton, Clay, Jackson, Calhoun, and Crawford were all canvassed; but, in the end, Clinton and Calhoun were dropped out. There were then no great or interesting political issues. The administration of Mr. Monroe had been one of perfect calm, except some casual controversies about contracts and offices, which interested the nation scarcely at all. But the cabinet of Mr. Monroe was like a powder magazine, which only needed a spark of fire to make an explosion and a conflagration. It was made up, as was said of an English ministry, of "all the talents;" and, of course, all the talents must be ambitious. There were plans, schemes, and counter-schemes which were never fully known until twenty years afterward.

John Quincy Adams, William H. Crawford, John C. Calhoun, and John M'Lean were all members of Monroe's cabinet, and were all afterward proposed for the presidency. Henry Clay had just been the distinguished Speaker of the House of Representatives; De Witt Clinton was mounted on the Erie canal, and had just triumphed over his political enemies; Andrew Jackson was at the Hermitage, with his laurels, fresh, green, and glorious, from the battlefield of New Orleans—as Counselor Sampson called it, "that death-bed of British glory." In fine, there was then upon the political stage a galaxy of talent, genius, and brilliancy which, I think, may be fairly said, had not been exceeded in a previous period, and has not been equaled since. The canvass for the presidency was conducted, not upon any general principles, or in reference to any special policy, but with reference to individuals and to their localities. Mr. Adams was a favorite in New England, Mr. Clay in the West, Cal-houn and Crawford divided the South, while Jackson had an under-current of popularity, which pervaded all parts of the country, and was produced by his military exploits, and not a little by the boldness of his character and the audacity of his conduct. De Witt Clinton was dropped, and confined his operations to New York. Calhoun, living near Crawford, was also dropped; and John M'Lean was not proposed until many years after. The others, Adams, Clay, Crawford, and Jackson were voted for. Neither of the candidates had a majority, and the election was made by the house of representatives.

Governor Wolcott said: "We don't need to have brilliant talents. There is old Sitgreaves, of Pennsyl-vania, will make as good a president as anybody. You want a man of business and integrity to take care of the business of the government." Sitgreaves was a member of congress from Eastern Pennsyl-vania, and interested in statistics.* Whether Wol-

---

* See Chapter IX.

cott's theory was right or not, the American people have practically acted upon it. Such men as Monroe, Van Buren, Polk, Taylor, Pierce, Buchanan, and Grant have been elected, while Clinton, Clay, Webster, and Calhoun could not be.

JOHN QUINCY ADAMS, who was elected by the house, in 1825, had much claim to be considered a man of genius and learning. Except Jefferson, he was the only one of all our presidents who was really a literary man. He was once a professor of belles-lettres in Harvard College, and his public addresses are both able and ornate. He occasionaly wrote poetry, although that was certainly not his forte. His lines to "A Bereaved Mother" are really good:

> "Sure, in the mansions of the blest,
> When infant innocence ascends,
> Some angel, brighter than the rest,
> The spotless spirit's flight attends.

> "Then dry henceforth the bitter tear;
> Their part and thine inverted see:
> Thou wert their guardian angel here,
> They guardian angels now to thee."

Mr. Adams, like his father, was a Federalist, but in consequence of their revolutionary companionship, Jefferson favored the Adamses, and put John Quincy in the way of political promotion. He began in the diplomatic service and was abroad many years, and at one time Minister to Prussia. At the time of the election in 1824, he was, undoubtedly, the best diplomatist, the best acquainted with our foreign affairs, and most experienced statesman in the country. He had been, from boyhood up, drilled in public affairs. He had an educated mind, and was thoroughly quali-

fied for public business. After his term in the presidency expired, he made the novel experiment of a retired president serving in the house of representatives,
and it was the most successful, although not the most
practical part of his life. He was called by the notorious
Tom Marshall, the "Old Man Eloquent," and he used
his eloquence with a power which few could resist.
He took part in the earliest and greatest discussions
upon the right of petition and human freedom. In
those days, the slave power was largely predominant.
It seems wonderful at this day, when the whole tone
and temper of the nation are different, that such an
abject spirit should have been exhibited by a large
part of the Northern people, aptly and truly called
Dough-faces. But so it was, and not till the discussions on the right of petition had reached the conscience, as well as the spirit of the North, was there
any recovery from the abject submission, which the im-
perious slave power demanded of the Northern representatives. Mr. Adams' speeches from 1833 to 1842,
on the subject of slavery and right of petition, and
the annexation of Texas, were the best, the ablest, and
the most effective made in the country. For his course
in the anti-slavery movement, for his clear views of
the constitution, and his defense of human freedom,
he will be remembered in after ages. He was never
popular with politicians, nor even regarded as a party
leader. No man ever questioned his integrity. No
man ever doubted his patriotism. Of him, with more
truth than of Chatham, it might be said : " The secretary stood alone. Modern degeneracy had not
reached him." Mr. Adams knew that he stood alone,
and among his methods of self-defense and asserting

truth was his " Diary," which has become memorable in the history of the country. With it, he demolished Jonathan Russell, a colleague commissioner in making the Treaty of Ghent. Russell, as well as some other people, was willing to insinuate that Mr. Adams wished to give up the exclusive rights to the Mississippi. Mr. Adams, by the use of his Diary, showed such complete detail of dates and circumstances, as put an end to that charge. There was another little historical incident worth remembering, though history will not record it. Mr. Clay was also a commissioner at Ghent, and when in the canvas of 1824, the newspapers intimated that Adams was inclined to give up the exclusive right to the Mississippi, Clay came out with a card, saying, he had something to say on that subject in a future time. Mr. Adams wrote a card of five lines, saying, " *now* is the day, and I defy the test of time, of talent, and of human scrutiny." It is enough to say, that the future time never came, when Mr. Clay was willing to utter another word on the subject. The fate of Jonathan Russell was not one he wished to share. Mr. Adams died in the hall of the house of representatives, the theater of his last and greatest glory. Falling into the arms of a friend his last words were: " This is the last of earth!" I know not whether any monument was erected to him ; but he needed it not. For, whether the ages to come shall hear of him or not, he could have said with Horace—

" Exegi monumentum ære perrennius."

In the election of 1824, although I did not vote, my sympathies were all with Adams. Perhaps they would not have been had De Witt Clinton continued a candidate; for, in spite of Governor Wolcott's opinion, I did admire genius and learning, and De Witt Clinton was undoubtedly among the most brilliant of our public men. When the election of November, 1824, came on, I had no vote; but, on arriving at Cincinnati, in the summer of 1825, found my friends and the public generally excited over the state of public affairs. The election which had just taken place was the second one in which the house of representatives had been called upon to take part. The first one was the celebrated case of Burr and Jefferson, which caused so much danger and controversy, that an amendment to the constitution was made, being the twelfth of the additional articles. In the original constitution it was provided that the electors should vote for two persons, and the one having the highest number of votes should be president, and the person having the next highest be vice-president; and, if a tie, the house should choose the president. In this no allowance was made as to whom the people may have intended for president and vice-president. This made no difference in the election of Washington or John Adams, both of whom had the highest vote at the time of their respective elections. In the summer of 1800, there would have been difficulty if the Federal ticket had been elected, for it was arranged that CHARLES COLESWORTH PINKNEY (of S. C.) should receive one vote less than Mr. Adams, and he did. But the Republican ticket had the majority of electors, and on that Jefferson and Burr had the same number of votes. Jefferson, however, was intended, and nobody dreamed that Burr would be seriously set up as president. The Federalists hated Jefferson, and took the opportunity

of voting in the house of representatives for Burr.
There the vote is by states. The Federalists held
states enough, with two or three equally divided, to
prevent the election of Jefferson. The balloting went
on for several days, amidst an intense excitement. At
length Mr. BAYARD, of Delaware, with half a dozen
others, holding the votes of two states, determined
to make an election, but determined also to make
an "arrangement" with Mr. Jefferson for re-
taining some friends in office, which was done,
and the election was made. This transaction caused
the almost unanimous adoption of the twelfth additional article to the constitution, which provides that
the electors shall specify the president and vice-president. Under this article the election of 1825 was
made. Four candidates had been voted for : Jackson
receiving 99 electoral votes; Adams, 84; Crawford,
41, and Clay, 37. Jackson had a *plurality* a little over
one-third of the whole number; but it was assumed
in the popular mind that, because he had a plurality,
he ought to be elected. Such was not the fact. Mr.
Adams was elected by the votes of thirteen states;
ten having voted in whole or in part for Mr. Adams,
and three (Kentucky, Ohio, and Missouri) which had
voted for Mr. Clay. Mr. Clay's friends had consulted
together, and voted in a body for Mr. Adams. This
surprised the enthusiastic friends of Jackson, and dis-
pleased those of Crawford. The result was that there
was a combination of the friends of Jackson and
Crawford against Adams and Clay. The jealousy,
which has ever existed in the South against the
Northern men, broke out with new force. Adams was
assailed with a malignity which is scarcely equaled in

the fierce conflicts of this day. John Randolph, of Virginia, said that John Quincy Adams was only serving out his father's time. Mr. Adams, however, was the last man to put himself out for the scolding of Thersites or the gossip of Mrs. Grundy. All that can be remembered now of Randolph, so much talked about in his day, is the " REMORSE " written on his card when death was near. Who would live a brilliant wit or a proud aristocrat, only to feel at last " remorse ?"

In the formation of his cabinet, Mr. Adams made MR. CLAY secretary of state. Then the storm burst forth, and from one end of the country to the other, "bargain, intrigue, and management," was shouted forth. It was declared that because Clay and his friends voted for Adams in the house, and Mr. Adams made Clay secretary of state, that therefore there was a bargain between them. It happened, however, that Clay had declared to several gentlemen before the election, that if the election in the house should be between Adams and Jackson, that he should vote for Adams, on the ground of his superior civil qualifications. He said this to my friend Dr. Drake, who, as others did, published that fact. This ought to have satisfied anybody; but politicians, like wolves of the prairie, never leave a scent until they destroy their victim. They did not destroy Mr. Clay, but they created that intense party spirit which has divided the country ever since. Mr. Clay has long since been acquitted of anything dishonorable in his vote for Mr. Adams, but never was a noble bird more hawked at by mousing owls, or beset with buzzing insects, than was this greatest of political warriors. Fortunately he was made by nature with all the courage, boldness, and strength, which was necessary for a conflict with the combined array of ambitious rivals, political hyenas, and ignorant mobs, which were arrayed to overthrow his power and blacken his name. Nevertheless, brave and strong as he was, it took all his strength, courage, and eloquence to meet his assailants successfully, even in the West. Here Jacksonism was strong, and took a popular hold on many people not inclined to it, by the plausible argument that Jackson having received the most votes ought, therefore, to have been elected by the house. In Cincinnati, in 1825, the popular current was for Jackson, the next strongest was for Adams, and the last Clay. At the time I came out there were not more than two hundred and eighty original Clay men in Cincinnati, four times as many for Adams, and much more than both for Jackson. The Adams and Clay men, however, fused together after the appointment of Mr. Clay to the cabinet. The combined forces made a formidable party, which in 1833–1834 made the basis of the great Whig party of the next twenty years. Mr. Clay found it necessary to defend himself against the charge of "bargain, intrigue, and management." One of his defenses was a speech made at Cincinnati, in the summer of 1825. A large number of the gentlemen of Cincinnati, originally friends of either Adams or Clay, gave him a public dinner at the Cincinnati Hotel, then kept by Mack, at the corner of Broadway and Front street. There were about two hundred present, and they were the *elite* of the city. I was fairly startled by the speech, which was the most eloquent one I ever heard, in fiery utterance and energetic action. It was utterly unlike that of Corwin or Webster, not superior, but unlike. Mr. Clay was not like Adams or Webster, able to write a polished or eloquent argument, nor like Corwin, able to adorn his speech with wit and humor; but he had more real soul than either. The power of personal magnetism, through eloquence, was greater than in any of his great rivals. His speech at the Cincinnati Hotel was not wholly on politics, but when he came to defend his vote in the house for Adams he fired up, his tall person seemed taller, his head and expression assumed a lofty bearing, with his foot advanced, and his arm raised, and his eye flashing, he seemed to defy, in his mere presence, the whole pack of hounds, who, under the name of Jackson, had yelped at his heels, and snarled at his fame. He said that he was compelled to choose between two distinguished citizens. " On one hand was a civilian, a statesman, versed in foreign affairs, and acquainted with business. On the other a military chieftain, practiced in war, and acquainted with armies. I would not, I could not, and I did not hesitate." I saw Mr. Clay at other times, and followed his political fortunes with unflinching fidelity, because he was a, I might say the only, leader of the Whig party ; but I never thought him equal to Mr. Webster, nor ever liked him personally. This seems strange to myself, for there is no one man in public life who attracted so strongly so many personal followers. Horace Greeley stuck to him with the tenacity of Jonathan to David. On his defeat, in 1844, I saw strong, intellectual gentlemen ready to weep ; and I dare say some did. Mr. Calhoun was the only man who in personal following could rival him. Calhoun was said to have been exceedingly attractive to young men, and he always paid great attention to them. While I admired as much as anyone the splendid bearing of Mr. Clay, and adopted to its full extent his American policy, I had no personal sympathy with him. He belonged to the Southern school of politicians, and had an arbitrary, antagonistic way, which seemed to look down upon the quiet and unobstrusive class to which I belonged. Mr. Clay had, however, in that very class many of his warmest admirers. In after years, I found that Webster had much of the same sort of bearing, and my admiration for him ceased with his speech on the 7th of March, 1850, when he undertook to prove that the laws of nature would keep slavery out of the territories of the West, and it was a matter of indifference whether we legislated upon it or not. Neither Clay nor Webster were men who had the moral courage to take a stand upon human rights, and defend it upon the ground of moral law. The Spirit of Laws (Montesquieu) had been written nearly a hundred and fifty years before, and yet these two great American leaders were behind that great work in the perception of moral justice. Mr. Clay deserves great credit, however, for being in favor of the gradual emancipation of Kentucky. This is part of his early record, and perhaps his early record is the best.

Returning to the dinner at Mack's, his speech was very effective, and, while the unfitness of Jackson for the presidency was made clear, so also the charge of "bargain, intrigue, and management" was entirely disproved by the facts brought before the public. Nevertheless, neither facts nor argument had much effect on the great multitude of people, who are seduced by the glare of military glory. Jackson was elected in 1828, and the eight years of his administration were filled with the most extraordinary mixture of folly and patriotism, of domestic factions, and national boasting; of political wisdom in some things, of social scandal in others; of the most extraordinary financial schemes, and the most extraordinary financial disasters.* Mr. Clay resigned from the administration of Mr. Adams, and soon after re-entered congress.

He, like Webster and Calhoun, always thought himself the proper man to make a president—was four times a candidate, and three times voted for in the electoral college. He was voted for in 1824, 1832, and 1844. In 1840, he was a candidate before the Harrisburg Whig Convention, and defeated by Harrison. He thought, and perhaps history will show, that the Whigs made a great blunder in not nominating him. He would have been elected, and, unlike Harrison, would in all probability have lived, and presented to the country and the world a far different and far better administration than that of the weak and prevaricating Tyler. In the election of 1844, Mr. Clay was defeated by the anti-slavery vote given to Birney, which operated directly in favor of Polk, the Democratic candidate. New York gave Polk only 5,000 majority, while 15,000 were polled for Birney, the Abolition candidate. It was fatal to Mr. Clay, and fatal to the Whig party, which, although successful in 1848, went to pieces for this very cause.

The world can not fail to admit and admire the

* See journals of the day.

stern heroism and the moral courage which induces some men to leave all forms, parties, and organizations, even friends and sound policy, to vote against popular opinion, and maintain for conscience's sake a small and powerless faction. But, whether this is wise; whether it is for that general welfare, which is the object of all good government, will remain doubtful until eternity has passed its judgment. Except to stir up the hostility, and finally the open secession of the slaveholders, it is impossible to see any good in the defeat of Mr. Clay by a side faction. BIRNEY and his followers were conscientious, upright, and many of them able men; but it is certain they accomplished nothing until Providence afflicted the South with that insanity, described in the proverb—" Whom the gods will destroy they first make mad."

I fully and always sympathized with the anti-slavery party, but believed that it was safer to follow John Quincy Adams, who was the foremost, boldest, and ablest opposer of slavery, in a great and powerful organization, than to follow a small, however conscientious faction, which, in itself, could not be successful. Mr. Clay was one of those, both North and South, who made the celebrated compromise of 1850. It is useless to say, that in my opinion, that compromise was infamous, a thing not to be endured by any man who believed in human rights or Christian principles. Compromises are always false to principle, even in a constitution of government; but when they compromise humanity, morals, and rights, they give just cause for resistance in all forms. Mr. Clay was then in the senate, and survived this transaction but a short time. His character is easily understood. He was born poor, and brought up with little regular education, and, for that reason, was never able to shine as a writer or as a disciple of Cicero, with the *ore rotundo* of a Roman senator. It would be as great an error to compare him to Demosthenes, for the Greek orator was an accomplished scholar. The art of Demosthenes was not the wild utterance of nature, but the skillful art of the student—studious to shine in an audience of scholars. Clay's eloquence was natural, and the only art he had was to adapt it to his audience, and this he did with great skill. Whether he spoke to the polite hearer in the senate, or to the untutored hunters of Kentucky—he knew well to whom he was speaking—and studied the means to convince or to please them. Brought up among slaveholders, where the passions predominate more than the reason, he was fiery and impetuous, but, at the same time, possessed of that strong sense which pointed out the necessity of courteous manners to a public man, and the policy of pleasing the multitude. Upon the whole, Henry Clay was one well calculated to be a leader among men, and to attract the unmingled admiration of his followers. If he had been more of a scholar, and more of what the world calls a moralist, he would have had fewer followers and admirers among the Western people, who loved more the frankness, courage, and gallantry of their chief, than they did the acquirements of a scholar, or the strict manners of a moralist. Mr. Adams had both these, but never, even in New England, had half the personal popularity of Clay. This difference of mind and manners made their political union very surprising to the public, and gave rise to some of the severest political taunts which were ever

uttered in public life. One of these, and perhaps the
bitterest ever uttered, was that of John Randolph.
He said, in the senate, that the union of Adams and
Clay was the "union of Black George and Blifil—of
the Puritan and the black leg."* On this Clay challenged him. A duel was fought, Randolph, I believe,
firing in the air, and acknowledging himself clearly
in the wrong.

But few anecdotes of Clay remain. Two I will
mention as illustrating a species of wit which Clay
had and used very aptly. The first occurred in
his well-known speech to the hunters of Kentucky.
In 1816, he had been one of a majority in congress
who repealed the per day compensation of members
of congress, and substituted a salary.. Young politicians will be astonished to learn that the salary was
only the humble sum of $1,500 a year, while now they
have modestly voted themselves $5,000. Small as this
sum was, and innocent as was the act, it raised a storm
of excitement and indignation. Of the majority
which passed that act, I think only two were re-elected.
Those two were William C. Lowndes, of South Carolina, and Henry Clay, of Kentucky. Mr. Lowndes
was a very able and eminent man of his day. He
came to West Point to place a son there, and I heard
him tell my father that the act was right, and he never
gave a more conscientious vote in his life. The aristocracy of South Carolina made no complaint, and
Lowndes was easily re-elected. It came near being
very different with Mr. Clay. His district ran back
from Lexington, where he lived, into the mountains,

---

* Black George and Blifil were two villains in Fielding's
novel of Tom Jones.

and among the frontiersmen. This class—called the
" hunters of Kentucky "—had been very much attached to Clay, but this act disgusted them. In their
simple lives, and limited views of life, they thought
such a salary enormous, and especially as its members
voted it themselves. Mr. Clay foresaw the storm, and
called a meeting. At that meeting many of the
" hunters " were present, with lowering brows. In
the course of his speech Mr. Clay said, fixing his eye
on one of his old supporters : " Suppose, my friend,
you had an old rifle, which you had borne through
the hills many a day, and it had never failed you, but
now you put it to your shoulder, and it snapped, but
hung-fire, would you break the stock and throw it
away, or would you try it again ?" " I would try it
again ; we 'll try you again, Harry Clay," shouted the
hunters.

On another occasion, toward the close of his life, he
had a party of friends to dine with him at Ashland.
While at dinner, a servant called him out to see a
gentleman. He apologized to the company. His caller
was an old client. When he returned he told what
had occurred. His client had asked him to plead his
case before the Bourbon County Court. Mr. Clay
said that he had retired from business, and did not
like to take any case. But his friend said he really
must, for he had always been his attorney. " But,"
said Mr. Clay, " if I come, I must charge you a fee,
which you will perhaps not be willing to pay." " How
much, Mr. Clay ?" " Four hundred dollars." " Then,"
said his client, " you are engaged." " Ah !" said
Clay to his guests, " when we are old we are like the

tortoise.　You must put coals of fire on our backs to make us move."

Toward the close of his life, Mr. Clay joined the Episcopal Church, and died in peace with all mankind.　In England he would have been called, what he was—the GREAT COMMONER.

CHAPTER XIV.

Thomas Corwin; his Genius, Career, Eloquence, and Character—Jackson; his Canvass for the Presidency—"Truth's Advocate"—Burr and Jackson.

In the summer of 1825, I took a short journey through the Miami country on horseback. I was riding alone in a piece of woods, between Hamilton and Lebanon, when I overtook a young man also on horseback. There was something in his appearance which struck my attention. He was very dark in complexion and hair, with a sort of swarthy look, more like an Indian than the whites. He was full-fleshed, with a quick, piercing eye, and pleasant expression. We made ourselves known, and I found that he was Corwin, afterward known as Tom Corwin, the " wagon-boy." He got this *soubriquet* from the fact that he had driven wagons in his youth. He was now at the bar, and was returning from the court at Hamilton to his home at Lebanon. As there is, I believe, no memoir of him, and as few men were so deservedly distinguished, I will here relate what I know of him, and what came to my ears from authentic sources. He was born in Kentucky, near Maysville. Thence his family moved, at the close of the last century, to or near the present town of Lebanon. They were among the oldest and best pioneer settlers of Warren county. There he grew up, with only the primitive education which was given in the family and log school-houses. But, where there is a native vigor, brightness, and quickness of intellect, with an ambitious spirit, it does not take a great deal of classic learning to give education, or make a successful life. Corwin had all the vigor and vivacity of intellect required, and the great talent of a taste for reading. Reading gives both fullness and breadth of mind. Corwin, in after years, had both, but the brilliance of his eloquence, his wit, and humor were due to other and even better qualities. He had a most genial disposition, kind feelings, and an almost marvelous susceptibility to the humorous points of men, society, and situations. No man better understood the keenness of irony, nor the power of an argument when feathered with wit and made pleasing by humor. In fine, he stood alone among orators, by the peculiar and remarkable character of his mind. Perhaps the best way to give some idea of him as an orator will be by practical illustrations. His first public appearance was in the Ohio legislature. That was near fifty years ago, when some of the primitive laws and institutions still remained in Ohio. Among others, the whipping-post still remained, whipping being an old New England punishment for small offenders. Some member had introduced a bill repealing the whipping law. Upon this, a member from Trumbull county rose and said he saw no objection to the whipping-post. He always observed that when a man was whipped in his state (Connecticut) that he immediately left the state. Corwin arose and said that " he knew a great many people had come to Ohio from Connecticut, but he never before knew the reason for their coming !" A few years after this, Corwin was a member of congress

from the Warren county district. There was also in
the house a General Crary (general in the militia),
from Michigan. Crary made a pompous speech on the
boundary question, flaming with the eloquence of war.
Corwin answered with a description of the heroism,
victories, experiences, and accomplishments of a militia general. He represented the gallant militia assembling on training-day, some with cornstalks, some
with canes, and some with umbrellas, flanked on the
right with wagons of watermelons, and on the left
with carts of gingerbread, the whole inspirited with
the rattling drum and squeaking fife. Then appeared
the heroic general heading his troops in a tremendous
charge on the watermelons. His nodding plumes at
at the head of the column, while rusty swords and
broken firelocks slew and slashed the watermelons!
From scenes like these the illustrious general of Michigan had returned, flushed with glory and full of
heroic experience, to lead an army against the invaders
on the border! The house was carried away with
mirth, and General Crary was heard of no more.
Corwin continued in congress, and a short time after
appeared as one of the orators of the great Harrison
campaign, in 1840. He was known then as "Tom
Corwin, the wagon boy." That campaign was signalized, among other remarkable features, by giving
soubriquets to the political chiefs, which signified some
alliance with common people. Governor Metcalfe,
of Kentucky, a strong friend of Harrison, was known
as "old stone-hammer," because he had been a stone-
mason. So Corwin was called the "wagon boy." He
appeared at almost all of the great meetings in the
state, and was everywhere attended by crowds. He

used to relate with much humor his reception one afternoon at Poland, Mahoning county. The Western Reserve (at least a large part of it) is laid out with roads at right-angles, and on straight lines, meeting in the center of the township, where the town must be, whether or no. Such was Poland, and Corwin was put at the head of a procession marching on a straight line to Poland. The hour was late. There had been a delay. They could see the town-green filled with people, and the platform erected. The deacons of the churches were the principal men, and managed the business. When Corwin arrived, one of the deacons arose, and said : " Brethren, this is Brother Cor-wine. Let us give Brother Cor-wine three cheers. One—hurra ! Two—hurra ! Three—hurra !" All were given as regularly as the clock strikes, and Brother Corwine was much amused.

It would be unsafe to judge from such examples that Corwin was not forcible in argument, for he was. But he chose, and perhaps rightly, to illustrate his arguments with those touches of wit and humor which kept the people in good temper, and fixed their attention. On one occasion, in the heated canvass of 1844, I was present at one of the best exhibitions of his peculiar eloquence. It was at Carthage, near Cincinnati. A grove of trees near that village had been a popular place for political gatherings. The nomination of POLK and the Texas question had excited the Whigs, and they put forth their full strength to elect Henry Clay, which they confidently expected. The meeting at Carthage was a very large one. I estimated at the time that there were near 8,000 people present. However that may be, it was a large and spirited meeting. The orator of the day was Corwin. The day was fine, the trees green above us, and the audience intelligent. Corwin began with what few orators dare do at that time—for the Democrats had made the name of Federalist odious—a splendid eulogy on Alexander Hamilton. In this he was grave and courteous, pointing out the great abilities and services of Hamilton, in giving success and stability to the treasury. From this he proceeded to the Texas question and all the matters of public policy. At last he came to the nomination of Polk, who was comparatively an unknown man. He had been selected as a sort of nonentity to defeat Van Buren, who ought to have been nominated. It was one of those blunders which the Democratic party frequently makes. The friends of Cass, in the convention of 1844, had defeated Van Buren, and in turn the friends of Van Buren defeated Cass in the election of 1848, when the Whig candidate (Taylor) was elected. When Corwin came to mention Polk (the unknown) it was done with a humor which I have never seen surpassed. " And *who* have they nominated? James K. Polk, of Tennessee? (Then he paused, and turning his head slowly from one side of the audience to the other, with the most surprised expression.) *After that,* who is safe ?" He closed his speech with the most rapturous applause.

It was about two years after that the war with Mexico came on, and Corwin took part against the war. This is always a dangerous thing for a public man; for in a war with a foreign country almost all men sympathize with their own country, however wrong it may be in a moral point of view. Few men who examine the question will think we had just cause of

war with Mexico. Yet, looking back over the thirty
years which have elapsed, no man can doubt that we
have derived great and immense advantage from it.
We got California and Nevada, with security for
Texas, by the war with Mexico. If all moral ideas
are to be excluded from the conduct of nations, and
they have by common consent a right to aggrandize
themselves at the expense of their neighbors, then a
war to acquire California is as justifiable as a war for
independence. Mr. Corwin did not take that view of
it, and made a speech in the senate, which, in real
vigor and excellence, has, perhaps, not been excelled
in the American senate. He had been, as I have
said, a reader, with a good library. The examples of
history were before him, and he used them with signal
effect. He said the country was large enough, and a
war of ambition and conquest could only serve to de-
moralize the people; that the war was unjust, and
that if he were a Mexican he would receive the invaders with " bloody rites and hospitable graves."
The last phrase was unfortunate, for his political opponents seized upon it as a want of patriotism. He
had been talked of for the presidency, but after this
he was seldom mentioned in this connection. Nevertheless, his speech was one of the best examples of
American oratory, and he remained in public office
until the close of his life.

The following letter from Henry Wilson, late Vice-
President of the United States, to Joshua Giddings, of
Ohio, shows what an extraordinary effect was produced on the public mind by Corwin's speech on the
Mexican War, and how the anti-slavery feeling was
rising against the compromise measures of Webster
and his friends :

" Natick, *February* 24, 1847.

" *Hon. J. R. Giddings:*

"Dear Sir :—I have received your favor of the 12th inst., and am very much obliged to you for the information communicated. There is a strong feeling here in Massachusetts in favor of bold action, and the course of yourself and others, especially the Whigs from your state, meets the approbation of the great mass of our people. We are much pleased with the speeches of Hudson and Ashman, but the people are delighted with the speech of Corwin. He has touched the popular heart, and the question asked in the cars, streets, houses, and everywhere where men assemble, is : Have you read Tom Corwin's speech ? Its boldness and high moral tone meet the feelings here, and the people of New England will respond to it, and tens of thousands want to hear more from him. Tell him to come out, though, in favor of the Wilmot proviso. We all hope and expect it of him. We can give him every state in New England, if he will take the right ground against slavery. How I should like to vote for him and some good non-slaveholder for vice-president in 1848. * * * I suppose that Webster, Clayton, Mangum, and Crittenden will be against him, for his speech was a terrible rebuke to them, and I am much mistaken if some of them very readily forget or forgive him. Their position is a most disgraceful one, and I do not see how they are to get out of it. I hope you will continue to use every effort to bring our friends right. * * *

"Yours, truly,

" Henry Wilson."

Horace Greeley wrote at the same time to Giddings, saying that Corwin was his first choice for the presidency, and Seward for vice-president! Reversing the order in which the distinguished New Yorker was held, and anticipating exactly what Greeley did when he defeated the nomination of Seward in the Chicago Convention of 1860.

For twenty years after this, Corwin continued in public office. He was embassador to Mexico, and member of congress from his old district, and finally a member of the Peace Convention. Just before his death, sitting in a large party, he said, with some bitterness, that he would be remembered only as a jester or a humorist. In this he did himself injustice. He did use wit and humor to illustrate his points and conciliate the people; but behind these always lay great principles of truth and justice. We can not place Corwin on the same level with Hamilton, Adams, or Clinton; but we can say that no man among them was animated with a better spirit, or saw truth in a clearer light, or more steadily advocated the best interests of his country. He was a fine specimen of that sort of a man who sprung up in the pioneer age. With no great education, with no society of the great, he was the peer of those who had, and lived in a republican country with just ideas of what a republic should be.

On the accession of Fillmore to the presidency, in 1850, Corwin was appointed secretary of the treasury, and remained until the accession of Pieree, in March, 1853. In the summer of 1852, Mr. W. D. Gallagher and myself were appointed by Mr. Corwin, under a resolution of the senate, to report the statistics of our steam marine. In the course of that time, and while Corwin was secretary, I got a striking evidence of what is called "red tape," and the necessity of what I would call a business, rather than a civil, reform. I wanted the steam statistics of New Orleans, and went to one of the bureaus of the treasury department, where they should be, because it was the duty of the collectors of the ports to report them quarterly. There I found the head of the bureau talking with a friend on the price and virtues of partridges, evidently thinking the partridge question of more importance than any public business. I asked him for the last report of the steam navigation of New Orleans, and he pointed me to a pigeon-hole in a bureau. I got hold of the collector's report, and, after an examination, found that it was wholly wrong. There were many more steamboats reported at New Orleans than existed there, or had been there for years. What was the matter, I could not see, until, after comparing several reports, I found that the collector, or his clerk, had regularly copied into the last report all that was in the former one; so that in his report of what should be the then steam marine of New Orleans, he had put fifty or a hundred steamboats destroyed or lost years before. In the same office I found another error of the same description. I wanted the shipments of vessels owned on the Atlantic. It was a part of the same inquiry. The collectors of the ports were to report them. It could be done, because all vessels of the United States are registered, and, if they were lost, it would, after a time, be known. I turned in the same office to a book containing these reports. I took up that of Portland, Maine, and found at one glance that it was totally deficient, and was obliged at last to resort to the shipping lists and insurance companies of New York. Here, it is very evident, is a want of reform in the very business of the department. It was the duty of the bureau officer to have these returns corrected. But what did he know about it? He was much more interested in partridges. The difficulty in these cases is the want of a supervising officer. It is impossible for the secretary to supervise these bureaus; for his whole time is taken up with members of congress and the general business of the treasury. It took me hours to get into Corwin's office, and years after it took a long time to see Mr. Chase. Whether this evil has been corrected, I know not; but it is certain if ever civil reform is undertaken, it must consist in a great deal more than in the mode of appointment. That is the least part of the evil. Appoint the minor officers as you may, who is to supervise the detached bureaus and see the whole machinery of work kept up to its whole duty.

The canvass for the presidency in 1828 was conducted with great bitterness. Other elections since have excited more national feeling, but none have brought out more bitter personal assaults, defamations, and controversy. The reason for this is found in the personal characters of Jackson and Clay, who were the real opponents, although Adams was the candidate against Jackson. Both these men had been brought up among slaves, and imbibed all the spirit of Southern aristocracy. They were both courteous men in society, and sometimes kind and generous, but impetuous in controversy, and despotic in bearing. They lived in the age of dueling, and both had fought duels. Jackson was called by his enemies, with almost literal truth, "the hero of two wars and forty frays." He and Benton had fought in the streets of Nashville, and he had killed two or three men in duels. He had commanded in Florida, when two men (Arbuthnot and Ambrister) were taken, as he claimed, as spies, and he hung them both up without any authority. On another occasion, he had tried and shot six militia-men. With many good qualities, especially courage, boldness, and enterprise, he was arbitrary and despotic. Jefferson was alive when Jackson was first mentioned for the presidency, in 1824, and said he was just as fit for the presidency as a cock for a sailor. In fact, the Battle of New Orleans, which Counselor Sampson called "that deathbed of British glory," was his single, and, as it proved, his most successful claim to be president. He was first nominated somewhere in Western Pennsylvania, by some men who were, as politicians always are, hunting for an available man, and afterward came forward claiming the merit of having discovered Jackson. In Pennsylvania, and two or three other states, his nomination took like wild-fire, while the Southern states were carried for him by the friends of Crawford. Mr. Clay was unable to carry for Adams any one of the states which had voted for himself. Mr. Adams held and carried all his own strength, while he derived none from Mr. Clay. The causes of this were very obvious. The Western states, which had voted for Clay, were composed of exactly those people who are most susceptible to the idea of military glory. In fine, they were carried by the Battle of New Orleans.

In the meanwhile, the canvass of 1828 was conducted, as I have said, with extreme bitterness. The bitter taunt of Randolph, in the senate, upon Clay, and the duel which followed, were typical of the continued assaults upon Clay for the next four years. The attack upon Jackson was equally bitter, with a good deal more material to support it. This was before the formation of the Whig party proper, and we who opposed Jackson were merely called anti-Jackson men. The basis of this organization was the combination of the supporters of Adams and Clay in 1827. We were abused as a " coalition " formed to keep office, while the people, it was said, were for Jackson. Before this, CHARLES HAMMOND had come to Cincinnati, from Belmont county, where he had practiced law, and was a strong friend of Clay. This reminds me of the first time I saw Hammond, and the disgust I had for his manners, although in fact no man could be better behaved than Hammond. He was sitting on a dry-goods box, at the corner of Main and Third streets. A young man was sitting beside with his arm around Hammond's neck—cheek-by-jowl. To see a young man thus treating a comparatively old man of high standing was a scene to which I was utterly unaccustomed, and was contrary to all my ideas of good breeding. This was not the only case, by any means, in which I found that the veneration for age and station, which was taught in New England, was not felt in the West. The young man who was thus hugging Hammond was William H. Harrison, Jr., the eldest son of Gen. Harrison, who soon after died.

Hammond, as I have said, had come to Cincinnati politically the friend of Clay. In point of law, information, and skill in writing, he was the superior of Clay. He and a few Adams men devised a monthly publication against Jackson, called "TRUTH'S ADVOCATE," and it was terribly severe on Jackson, chiefly because it was *truth* that it stated and proved. But of what value is truth when opposed to human passions? The impression left upon me is that in politics men neither want to hear truth nor care for it when it is told. In this case it may be said that the force of "*Truth's Advocate*" was broken by an apparent attack on Mrs. Jackson, which reacted. But in fact it was not an attack on Mrs. Jackson, but on Jackson's marriage with her. The facts were these: Mrs. Jackson, when young, was married to a man in East Tennessee, who used her ill. At that time Jackson became acquainted with her. Soon after she commenced a suit for divorce from her husband. The country was very thinly settled. The courts sat at great distances from the parties. It was known that the divorce suit was commenced, and it was confidently reported the decree of divorce had been granted. On that, Jackson was married to the divorced lady. It turned out that the decree had been delayed, and that at the time of the marriage, Mrs. Jackson had not been legally divorced. The marriage was innocent in intention, but illegal in fact. The decree of divorce was made a few days after. This transaction was set forth in *Truth's Advocate*, not certainly to injure Mrs. Jackson, but to show the character of Jackson, as regardless of law, when interfering with his purpose. Mrs. Jackson was always esteemed a kind, Christian woman, and at her death Jackson lamented her with deep grief.

Another transaction, described accurately in *Truth's Advocate*, was Jackson's connection with Burr. It was known that Burr had boats built on the Cumberland for his expedition, and that Burr visited Jackson at Nashville, and that Jackson had something to do with the boats. But it was not proved that Jackson knew anything of the object of the boats beyond an emigration to Western Louisiana; nor has it ever been proved that Burr's expedition had anything more treasonable in it than afterward took place in the emigration to Texas and the seizure of a Mexican territory. It is true, however, that those who knew Burr in the West, believed the object was the separation of the Western States from the Union. It is one of the mysteries of history that Burr should be able to organize a great expedition; should have talked to hundreds, if not thousands of people on the subject; should have enlisted able, public men in its favor, and yet that it should never be revealed what was the man's object. Nothing can better illustrate the artfulness of Burr's character. No man of his times has been more talked about than Aaron Burr. No man has had more enemies, or left the world in much worse odor. And yet Burr had come of a very religious, Christian family; was a man of shining talents; had served reputably in the war of the Revolution; had been in the family of Washington; was an able lawyer, and among his last public performances presided over the Senate with great dignity. The licentiousness which was so strongly charged upon him, was shared with many officers of the Revolutionary army. In fine, up to his duel with Hamilton, his career seems to have been approved by the public,

and his vices covered with the mantle of admiration
for his ability. Here we come to another historical
enigma. Why should his duel be charged upon him
as so much greater crime and disgrace than upon
Hamilton? As a duel, it was shared equally between
them. If Burr was known to be vicious, Hamilton
was by no means spotless. But if we were to judge
by the splendid sermon of DR. NOTT in his eulogy, we
should think the world had lost an unequaled apostle
of virtue. Hamilton was, in the common phase of the
world, a great man, and compared with Burr, was an
example of honor and morality. But the main cause
of the public judgment in this case was political and
social. Hamilton had married Miss Schuyler, associated with the best and proudest aristocracy of New
York. He was the friend and associate of Washington. He was really great in his management of the
treasury department, and more than that, he was the
bright, particular star of the Federal party, its apostle
and leader. He had quarreled with John Adams,
and if anyone wants to see an account of Hamilton
quite different from Dr. Nott's, he need only read a
letter from Adams to Jefferson, contained in the life
and correspondence of Adams. In that, he says,
among other things, that it is only necessary in the
future to have two such adventurers as Hamilton and
Burr, with their talents and ambition, to rise at the
head of factions, in order to destroy the government
and Union. How near this came to be fulfilled in the
war of the Rebellion, is well known. Adams hated
Hamilton, and Jefferson hated both Hamilton and
Burr. When the snows of eighty years had passed

over their heads, their memories were yet heated with the fires of political rivalry.

But I must return from this episode to my subject. Burr did visit Jackson on the Cumberland, and, in some respects, they were not unlike, but, in all that regards patriotism and profound interest in his country and countrymen, Jackson was far the superior, and also in that broader view of policy which discarded all artifice, and openly and boldly pursues its objects. It is reported that Burr afterward said that he had found in Jackson, on the Cumberland, a man who was fit to be a leader and commander.

Truth's Advocate published all that was known of Jackson and Burr in this boat-building business, but there was nothing in the affair which really indicated any want of patriotism or duty on the part of Jackson. These, and many other matters were published in *Truth's Advocate*, but whether it did more good or harm is doubtful. The world does not seem very anxious to learn truth, and still less to be judged by it. It may, however, be safely said that the publication of truth, in regard to Jackson, greatly diminished the popularity with which he came into office, and his arbitrary acts in office made it impossible for his successor (Van Buren) to be either popular or successful.

The canvass of 1828 was, as I said, conducted with great personal bitterness, but far more honestly than elections are now, and with far more truth in the statements made. It is true that the charges against Mr. Clay, of " bargain, intrigue, and management," had no just grounds, and that the illegality of Jackson's marriage made no moral crime, but, after all, there were no charges made which had not some appearance of fact, and there was no attempt to corrupt the public mind, or to make the offices of the country the spoils of party. That was reserved for the second administration of Jackson, when the corrupt New York politicians, of the Tammany class, had got his ear and confidence, through what was called the "Kitchen Cabinet." The scenes which then occurred are the most remarkable in our history, and, in some respects, the worst. Private scandal and public corruption then began that influence in public affairs which have pervaded politics ever since.

Apparently Mr. Adams was defeated by a very large majority of the electoral vote, but really the majority was comparatively small. Jackson had received a popular majority over Adams, in 1824, of 50,000, in a vote of 350,000. In 1828 he received a majority of 138,000, in a vote of 1,156,000, not so large, in proportion, as before. In 1824, five states chose electors by the legislatures. Anyone can see, by examining the votes of 1828, how little the strength of parties has changed since. The truth is, that politics, like religion, descend from father to son, with little variation. In two hundred years of English history, we see only alternation between the great Whig and Tory parties.

CHAPTER XV.

Nullification—Calhoun's Theory—Hamilton's Speech—
South Carolina Volunteers—Curious Incidents in South
Carolina—Webster's Speech—Jackson's Position—The
Proclamation—The Tariff—The Compromise—Failure
of Oratory—Success of the Republic.

THE presidential election of 1828 was scarcely over,
when there arose another controversy of wider and
deeper significance. In 1828, was passed a new tariff
act, which adopted and enforced the principle of pro-
tection to certain interests, especially with a view to
encourage and support American manufactures. Wool
and woolens were particularly protected. This act
gave great offense to the cotton states, which now
adopted, under the lead of MR. CALHOUN, the doctrine
that to diminish the imports was to diminish the ex-
ports, and, consequently, to diminish the value of the
cotton crops. They claimed to raise the cheapest and
best cotton in the world, and yet asserted that they
could not export it in proportion if we did not import
freely. I do not argue this point. It was quite plausible. But I wish to recall some of the consequences.
The tariff, of 1824, was pretty high, and the tariff of
1828 higher. Then the orators of South Carolina came
forth to proclaim the ruin and destruction which must
follow in the South. GENERAL JAMES HAMILTON, a
most eloquent man, proclaimed in public meetings the
ruin, devastation, and foreshadowed doom which at-

tended this terrible tariff, in South Carolina. According to him the homes were desolate, the beautiful villas and gardens of the planters were going into ruin. Whether true or not, this alarming picture startled the imagination of the people. The politicians fanned the flame, and loudly asked, what is the remedy? It was then that the genius of MR. CALHOUN formed a theory to suit the case. He said that the constitution was made by the states, not the people. It was a compact, to which the states were the only parties, and that, therefore, they were the only judges of whether there had been an infraction of the constitution, and if there had been, so the STATE could *interpose* its powers and authority to arrest the supposed unconstitutional laws of the general government. This is what was popularly known and correctly defined as NULLIFICATION—a practical nullification of the national government. Had it been possible to have carried this theory into effect, there would be no national government at this time. The most singular idea of Calhoun, and it is still stranger that it prevailed in the beginning of secession, was that this proceeding, by which the authority of the national government was to be overthrown, would be a peaceable measure! How could it be peaceable, if there were any people, even a minority, who were willing and able to support their government? It is probable that this very idea of a peaceful nullification, or secession, had great influence in favoring secession until the war actually came on. But the people of South Carolina, in 1828–1832, when there was great excitement on the subject, did not quite believe the doctrine of peace when rebellion was attempted. So, when they found the government would collect its revenue, through its officers, unless some resistance was made, the legislature of South Carolina passed an act to raise a body of 12,000 volunteers, armed and equipped. Here came in a part of unwritten history, which I knew myself, and always seemed to me supremely ridiculous. The nullifiers were foaming with rage, especially against American manufactures and ship owners, who, according to their theory, were defrauding the cotton-growers, by a tax on imports. They declared they would buy no American cloths or goods, but would go to England for everything. When, however, they must clothe the 12,000 volunteers, they determined to have the best. So they made a contract for blue uniforms and brass buttons. It happened that I was then traveling in New England, and, among other places, stopped at Waterbury, Connecticut, where my friend, Mr. Scoville, had then just began one of that series of factories which have made Waterbury a city. It was a button factory, and he showed me the works and the very ingenious machinery employed. Then, taking down some packages of finished brass buttons, very fine of their kind, he, with a laugh on his face, showed me the very buttons which were to be used by the volunteers of South Carolina. To me nothing could seem more ridiculous. There were the emblems of South Carolina, with its motto—*Nemo me impune lacessit*—on buttons made in Connecticut, to uniform the troops with which that little state was to defy the government, and boast that it would use no Yankee manufactures! In the many years which elapsed from nullification to the war of the Rebellion, many things of this kind occurred. The Southern people seem to have been really unconscious how largely they were dependent on others, not indeed for the bare necessaries of life, but for nearly all that made life comfortable.

The debate, the excitement, the threatenings, and the fears on the subject of nullification continued three years—indeed through all the first administration of Jackson. In the meanwhile there were several memorable occurrences.

I have mentioned the picture of desolation in South Carolina (attributed to tariff) drawn by Major James Hamilton, who had been a member of congress. It was really eloquent and beautiful, but terminated with the idea which afterward culminated in secession and rebellion. Speaking at Walterborough, South Carolina, he said :

" Where are now those beautiful homesteads and venerable chateaus which once adorned the land of our fathers, the abodes of hospitality and wealth, from which the most generous benefactions were dispensed to contented labor—by which slavery itself lost half the burden of its chains, in the kindness with which they were imposed? Gone ; fallen into irreversible decay. On the very hearthstone where hospitality kindled the most genial fires that ever blazed on her altars, the fox may lay down in security and peace ; and from the casement of the very window from which the notes of virtuous revelry were once heard, the owl sends forth to the listening solitude of the surrounding waste her melancholy descant, to mark the spot where desolation has come."

Was this picture true, or was it only fiction ? I suspect the orator, like the Fourth of July orator, had something to go on, but colored it with the visions of fancy.

Such were the strains by which South Carolina was called to believe herself deeply injured, her feelings outraged, and her rights violated. " But how," says the orator, " are we to interfere for the purpose of arresting the progress of the evil?" To this he replies: " A nullification, then, of the unauthorized act is the rightful remedy."

This doctrine was professedly founded on the Virginia and Kentucky resolutions of 1798, and it was defended as a peaceful measure. Those resolutions of 1798 were generally embodied in the proceedings of Democratic conventions, from 1828 to 1840. They were a part of the regular stock-in-trade of the party. How they came to be so, since they were never adopted but by two states, is a political enigma. The truth is, however, that all the original leaders of the Republican,[*] as it was first called, and afterward the Democratic, party, were Anti-Constitutionalists; opposed to the adoption of the constitution, fearing that it might lead to the foundation of a national or supreme government, in opposition to the rights of the states. There is no doubt the founders of the constitution intended it to be a national government; and no doubt it has become so in fact. But to this the Anti-Federalists were opposed, and so, for half a century, they continued to indoctrinate the Democratic party with them, and to infuse them, as far as possible, into the Democratic conventions. In the meanwhile, however, there was a counteracting force, which ulti-

---

[*] See Proceedings of Democratic Caucuses in 1808, 1812, 1816, and 1824.

mately proved politically omnipotent. This was nothing more or less than the patriotic *feeling* of the people. Men profess to be governed by reason; in fact, they are governed by feeling and interest. *This* feeling of nationality grew up at first under the insults and injuries of European powers. France brushed with us in 1798; the British fired upon the Chesapeake in 1809 ; Napoleon confiscated our ships in the port of Antwerp, under the Berlin and Milan decrees; the British seized our ships, under orders in council—they impressed our seamen in our own ships, with a sublime indifference to our rights and feelings, which in these days would seem incredible and impossible. The war of 1812–1815 began with the celebrated motto, " Free Trade and Sailors' Rights," and ended with that famous battle of New Orleans, which Counselor Sampson, not inaptly, called " the death-bed of British glory." It was certainly the death-bed of British pretension toward us. In the meanwhile, English travelers, reviewers, and writers were abusing and sneering at the American people. Some time after this, Robert Walsh wrote his " Appeal." At this time it is difficult for an American to realize this state of things, and the opposition and contumely, and even humiliation, under which this country grew up into a real and solid nationality. It was in this way nationality was cultivated, and the people began to *feel* there was a nationality, long before the gentlemen who were asserting state rights realized that fact. Against such a feeling all the arguments and casuistry of political philosophers are in vain. The resolutions of 1798 are no longer heard of. The war of the Rebellion buried them. Thirty-eight states and fifty millions of people can not be controlled by an abstract philosophy, or paper resolutions. The government is, and must henceforth remain, what the practical necessities of the country make it.

But let us return to nullification. At the same time that Hamilton was rousing South Carolina with fiery speeches, public meetings, both in Carolina and Georgia, were passing contra-resolutions against the supposed offenders. Kentucky and Ohio were strong tariff states, under the lead of Henry Clay. In Laurens and Edgefield counties, South Carolina, and in Baldwin and Montgomery counties, Georgia, it was resolved not to consume or buy the hogs, cattle, mules, bacon, etc., of the Western States.* When the legislature of South Carolina met, in December, this feeling was strongly developed. PRESTON, THOMPSON, HOLMES, and other members offered resolutions, the substance of which was that the tariff acts were palpable and dangerous infractions of the constitution, and that the state had a right to interpose and arrest them. How a tariff act, which is passed under the most direct and explicit power conferred by the constitution† on congress, can possibly be an infraction of the constitution was not explained then, and has never been explained since. Among the proceedings of the legislature of South Carolina was an act requiring citizens of South Carolina to take a test oath of exclusive allegiance to the state.‡ This test oath was the very essence of rebellion, although enacted thirty-two years before actual rebellion begun.

---

* See Niles' Register, 63.

† Constitution, article 1, section 8.

‡ South Carolina Ordinance, November, 1832.

The Court of Appeals in South Carolina, to their honor be it said, with great personal disinterestedness and moral independence declared the ordinance of the state on this point unconstitutional.*

In the meantime, JAMES MADISON, ex-president of the United States, had written two letters, published by a friend, declaring the tariff constitutional. These had a sedative effect, and the public mind was soon after turned to another subject. Practical nullification was not attempted until four years after. Let us, however, follow it to the end.

In May, 1832, congress again revised the tariff, not for the purpose of increasing duties, but that of remodifying them and rendering them more agreeable to the Southern States. That this was a fact was declared by COL. DRAYTON in an address to the people of South Carolina exhorting them to sustain the Union.† The very fact that such exhortation was made, and that nullification of the laws of the United States was considered a just and constitutional remedy for supposed evils is positive proof that the seeds of the Rebellion of 1861 were sown and alive twenty-eight years before. The modification of the tariff proved unsatisfactory. The excitement was again renewed. The imaginations of the people were inflamed with the idea that they were imposed upon by the majority in the Union. Inflammatory toasts were drunk, and the most distinguished public men supported measures, the sole object of which was to resist the laws of the Union.

MR. JOHN C. CALHOUN, in a letter, dated "Fort Hill,

---

* Decisions of South Carolina Court of Appeals.
† 45 Niles' Register.

30th of July, 1832," declared that nullification was a peaceful remedy, and necessary to the preservation of others.* He said, that he had entire confidence that the time would come when this principle would be regarded as "the great conservative principle 'of our admirable system of government," and those who maintain it among "the great benefactors of the country." If Mr. Calhoun believed this, the history of the next thirty years proves him to have been among the most deluded and mistaken of men. It is true, that a casuist may say, that nullification and secession were not the same. But they both had the same root. If a state nullified or resisted the laws of the United States, then the revenue could not be collected without force ; and, if a state seceded, then the revenue could not be collected without force. It came practically, and, in the view of common sense, to the same thing. It was resistance to the supreme laws of the Union, which could only end in a final conflict. The doctrines of Calhoun, McDuffie, Major Hamilton, and others were not destined, however, to be accepted even in the South, without a stern opposition. JUDGE SMITH, who had been United States Senator, in an address to the people of Spartanburg (S. C.),thus wrote: " To say that you can resist the general government and remain in the Union at peace is a perfect delusion, calculated only to hoodwink an honest community, until they shall have advanced too far to retrace their steps, which they must do, and do with disgrace and humiliation, or enter upon a bloody conflict with the general government. The general government can

* 43 Niles' Register, 56.

not bow its sovereignty to the mandates of South Carolina while the Union is worth preserving."* Was there ever prophecy more perfectly fulfilled? The delusion continued, the people of the South were hoodwinked, the government was resisted, the bloody conflict came on, and the South ended it in disgrace and humiliation. But all this did not happen just then. The usual debates, controversies, and compromises took place through nearly thirty years, in which nothing was settled, and nothing could be settled while it was considered debatable whether the national government was supreme.

This was the state of things, when in October, 1832, the legislature of South Carolina passed an act " calling a convention of the people " of the state. The convention elected under this act assembled at Columbia, the 19th of November, 1832, and there passed an act for nullifying† certain acts of Congress, called the tariff acts. It is unnecessary to say more of the ordinance, than that it pronounced the tariff acts of 1828 and 1832, " null and void," and not binding upon the state, its officers, or citizens; that it was unlawful for any constituted authorities to enforce payment of said duties ; that if the general government should employ force to carry into effect its laws, or attempt to coerce the state by shutting up its ports, that South Carolina would consider THE UNION DISSOLVED. This was a frank, open resistance to the laws of the Union. But it met with no help or great sympathy from the other anti-tariff states. Governor Gayle, of Alabama, condemned nullification. The legislature of

---

* 43 Niles' Register, 219.
† 43 Niles' Register, 219.

Tennessee passed resolutions unanimously condemning it. The legislature of Georgia, a strong anti-tariff state, also condemned it. Nevertheless, South Carolina persevered; called out a great number of volunteers, and the whole state was a great camp, filled with fire and fury.

Such was the state of things when, on the 10th of December, 1832, General Jackson issued his now famous PROCLAMATION, one of the ablest and most important documents in our history. Its composition was attributed, and, no doubt correctly, to EDWARD LIVINGSTONE, then secretary of state. The sentiments were, doubtless, those of Jackson. It was filled with that LOVE of UNION which, in all times and circumstances, has been a leading element of the American character, and it was received almost universally with approval and applause. One paragraph only is necessary to show the constitutional ground taken :

" I consider then," says the President, " the power to annul a law of the United States, assumed by one state, incompatible with the existence of the Union; contradicted expressly by the letter of the constitution; unauthorized by its spirit; inconsistent with every principle on which it was founded, and destructive of the great object for which it was formed.

" No act of violent opposition to the laws has yet been committed, but such a state of things is hourly apprehended, and it is the intent of this instrument to PROCLAIM, not only the duty imposed on me by the constitution, ' to take care that the laws be faithfully executed,' shall be performed to the extent of the powers already vested in me by law, or such other as the wisdom of congress shall devise and intrust to me for that purpose; but, to warn the citizens of South Carolina, who have been deluded into an opposition to the laws, of the danger they will incur by obedience to the illegal and disorganizing ordinance of the convention."

This proclamation had a most extraordinary effect on the public mind. That which was wanting in 1860 was present in 1832—the manifest determination of the government to put forth all its power to suppress insurrection and punish traitors. JACKSON was a man of iron will, of keen intellect, and burning patriotism, whom no sophistries could deceive and no demagogues could intimidate. The heart of the nation responded to him. Happily the war of the Rebellion was put off for thirty years, when it could be more decisive, and vindicate the justice of Providence more clearly to the intelligence of mankind.

In connection with this proclamation must be taken another document, not less striking or effective. This was the speech of DANIEL WEBSTER, delivered in the senate, January, 1830, on the doctrine of nullification.

In the discussion on Foote's resolutions, COLONEL HAYNE, of South Carolina, advanced the whole doctrine of nullification, as created (I may say) by John C. Calhoun, and held by South Carolina. The reply of Daniel Webster, on the 26th and 27th of January, 1830, was the most celebrated speech ever delivered in congress, and more than equal to the great speeches of Chatham and Burke. Of course the subject of constitutional law and political theories did not admit the fiery eloquence of Chatham or the splendid diction of Burke, but it was far superior to them in the closeness of logic, the dignity of the subject, and the imposing strength with which he carried a nation with him. The precise meaning and power of that speech was not so apparent then, even with all its popular success, as it was in the war of the Rebellion. The young men who were then coming upon the stage of action, got their idea of constitutional law from Webster, and they were just of the age to become the actors and leaders when secession began. The attempt at nullification and the argument of Webster, kindled thousands of minds into the ardor of patriotism and the study of constitutional law. I was one of them, and my little work, the " Political Grammar,"* published in 1834, was one of the consequences. It was one of the few things which have satisfied me that I had not lived wholly in vain.

When Webster's speech was delivered, I was crossing the mountains (as the phrase then was), on the death of my father at New Haven (Conn.), and I received the speech in the *National Intelligencer*, I think, at Somerset (Penn.), and I was completely startled and surprised. It seemed to me to embody all that grand idea of the American Republic, with its glory and strength surviving, as I believed, and do believe it will do until the sunset of history; giving to the nations light, freedom, and righteousness. No speech before or since, has produced such an effect on me. I asked my friend, JUDGE BURNET, then senator from Ohio, how it was delivered and with what effect on the senate ; for, when I heard Webster he was rather a cold speaker. Judge Burnet said, it was delivered with a warmth and energy worthy of the subject, and

* Published by the Harpers, in 1834, and still in circulation.

the effect was most striking. Such a speech had already prepared the public mind for the proclamation of 1832. Both have gone to the world and remain to-day among the greater documents in political history; and of them, their authors might have said with Horace and with Tacitus, that they would survive to other ages, when brass and stone had decayed.

Here let me remark on the decline of American oratory. At least, that decline seems very evident to me, and the causes equally evident. We hear to-day of immense audiences gathered to hear Moody and Beecher, John Hall, and many others; but taking the evidence of what they said, and how they appear in print, would any one compare them with Dwight, and Mason, and Nott? The actors, it is said, went to hear Dr. Mason preach in order to learn his gestures. The sermon of Dr. Nott on the death of Hamilton has never been equaled by any of the Beechers, Halls, or McCloskys of the day, and I could pick out twenty of Dwight's sermons which are not equaled by any of the popular preachers of the present time. We need not cite Whitfield, for he was a prodigy. It is exactly the same thing with political oratory. What man in public life of any sort equals Webster or Clay? You will say Corwin, but Corwin is not of this generation. He is dead. Besides he never did rise to the level of Webster and Clay. But justice to him requires me to say that his oratory was peculiar; it was his own; not borrowed from either ancient or modern school. It is beyond all doubt or question that we have no orators of this day equal to those of the last generation. But the question arises, why? This is a boasting generation; why should there not be orators as well as machinists, telegraphs, or railroads ?   The answer is very simple and the reason plain, though not a sufficient one to account for a lack of ambition on the part of men to win the fame of an orator.

The reason is this, that a public speaker now is not ambitious of fame from posterity, but how he shall appear before his present and temporary audience. The facts and the reasoning are made plain to the voters, but the oratory is wanting.   He is talking for the newspapers.   It may not be a mistake, but it is a fact.   The newspaper has killed the great orator.   How killed him ?   Because, he is anxious to appear in the newspaper and be popular before the people, and what is required to make a man popular in the newspaper is a very different thing from what is required for a great orator.   What do the ordinary readers of newspapers care for classic language, splendid figures, profound learning, or deep sentiment ? Nothing.   Hence, the pulpit orator and the political orator, perceiving this, fall, at once, into that colloquialism which is the ruin of all oratory, of all eloquence, and of all future fame.   But worse than this, when he who should have been the great orator of the pulpit, the bar, or the senate comes into the newspapers, he is beaten by the newspaper writer.   He thinks he is telling the world a good deal in most splendid language, but finds that the newspaper writer is ahead of him. The public writer of the newspaper is a well-informed man, who knows the people well, and who knows how to speak to the people in old English—the Anglo-Saxon tongue. Now, what is the result ? The orator of the pulpit and the senate, after sacrificing all true oratory, the classical and

the poetic, the fervent and the grand, for the sake of
newspaper notoriety, finds that it is not he, but his
newspaper friend, who appears before the public as the
great man of the occasion! But let us return to the
thread of history. The speech of Webster and the
proclamation of Jackson silenced the conspirators.
South Carolina was a camp, and the beautiful uniform
of the volunteers shone with the buttons made by Mr.
Scoville, at Waterbury, Connecticut. In this condition
of affairs, congress passed what was called the " force
bill," the meaning and object of which was to enforce
the collection of and the execution of the laws in any
state or states attempting to nullify the laws of the
United States. At this time of great emergency, to
save the nullifiers, if possible, from the effects of their
wild and insane proceedings, Mr. Clay proposed his
compromise bill—a compromise which caused the loss
of fortunes to thousands of persons, and which ultimately threw the country into the worst commercial
convulsion it has ever known, and did not abate one
whit the causes of that political antagonism which
existed and must exist between slavery and freedom,
and which at last Providence settled by the war of secession. Mr. Clay was not at that time on speaking
terms with Mr. Calhoun, but his friends proposed the
plan to the latter, and it was accepted. The plan was
that the tariff should be reduced a certain per cent.
each year until it fell to twenty per cent. This compromise was adopted. South Carolina suspended her
aggressive operations, and the country returned to an
apparent peace—apparent only. How delusive, how
uncertain, and how utterly inefficient, we shall see
when we examine the subsequent debates on the right

of petition, the after compromise of 1850, and the secession war of 1861. Why were the people of that
day so deluded? In fact, they were not. The real
statesmen of that day knew well that the political vol-
cano might burst forth at any moment.

In another chapter* I have noticed the Missouri question, the compromise of 1820. From that time on for
forty years, statesmen of all parties were engaged in
constant, cautious, fearful attempts to compromise the
great crime of the country. They were trying to use
the language of an exorcist, " to lay the ghost!" But
the ghost was impracticable. There was no human
power capable of laying it.

The more the southern slave states grew in numbers,
in cotton products, in wealth and political influence, the
more they felt the necessity—an honest necessity—of
protecting slavery and extending its domain; the more
grew the necessity of the non-slave states, the more
the church was excited to inquire into it, and the more
northern demagogues found a fruitful field in which to
play upon the passions and the prejudices of the
people.

The conflict was inevitable. We see it now; but
thinking people saw it long years before it came to
pass. In 1828, however, the disease was not called by
its right name. As we have seen, they called it the
wrong of the tariff; but behind the tariff lay cotton,
and behind cotton lay slavery. We shall see later how
it at last took its proper name. I have here traced
one chapter in the history of political slavery, and have
done it not so much for the curious interest of the
reader as to put on record what I know to be—brief

* Chapter VI.

as it is—an accurate view of one of the most interesting periods of the social progress and political revolutions through which our country passed. The time was four years, but it was a complete microcosm of what followed in the war of secession.

I may remark here that I know of no more signal example of the interposition, wisdom, and mercy of the divine Providence than that by which the rebellion was averted in 1832, and by which it was brought on and conquered in 1861. If there had been actual rebellion in 1832, it would have been called a tariff war. South Carolina, or any state which joined her, would have been easily conquered, but slavery would have remained untouched, and the South would still have believed itself the dominant power. Thirty years afterward, however, the real cause was slavery, and the whole power of the South was arrayed in its defense, and slavery and secession were both destroyed. God justified His ways to men. The great republic, after one hundred years of struggle, stands literally regenerated and disenthralled. Storms and darkness have fled from her horizon, and nothing but the wrath of God upon disobedience can ever again cross her splendid career.

CHAPTER XVI.

*The Cholera—Its Advent, Progress, and Mortality—Dr.
Drake's Literary Parties—General King—Mrs. King
(Mrs. Peters)—Catharine Beecher—Harriet Beecher
(Mrs. Stowe)—Professor Stowe—Judge Hall—Mrs.
Caroline Hentze—College of Teachers—Albert Pickett
—Joshua Wilson—Alexander Kinmont—James Per-
kins—Dr. Beecher—Alexander Campbell—Thomas L.
Grimke.*

In 1832 the Asiatic cholera visited the United States.
No great epidemic or general disease has before or
since prevailed in North America. The yellow fever
had appeared locally in New York, Philadelphia, and
Charleston. In 1699* the yellow fever appeared in
Philadelphia, and swept off a great number of people.
In 1728 it broke out in Charleston, and swept off many
inhabitants. The planters would suffer no persons to
carry supplies into the town, and the numbers of the
sick were so great that white persons were scarcely to
be found sufficient to bury the dead. The yellow fever
again appeared in New York and Philadelphia in
1793, 1797, 1798, and 1823. These visitations were,
however, local, and did not extend to other places.
In 1832 the Asiatic cholera became general throughout the United States, and for this reason, and because
I was present where it prevailed in every season, it
may be interesting to give some of the leading facts

* Holmes' Annals.

of those times. The cholera arrived at Quebec in an emigrant ship, and immediately proceeded by the Champlain canal and Hudson river to New York city. On the other hand, it ascended the St. Lawrence, entered the basin of the lakes, and swept around the upper Mississippi, whence it entered the valley of the Ohio. From Buffalo it was carried by Scott's troops, then on their way to engage in the Black Hawk war, to other places. Among these troops, it broke out on the bosom of the lakes, and, by the time they reached Chicago, they had already been decimated by death, and a large number of those left were immediately consigned to hospitals. General Scott, his staff, and about two hundred and twenty men, embarked in the steamboat Sheldon Thompson, in which, on the 8th of July, the cholera broke out. The boat arrived on the 10th inst. at Chicago. In these two or three days, out of two hundred men, one officer and fifty-one men died, and eighty were left sick at Chicago. The fate of those in the other boats was even worse than that of those on the Sheldon. On landing the troops, many of the soldiers deserted, and their fate was terrible. Mr. Norvell, of Detroit, wrote to the Philadelphia *Enquirer:* "Of the deserters scattered all over the country, some have died in the woods, and others have been devoured by the wolves. Their straggling survivors are occasionally seen marching, some of them know not whither, with their knapsacks on their backs, shunned by the terrified inhabitants as the source of mortal pestilence." Such were the scenes and horrors which attended the cholera in its first progress through the northwest. At its first appearance from Quebec to New York, I was at West Point, on the Hudson. From Albany to New York, in the small villages, and especially at West Point, it appeared only in the premonitory symptoms, and was not violent; but in the city of New York it was violent and fatal. The newspapers published the cases and deaths daily, and they were looked for and read with the deepest interest. In New York, as in nearly all cities and towns, the disease appeared in low places and in neighborhoods where filth prevailed. The same fact was noted in the city of London, and a parliamentary inquiry showed that it appeared in the same localities with the typhoid fever. These localities were where there were filthy sewers, cess-pools, and drains; but it is remarkable that neither in London nor in New York was this pestilence as fatal in proportion to their inhabitants as in many smaller places. It was also noted that no appearance of anything unusual in the weather or atmosphere was apparent. In the month of June, when the cholera descended the Hudson, the weather was most beautiful, the temperature mild, and the air calm. While this pestilence was terrifying humanity, nature remained the same.

In the month of October, 1832, when the cholera had apparently left New York, I determined, after nearly four years' of absence, to return to Cincinnati, and resume my profession. We returned by way of Buffalo and Erie to Pittsburg. At Erie, Pennsylvania, we took the stage to Pittsburg, and at Pittsburg took a steamboat down the Ohio. When we arrived at Pittsburg, we were surprised to find that the Ohio river was covered with the cholera, almost every steamboat having it on board. It had arrived at Cincinnati about the 20th of September, but we had supposed that by this time (October) it had abated, and we took a steamboat for Cincinnati. At Wheeling we found boats with the cholera on board, but determined to go on. On the way down, my wife had a slight attack of cholera, but soon recovered. At Marietta island, a singular incident occurred. We reached there about dark, and the captain dropped anchor, intending to remain for the night. Just then a steamboat came up the river, and stopped at the island near our boat. On asking for the news, the captain said they had four or five cases of cholera on board, and were about to bury one of their dead on the island. This at once gave the alarm. Captain, crew, and passengers of our boat were all excited; ladies were using camphor bottles; and the captain and crew appeared the most alarmed. The anchor was immediately lifted, steam started, and we went down the river. The fright soon subsided, and the next morning the sun rose bright and beautiful on one of the loveliest of October days. Here I may again remark that never was the weather brighter or better than during the prevalence of the cholera. We proceeded on our journey, but many of the passengers, including myself, decided that it was dangerous and unwise to go to Cincinnati. My main motive for going there had ceased to exist, for I found by a letter at Wheeling that my mother, who had been left almost alone at Cincinnati, had left there and gone to Oxford. I decided, therefore, to land at Gallipolis, and go to Oxford. Among the ladies on our boat was Mrs. Jonathan Bates, who still survives, almost the only one of that period who can remember and relate the facts I have here stated. She is now past eighty years of age, and has lived the nearly half century since, to be a most useful and respected member of society, honored in the church, and admired by her friends. She, myself, and others proceeded across the country by stage to Chillicothe. At Chillicothe, we took a carriage to Oxford. At Oxford I found my mother, and remained a month in that pleasant village. Then and at several subsequent visits, I became interested in Miami University. In 1835, I delivered a literary address before the societies there. Here I may say that no western institution of the same means and age has done more for the cause of education, or sent forth more able and intelligent men, than Miami University. It is to be regretted that its means have been crippled by the early lease of its lands at a comparatively nominal rate. There is now a prospect of its revival, with increased strength, and it is hoped that it will yet become one of the most valuable of our institutions.

Our visit at Oxford passed pleasantly and speedily away, and about the first of December we returned to Cincinnati. A snow had fallen, the streets were icy, and the gaslights dimly burning, presenting to our imagination the ghostly appearance of the departed cholera. The city was then healthy, and remained so until the following May, when the cholera again broke out among the Germans in the northern part of the city. It returned again in 1834, 1849, 1850, 1851, 1852, and 1865 (or 1866). In one of these seasons (1849) it was far more severe than in 1832, and, in all times of its appearing, alarming. That I may not return to this subject, I will here give a summary of some of its causes and effects. In September, 1849, the board of health in Cincinnati returned the following number of deaths between the first of May and the first of September, four months :

Deaths by Cholera,................................ 4,114
    "   " other Diseases,................... 2,345
    Aggregate,................... 6,459

If we add to this the number of deaths in the last two weeks in April, and from the first of September to the fifteenth of October, during which the number of deaths exceeded the average, we shall have, for six months, at least 7,000, of which 4,600 were from cholera. The mortality of the other six months, at the average rate, was only 1,500. We have, then, for 1849, a total mortality of 8,500, which (the population of the city being 116,000), made a ratio of one in fourteen. If we examine this mortality *socially*, we shall arrive at some extraordinary results. The division of the cemeteries of Cincinnati by nationalities and religions, is so complete, that we can easily determine how many Americans and how many foreign born died of cholera. Taking the number given above, of those who died between the first of May and the first of September, we have this result :

Germans, Irish, and Hebrews, ... 2,896
Americans, English, Scotch, and Welch,............. 1,218
    Total,................... 4,114

The ascertained proportion of Germans, Irish, and Hebrews, at that time, was 40 per cent. of the whole population. The residue of the population (Americans, English, Welsh, etc.), was 60 per cent. Now, making the comparison, according to these proportions, we find that :

Died of Cholera—Germans and Irish,	1 in 16
" " Hebrews,	1 in 64
" " Americans, English, etc.,	1 in 56
" " the whole population,	1 in 29

We thus see that the deaths among the German and Irish was within a fraction of being fourfold that of the Americans, and double those of the entire population, in proportion. Investigations like these, into the results of different modes and habits of life, would contribute something to the progress of social science, that science which will be of the greatest importance to the future. The causes of these results are probably various; but must, undoubtedly, be found in the different conditions of the people and different modes of living.

During the prevalence of this pestilence, a deep gloom and solemn fear pervaded the city. Many plans and suggestions were made to mitigate the disease. The greatest mortality was in the hot month of July, yet great fires were made in some streets, with the idea of driving off the poison; but the disease went on with its fearful fatality, and the "long funerals blackened all the way." At this time my brother-in-law, Dr. Worthington, died at our house, not of cholera, but of typhus fever, taken from exposure and fatigue from attending upon his patients. In consequence of this, and the deep gloom which pervaded the city and ourselves, we went for a few weeks to Xenia. Arrived there, we found that the cholera had broken out at about the same time. Our friends were alarmed and excited, and exposed through the same scenes, only on a smaller scale, as those seen in Cincinnati. Thus, we had passed through all the terrors and afflictions of the year 1849, fatal to Cincinnati. It was one of the saddest and least profitable years of my life. I have described it here, for the purpose of exhibiting, briefly, what seems unknown to this generation—one of the greatest calamities that can afflict mankind.

I will now return to the period in time when I left my personal narrative. January, 1833, found me in a small law-office, on Fourth street, near Main, Cincinnati. I had determined to resume my profession at any rate, for the purpose of doing something, however little. It turned out to be little; but the attempt was most valuable to me, for it made the remainder of my life useful and honorable, if not remarkable. It was in this office I formed the idea of writing " *The Political Grammar,*" a practical work on the constitution, much needed by young men, and which, for *forty* years, has been more or less in circulation. It is a brief compendium of the commentaries, legislation, and decisions of the supreme court in regard to the constitution. It was adapted to students, and has been studied in many of the academies and institutions of the country. It was really not published until two years after it was planned. In the meanwhile, and connected with this idea, I acquired a bent toward literary pursuits, which have occupied my mind and attention from that day to this. Circumstances, which I will now relate, encouraged that taste, and completed my transfer from the life of a lawyer to that of a public writer. It was in that year, 1833, my friend and relative, Dr. Daniel Drake, instituted a social and literary reunion at his house, which, to those who frequented it, possessed all the charms of information, wit, and kindness. These meetings were really formed for the benefit of his daughters, then just growing into womanhood. Those meetings are indelibly impressed upon my memory, and though others of similar character have been made memorable by literary fame, I am well persuaded that they were neither more instructive nor more pleasing than those of Dr. Drake, at his Vine-street home. The reunions were small enough to meet in the parlor, and the entertainment and instruction of a conversational character, so as to avoid the rigidity and awkwardness of a mere literary party. Thus, the conversation never degenerated into mere gossip, nor was it ever forced into an unpleasant or an unwilling gravity. We used to assemble early—about half past seven— and, when fully collected, the doctor, who was the acknowledged chairman, rang his little bell for general attention. This caused no constraint; but simply brought us to the topic of the evening. Sometimes this was appointed beforehand. Sometimes it arose out of what was said or proposed on the occasion. Some evenings essays were read on selected topics. On other evenings nothing was read, and the time was passed in the discussion of some interesting question. Occasionally a piece of poetry or a story came in to relieve the conversation. These, however, were rather interludes than parts of the general plan, whose main object was the discussion of interesting questions belonging to society, literature, and religions. The subjects were always of a suggestive and problematical kind; so that the ideas were fresh, the debates animated, and the utterance of opinion frank and spontaneous. There, in that little circle of ladies and gen-

tlemen, I have heard many of the questions which
have since occupied the public mind, talked over with
an ability and fullness of information which is seldom
possessed by larger and more authoritative bodies.
Nor were these meetings unimportant; for nothing
can be unimportant which directs minds—whose influence spreads over a whole country—and such were
these. I do not say what impressions they received;
but I know that persons were assembled there, of such
character and talent as seldom meet in one place, and
who, going out into the world, have signalized their
names in the annals of letters, science, and benevolence.

Dr. Daniel Drake was himself the head of the circle,
whose suggestive mind furnished topics for others, and
was ever ready to revive a flagging conversation. He
was a man of real genius, whose mind was fresh, active, ambitious, and intellectually enterprising. He
studied medicine with Dr. Goforth, the pioneer physician of Cincinnati, and for thirty years was a leader
in medical science and education. He founded the
Medical College of Ohio, the Cincinnati Hospital, and
was a professor in medical colleges, and a teacher, during the largest part of his active life. He closed his
career with a great work on the diseases of the Mississippi Valley, a work of great value, embodying
an immense amount of research, information, and
science.

General Edward King was another member of the
society, who, in spirit, manners, and elocution, was a
superior man, having the dignity of the old school,
with the life of the new. He was a son of Rufus
King, one of the early and able statesmen of our

country who did much to form our constitutions, and whose name will live in the annals of history. Gen. King was bred a lawyer, and came out to Ohio, as many aspiring young men did, to found his fortunes in what was then the New West. He married a daughter of Governor Worthington, practiced law at Chillicothe, and became speaker of the Ohio Legislature. Removing to Cincinnati, he became a member of our literary circle—both witty and entertaining. His wife, since known as Mrs. Peter, has become more widely known than her husband, for her great and active benevolence, and as the founder of institutions, and a leader in society. She had read a great deal, had a strong memory, and was remarkable for the fullness of her information. She wrote several essays for our circle, and was a most instructive member. The activity, energy, and benevolence of her mind accomplished in the next forty years probably more of real work for the benefit of society, than any one person, and that work has made her widely known both at home and abroad.

Another member of our circle was JUDGE JAMES HALL, then editor of the *Western Monthly Magazine*, whose name is known both in Europe and America. He also, in the long time that elapsed before his death, accomplished much and good work as a writer, citizen, and man of business. The *Western Monthly Magazine*, which he then edited, was an excellent periodical, to which many of the literary young men of Cincinnati contributed. But literary periodicals there have never been profitable. Many have been published, but soon perished. Judge Hall left the magazine to become cashier and president of the Commercial Bank, a much more profitable business. In the meanwhile, he published several stories, novels, and essays on the West, which made him widely known, and deserved the success they received, by their very pleasant style and pictures of Western life.

PROFESSOR STOWE, then a comparatively young man, was also present, and contributed his share to the conversation. He is the best Biblical scholar I ever knew. In recent years he has published his " History of the Books of the Bible," a work of great learning and of great utility. His first wife, a New England lady, quite handsome and interesting, also attended the reunions. His present wife, then MISS HARRIET BEECHER, was just beginning to be known for her literary abilities. Two or three years after this time, I published in the *Cincinnati Chronicle* what, I believe, was her first printed story. I had heard her read at Miss Pierce's school, in Litchfield, Connecticut, her first public composition. It surprised everyone so much that it was attributed to her father, but was in fact only the first exhibition of her remarkable talents. In the reunion I speak of, she was not distinguished for conversation, but when she did speak, showed something of the peculiar strength and humor of her mind. Her first little story, published in the CHRONICLE, immediately attracted attention, and her writings have always been popular. Notwithstanding the world-wide renown of "*Uncle Tom's Cabin,*" her real genius and characteristics were as much exhibited in her short stories as in her larger books. Her sister, MISS CATHARINE BEECHER, was a far more easy and fluent conversationalist. Indeed, few people had more talent to entertain a company, or keep the ball of conver-

sation going than Miss Beecher, and she was as willing as able for the task. For many years she was distinguished as an educator, and has published works
on domestic economy, metaphysics, and religion. Her
name is widely known, and she is distinguished as an
author and a philanthropist.

Conspicuous in our circle, both in person and manners, was Mrs. Caroline Lee Hentze, whom none saw
without admiring. She was what the world called
charming. And, though since better known as an
authoress, was personally quite remarkable. Her husband, Mr. Hentze, was a Frenchman, born in the
French Revolution. A man of such sensitive and retiring habits, as hid him from the public view. Yet,
he was a man of science, fond of entomology and
natural history. At the time I speak of, they were
keeping a popular female seminary on Third street,
and were among the most active and interesting of
our coterie. Soon after this, they moved to the South,
and established a female seminary there, and Mrs.
Hentze contributed several novels to the press. I
might name other persons whose wit or information
contributed to the charms of our intercourse, but I
should want the apology which public fame has given
to the mention of these. We had more than one
whose memory does not linger on the fame-covered
hill, but whose bright minds flowed in the vale below,
and sparkled as it flowed.

It is enough that I have mentioned out of a small
circle gathered in a parlor names which have been renowned both in Europe and America, and whose public reputation has contributed to the fame of our country. I have dwelt more particularly on these meetings

to illustrate what I think I've seen in other cases, and to which people in general seldom give due weight. I mean the influence of social sympathy in forming and developing individual minds.

Several years since, I heard one of the oldest and most experienced teachers in the United States enumerate a number of distinguished public men in New York, who had all been at the same time pupils of one school. Among them were the most eminent literary men of that state. I can not doubt that they greatly influenced one another in their tastes and studies, for I have seen that in other schools and societies.

About the year 1833, was founded what was called " The College of Teachers," which continued ten years, and was an institution of great utility and wide influence. Its object was both professional and popular ; to unite and improve teachers, and, at the same time, to commend the cause of education to the public mind. The former object might have been obtained by the meeting of practical teachers only, as is now done, but to popularize education required that gentlemen of science and general reputation, who had weight with the community, should also be connected with it. At that time, public education was just beginning, and almost all in the Ohio educational system, as I shall hereafter show, was created and developed after that period. To do this was the object in view, and, accordingly, a large array of distinguished persons took part in these proceedings. I doubt whether in any one association to promote the cause of education, there was ever in an equal space of time concentrated in this country a larger measure of talent, information, and zeal. Among those who either spoke or wrote for it, were ALBERT PICKETT, the president, and for half a century an able teacher; DR. DANIEL DRAKE, the HON. THOMAS SMITH GRIMKE, the REV. JOSHUA L. WILSON, ALEXANDER KINMONT, and JAMES H. PERKINS, PROF. STOWE, DR. BEECHER, DR. ALEX. CAMPBELL, BISHOP PURCELL, PRESIDENT MCGUFFEY, DR. AYDE-LOTTE, E. D. MANSFIELD, MRS. LYDIA SIGOURNEY, and MRS. CAROLINE LEE HENTZE.

With these were numerous professors, practical teachers, and citizens, zealous for the cause of education, most of whom contributed more or less to the transactions of the college. These transactions were for several years embodied in annual volumes, which can no doubt be found in public libraries, and which contain able and eloquent treatises on various subjects.

The duty of organization and publication—in fact, that of practically sustaining the association—fell mainly on the working teachers of Cincinnati, and for this reason, probably, it ultimately died away, and lost its popular character. It had, however, accomplished its object, in exciting popular interest in education, and impelling many persons to its support, who had the ability and influence, to found the present system of public schools in Ohio. Since that time, associations of practical teachers have taken its place, and are beyond doubt useful and instructive to teachers. Yet there is wanting some popular means of connecting teachers with the great public; and I am convinced that the College of Teachers, composed of both practical and literary men, was the best reunion of that sort yet devised, and for which no substitute has been found. The human spirit, like a plant, needs a genial soil, and draws nutriment not only from the earth, but from the atmosphere. In this place it is proper to mention some of those who took an active part in the College of Teachers, and nearly all of whom are dead.

ALBERT PICKETT, president of the College of Teachers, was a venerable, gray-haired man, who had been for nearly fifty years a practical teacher. He had for many years kept a select academy, in New York. He removed to Cincinnati a few years before the period of which I speak, and established a select school for young ladies. He was a thorough teacher, a man of clear head, and filled with zeal for his profession. He presided over the college with great dignity, and I never knew a man of more pure, disinterested zeal in the cause of education.

DR. JOSHUA L. WILSON was a pioneer in the church as well as in the settlement of Cincinnati. He was not the first pastor of the Presbyterian Church, but was the longest in service—I think about forty years. In the College of Teachers he was an earnest and zealous advocate of public education; but demanded that education should be founded on religion, and the Bible should be a primary element in all public education. In 1836, Dr. Wilson delivered an address, in one paragraph of which he sums up his reasoning on this subject (which is also an example of his style and sentiments): " But, to sum up what I have said, 'God has made of one blood all nations of men.' These natures of ours, which climate, custom, language, and religion have made appear so opposite, are formed after the same image, Is the rude Hotentot superior to the ape? It is because he is a man, and not a brute. Is the civilized man superior to the

Hottentot? It is because he is instructed and educated. Is the Christian superior to the pagan? It is
because he knows the Bible, and its Divine Author."

ALEXANDER KINMONT might be called an apostle of
classical· learning. If others considered the classics
necessary to an education, he thought them the one
thing needful—the pillar and foundation of solid learning. For this he contended with the zeal of a martyr
for his creed; and if ever the classics received aid
from the manner in which they were handled, they received it from him. Kinmont was a Scotchman, born
near Montrose, Angusshire. Having accidentally lost
one arm, he was left to pursue the bent of his tastes
toward learning. In school and college he bore off the
first prizes, and advanced with rapid steps in the
career of knowledge. At the University of Edin-
burgh, which he entered while yet young, he became
tainted with the scepticism then very prevalent. Removing to America, he became principal of the Bed-
ford Academy, where he shone as a superior teacher.
There he emerged from the gloom and darkness of
scepticism, to the faith of the " New Church," as the
church founded on the principles of Swedenborg is
called. His vivid imagination was well adapted to receive these doctrines, and he advocated them with all
the fervor of his nature. In 1827, he removed to
Cincinnati, and established a select academy for the
instruction of boys in mathematical and classical learning. The motto adopted was: " *Sit gloria Dei, et
utilitate hominum,*" a motto which does honor to
both his head and heart. In 1835, before the College
of Teachers, he was specially opposed to the doctrines
of Mr. Grimke, which were in favor of what he termed

an " American education," and in opposition to mathematics and the classics. On this he rose to the highest style of oratory, and seemed like one of those classical heroes whom he admired so much. Kinmont made a profound impression on those who knew him, and to me he had the air and character of a man of superior genius, and, what is very rare, of one whose learning was equal to his genius.

JAMES H. PERKINS took little part in the college, but was one of the literary circle of which it was mainly constituted. He was a New England man, highly educated ; came out to Cincinnati as a lawyer ; was a year or two editor of the *Chronicle ;* and finally a minister of the Unitarian Church in this city, where he made a strong impression. He died young, and was most profoundly lamented by a large circle of friends, and held in honorable remembrance by the community in which he had lived. As a writer, Mr. Perkins was remarkably graceful and easy, and some of his short articles were as popular as any written in the country. When editor of the *Chronicle,* I published one of Mr. Perkins' articles, called " *The Hole in my Pocket.*" That article, I think, must have been published in nearly all the newspapers in the country. Years after it was first published, I saw it in our exchange papers, floating about. He edited a work entitled " Western Annals," or " Annals of the West," the materials for which were mainly furnished by James Albach. It is the only complete book of its kind I know of, and the only monument which Mr. Perkins left to his literary labors.

DR. LYMAN BEECHER was one of the speakers in the College of Teachers, but contributed little to its proceedings. On one occasion he entered into the discussion of the question, whether excitement to emulation was an admissible means of education. On this subject there are various opinions. Dr. Beecher, and a majority of the committee, made a report against the admission of emulation in any form. The other members of the committee, being *Mr. Pickett, Dr. Drake,* and *President McGuffey,* made a counter-report. The college did not adopt either report, but simply passed a resolution, that rewards to merit were a right and proper means of education.

BISHOP PURCELL was present in several meetings, but took no active part in the proceedings.

Among others present, was DR. ALEXANDER CAMPBELL—a most remarkable man. He became, perhaps unintentionally, the founder of a large religious sect, called, in his time, Campbellite Baptists, but now known as *The Disciples of Christ.* I have heard Dr. Campbell preach, for the very purpose of ascertaining his doctrines. I can not be mistaken in two of his peculiar principles—the first, that the Bible alone is the only creed, and that no human creed is right; secondly, that regeneration is coincident with baptism that is, baptismal regeneration. On this account, he was at first excluded from the Baptist Church, but the opinions he held were in some degree popular, and the sect he founded has continued to increase. Campbell was a man of learning, keen intellect, and an instructive speaker. He was interesting in discussion and conversation. His name will probably live longer as the founder of a sect than that of many men of genius.

One of the most remarkable men who appeared in

the College of teachers was THOMAS SMITH GRIMKE, of South Carolina—a most devoted Christian, and a thorough American. He had formed some very peculiar theories of education, flowing from the ultraism of his ideas. The classics, he held, should not be taught as a means of education, because they were the literature of heathenism, and inculcated false principles. The study of Homer, he said, had given the heroic character to the leading men of South Carolina, so that they dwelt in the ideality of a false heroism, rather than in the plain, practical, Christian sentiment of America. Hence, he said, sprang the duel, dissatisfaction with the Union, and the outbreak of nullification—to which may since be added *the Rebellion.* Against mathematics he protested almost equally strongly. He thought it unnecessary to give so much time to the study of abstract science, when it could be employed on the Bible, literature, and political institutions.

In advocating these ideas he delivered a fine address before the College of Teachers. On the subject of the classics he was answered by PROFESSOR POST, in a very elegant discourse. On the subject of mathematics he was answered by myself, in a discourse entitled " The Utility of Mathematics." Parts of this address have for forty years been published in school readers. The peculiarities of Mr. Grimke did not diminish the high regard in which his character was held. He was an earnest Christian, a man of profound thought, of excellent learning, and of noble conduct. He carried us back to the days of primitive Christianity, and his discourses on science, literature, and religion were filled with the spirit of piety.

The Charleston Temperance Society declared emphatically that he was the father of the temperance movement in South Carolina. He was a member of the Episcopal Church, and adorned by his life and conversation the doctrines he professed. He held some peculiar opinions. He believed it the duty of every Christian, ecclesiastic or layman, to preach the gospel to every creature, and authorized to administer the ordinances of religion. He worked to make the world altogether righteous by means which supposed it already such.

> "Of those
> That build their monuments where virtue builds,
> Art thou; and gathered to thy rest, we deem
> That thou wast lent us just to show how blest
> And lovely is the life that lives for all."

Among the first subjects of interest which came before the College of Teachers was the inefficiency of the school system and the ignorance of teachers. These points were fully discussed until the principles necessary for improvement were determined. Looking to an efficient school law, the College of Teachers passed a resolution that it would greatly advance the interests of education in the West for teachers and friends of education to hold periodical conventions at the seats of government in the different states, during the session of the general assemblies.

In pursuance of this resolution, a convention of teachers and friends of education was held in Columbus, assembling on the 13th of January, 1836. Of this convention Governor Lucas was president; Dr. Hogue, vice-president, and Milo J. Williams, secretary. Prior to this time Governor Vance had appointed Professor Calvin E. Stowe an agent of the state to visit Prussia, and obtain information on the Prussian system of instruction. He had just returned, and was a member of the convention. The Prussian school system was discussed, lectures delivered, and debates held. The subject of common schools was referred to a committee, and on the 16th of January the committee reported, by E. D. MANSFIELD, pointing out the defects of the school law, and recommending amendments in relation to the appointment of a superintendent, the requisition of higher qualifications on the part of teachers, the greater responsibility and additional duties of examiners, the establishment of school libraries, and the collection of school statistics. This report was adopted in the form of a memorial to the legislature, and all its recommendations have since been embodied in the school laws.

The convention of the friends of education met again in the winter of 1836–1837, and recommended the substance of the act of March, 1838, which was adopted by the legislature, and made one of the most important school epochs of the state. In fine, the College of Teachers was the moving cause of that magnificent school system which has placed Ohio in the front rank of states who regard education as the defense of republican freedom.

In the proceedings of the College of Teachers I took an active part, as I did in all movements for education. Besides the discourse on " The Utility of Mathematics," I made several reports, and entered into nearly all the public discussions. Subsequently I delivered several lectures, and published a volume on

various topics connected with popular education. On
looking back upon this part of my life, I find nothing
to regret, but feel grateful that I was permitted to do
something for the promotion of the intelligence and
elevation of the people.

CHAPTER XVII.

Ormsby Mitchell—The Political Grammar—Dr. Lyman Beecher—John Quincy Adams—Abolition—Right of Petition—Bank of the United States—Removal of the Deposits—Storer and Lytle—Cincinnati College—Dr. McGuffey—Charles Telford—Cincinnati Chronicle—Benjamin Drake—Myself.

In the year 1834 I had my office on Third street, near Main. My partner in our professed law business was ORMSBY McNIGHT MITCHELL, a man so noted and so brilliant that I must mention him here. Mitchell was noted at West Point for his quickness and ingenuity. My father, who was professor of philosophy there, used to say of him: "Little Mitchell is very ingenious." He was more than that, for he was what you seldom see, a man of real genius. A great many people are spoken of as men of genius, but I never saw more than half a dozen in my life, and Ormsby Mitchell was one of them. Many of those who read these pages will remember him as the founder of the Cincinnati Observatory, as an eloquent lecturer on astronomy, and as a patriotic general in the war. I shall speak of him hereafter in each of these capacities. It is enough now to say that he was my partner in a profession for which I think neither of us was well adapted. We were really literary men, and our thoughts wandered off to other subjects. The scene in our office was often a remarkable one, though observed by no eyes but our own. Mitchell was fond of the classics, and instinctively fond of eloquence, which in his after lectures on astronomy he so brilliantly exhibited. The scene I refer to was this: Mitchell sat in one corner reading Quintilian, a Latin author on oratory. He was enamored of the book, and would turn to me and read passages from it. I, on the other hand, sat at my desk in another corner, writing my *Political Grammar* (now the *Political Manual*). Thus we were two students, each occupied with his own literary pursuits, and neither thinking of what both professed, the practice of the law. The consequence was, what might have been expected, Mitchell resorted to teaching classes, and I became a public writer. We both found our vocations, though, very different from what either had anticipated.

This was one of the cholera seasons, in which I finished my *Political Grammar*, and found relief from the anxieties of the season in my literary work. Literary work has been the theme of my existence, and I can say with Cicero, at however great a distance, that it has been with me, in the city and in the country, at home and abroad, a pleasure in prosperity and a solace in adversity. It has never been a labor to me, as some think, but a pleasant employment. In some form, whether of newspaper, book, or statistical work, it has compensated me as well as most professional employment. I can not complain of it, while I am thankful that it has done some good, and been of no little service to the public interests.

There were many things of interest in the year 1834, and to us as individuals, not the least was, that both Mitchell and I joined the Second Presbyterian Church. The pastor of that church was DR. LYMAN BEECHER, one of the most remarkable clergymen in the United States; remarkable for great abilities, great virtues, great power as a speaker, and no little eccentricity. I have known and heard many of the most able, noted, and eloquent preachers in the United States; but, taken all in all, I never knew the equal of Dr. Beecher in the Christian ministry. The pulpits and the places he occupied before the public will, in some measure, testify to his eminence. He was pastor of the church in Litchfield, Connecticut, when I was a law student. The students all attended his church, and it was there he delivered his six lectures on temperance, which were the origin of the first great temperance movement.

Thence, he went to Boston as the pastor of the Park Street Church, where he was engaged in the Unitarian controversy; from there he was called to the leading professorship in Lane Seminary, a theological institution just founded in Cincinnati. He was now also pastor of the Second Presbyterian Church; his mind was so active and industrious that he filled both offices with unrivaled success. At this time, 1834, there was a quiet but extensive revival in the Second Presbyterian Church; it was then that Mitchell, I, and perhaps forty others united with the church, of which I was a member during the whole of my residence in Cincinnati.

My Political Grammar, by Harper & Brothers, New York, subsequently published by Truman & Smith, was transferred to A. S. Barnes & Co., New York, who now publish it as the Political Manual. It was begun when the nullification question, the real origin of the Rebellion had just been discussed, and I was filled with the absurdity of nullification and with love of the Union. Under these circumstances the book contained very positive ideas on that subject, and was charged with being onesided; however that may be, it has remained before the public for forty years and met with the approbation of intelligent men and patriotic people. This year also saw the beginning of a controversy on the subject of slavery, which lasted until slavery was destroyed in the civil war. Perhaps, this is the proper place to mention how that controversy began. I have already in a former chapter mentioned the Missouri Compromise and the excitement which it caused; that had died away until the tariff of 1828 caused a new agitation in the South, which I have also described; this caused nullification, and the claim then strongly put forth, that a state had the right to interpose and nullify the laws of the United States. All these transactions had undoubtedly increased the feeling of thoughtful and religious people in the North; that slavery was the real cause of these agitations, and that unless some remedy for it could be found, either the Union would be destroyed or slavery become dominant in the whole country. Hence, arose abolition societies. The idea of an abolition society was not a new thing. The Society of Friends, Franklin, Rush, and numbers of enlightened and benevolent people had presented petitions against slavery in the early stage of the government; they were then treated with respect, but caused no public agitation; now, however, the abolition societies were regarded as political agitators, disunionists, and assailants of constitutional rights. In the North as well as the South, they were regarded as the enemies of the Union, of commerce, and of the constitution. At least, such was the coloring put upon them by all leading politicians, and almost all the press. They established papers to sustain their opinions, and in the controversy which ensued the leaders became martyrs to their defense of freedom. Garrison was imprisoned in Baltimore, Owen Lovejoy, in Illinois, was killed by a mob, and hundreds of others less noted were imprisoned, or exiled, or killed, or murdered. At this time, 1834, they had excited little interest, but had begun to present petitions to Congress. The right of petition was an undoubted constitutional right of every man, woman, or child, black or white, bond or free. It was so described and maintained by John Quincy Adams in his bold and vigorous speeches upon this question. Here it was that the South committed a great blunder, unless their leaders looked forward not only to civil war, but to success in it. They assumed that the abolition societies were the cause of a dangerous agitation, and, therefore, must be suppressed by negative if not positive law; that is, the right of petition must be denied altogether. This, they undertook to do. The controversy on the right of petition, for the next half a dozen years, exhibits clearly the purpose of the South to suppress all discussion on the subject of slavery. A few historical facts will show this clearly. In December, 1835, Mr. Fairfield, of Maine, presented the petition of one hundred and seventy-two women, praying the abolition of slavery in the District of Columbia; it was laid on the table, yeas, 180; nays, 31; the nays all from the North, and mainly Whigs. A few days after, Mr. Jackson, of Massachusetts, presented a similar petition, and it was laid on the table, yeas, 140; nays, 76. In the following year, Mr. Buchanan, of Pennsylvania, presented a similar petition in the senate, from the meeting of Friends, and he moved that the memorial be read and the prayer of the petitioners be rejected.

In December, 1837, finding that the agitation was not quieted, it was resolved by the house of representatives: " That all petitions, memorials, and papers touching the abolition of slavery, or the relations of slaves in any state or territory of the United States, be laid upon the table, without being debated, printed, read, or referred." This resolution was passed by yeas, 122: nays, 74; the nays being mainly, if not entirely, the Whig members from the free states. In December, 1838, Mr. Atherton, a Democrat from New Hampshire, introduced a set of resolutions, which caused great excitement and discussion at the time. The last clause was the one most important and most discussed; it was this: " That every petition, memorial, resolution, proposition, or paper, touching or relating in any way, or to any extent whatever, to slavery, as aforesaid, or the abolition thereof, shall, on the presentation thereof, be laid on the table without being debated, printed, or referred." This was called the Gag law; its object was to silence all discussion whatever; it passed by yeas, 127; nays, 78. It would seem that the house had now done all that was possible to silence the agitation of the slavery question. But in January, 1840, William Cost John-

son, of Maryland, *Whig*, introduced resolutions, the
last of which was:

" Resolved, that no petition, memorial, resolution,
or other paper praying for the abolition of slavery in
the District of Columbia, or any state or territory, or
the slave trade between the states or territories of the
United States in which it now exists, shall be received
by the house or entertained in any way whatever."

It will be seen that in these five years the house had
step by step arrived at the conclusion, not merely to
reject, but not even to receive any petitions on the
subject of slavery. This was so directly contrary to
the received opinions of the United States, on the
subject of constitutional freedom, that even some
Southern members voted against it. The resolution was,
however, carried by a 114 to 108; the majority being
made by Northern dough-faces, who had neither the
courage to resist, nor the sense to understand this violent abrogation of constitutional rights. Of the
twenty-eight Northern members who voted for it, six
came from Ohio; they soon passed into oblivion and
their names are now unknown, except in the political
record of the day. The controversy on the right of
petition was now ended until these usurpations were
all blotted out in the blood of the Rebellion. Even the
historian will scarcely notice them, since slavery and
all its attendant crimes are, we trust, destroyed forever.

We must now return to the year 1834, in which were
many subjects of political interest. One of these was
the removal of the deposits by Jackson. The Bank
of the United States then existed, and had been chartered for the very purpose of transacting the financial
business of the United States. The public deposits

were by law made in that bank, which also transferred
the government moneys, and in fact performed its
financial business. Jackson was opposed to the bank,
and greatly irritated by the conduct of Nicholas Bid-
dle, president of the bank, who very unwisely undertook to oppose and resist the influence of the president. In consequence of his own irritation and hostility, he undertook to remove the deposits. Finding
the secretary of the treasury opposed to his views, he
appointed Mr. Duane, of Philadelphia, secretary of
the treasury, but Duane was also opposed to his mode
of proceeding. In a brief time, Duane was removed
from office, and Roger B. Taney, of Maryland, afterward chief justice, was appointed secretary, and the
deposits were removed. This whole procedure shocked
the public mind, and was the real origin of the Whig
party. It is possible the term had been used before
this time, but it was first used as the collective name
of the great party opposed to Jackson. I was at a
meeting in the court-house of Cincinnati in the year
1834, and spoke and introduced resolutions in which
the term Whig was employed. It was the first meeting in which I ever heard it employed. The objects
of the Whig party were, opposition to arbitrary power,
as exhibited by Jackson, and in favor of legislation for
the "general welfare," embracing subjects of finance,
industry, and commerce. The term " general welfare"
is expressly used in the constitution to denote the general legislation of congress. The right thus to legislate
on these subjects, without a special grant in the constitution, was denied by the present Democratic party,
which began at the same time with the Whigs, and

which professed an adherence to state rights and strict construction of the constitution.

I say the present Democratic party, because the old Democratic party, in the time of Jefferson, did not call itself Democratic. It was a nickname, given it by its opponents from the Democratic clubs of France and the Democratic clubs formed in this country by Genet, the French ambassador, who was sent home by Washington for interference in politics. The party of Jefferson, now called the old Democratic party, called itself Republican, and all the official records of that party, down to the last caucus in 1816, show this fact. The present Republican party has the name of the old Democratic party, and it has proved its name to be quite as popular as that of Democratic. Thus we see that in 1834 the parties, or rather great factions, which had been formed under personal leaders, such as Clay, Jackson, Adams, and Crawford, were now consolidated into the great national parties called Whig and Democratic, which for the time being were separated by real principles.

The opponents of the United States Bank, who, after the removal of the deposits by Jackson, became hostile to paper money, proposed the doctrine of hard money, and Colonel Benton, then in the senate, said that gold would flow up the Mississippi. This was laughed at by the Whigs, and gold has not yet flowed up the Mississippi. But this idea gave rise to a curious incident in Cincinnati politics. ROBERT T. LYTLE (son of General William Lytle, a pioneer in this section, and a warm friend of Jackson's) represented Cincinnati in congress. He was a lawyer, and quite a brilliant man, ambitious of political honors, and a protegé of Jackson's. In fact, I was told that Jackson treated him almost as a son. Of course, when Jackson removed the deposits, Lytle sustained him by his vote; but in the meanwhile the business men of Cincinnati considered themselves injured and endangered by the attack on the United States Bank. In consequence of this feeling, Lytle was defeated at the next election, and was succeeded by BELLAMY STORER. At the end of Storer's term, he declined a renomination, and the Democrats nominated Lytle, but the Whigs were exasperated by Jackson's conduct toward the bank, and determined, if they could not elect *their* candidate, they would put a slight upon Lytle. There was a wild, good-natured young man, called Wash. Mason, whom they nominated for congress against Lytle, and called the contest " Gildibus against Goldibus." Strange as it may seem, " Gildibus" came within about fifty votes of being elected, a result which accomplished what the Whigs intended as a slight, but not a success. Lytle did not remain in Congress, and in a few years died. His son, General Wm. H. Lytle, was also a brilliant man, who was killed on the Union side in the war.

Perhaps this is the proper place to mention the final result of Jackson's war on the bank. The bank was not rechartered by congress, but was chartered by the State of Pennsylvania. It undertook to sustain the State of Pennsylvania in its great internal improvements and developments, and supply national currency. In one word, it undertook to do the business of a national bank, without its power. The result was, the bank failed, and caused a good deal of commercial disaster. About this time, great numbers of state banks were chartered, and, instead of a national currency, we had a state bank paper. Jackson, to avoid, as he thought, the effects of destroying the United States Bank, advised the state banks to issue currency and aid the merchants. This they did, and within three years the banks failed, and the greatest commercial disaster the country had ever known took place, and for six or seven years the commercial distress was greater than it ever has been before or since. Such was the result of what may fairly be termed ignorance and presumption.

Cincinnati College, which had been founded in 1818–1819, was revived in 1835, with an academic and medical department. The principal founder of Cincinnati College was General William Lytle, who proposed to some of the citizens that they should finish the building which had been begun for the Lancaster Seminary, endow it, and procure a college charter. Leading the way with a subscription of $11,500 (eleven thousand five hundred dollars), he was followed by as many as forty respectable citizens, whose contributions made a large amount. A charter was obtained which gave ample power to appoint professors, organize a faculty, and confer all the degrees which are usually conferred in any college or university in the United States. Under this charter classes were subsequently formed, and many of the prominent young men of Cincinnati were taught and graduated in that institution. A few years afterward the college was abandoned, and only a primary department retained. In the revival of the Cincinnati College there was instituted a medical department, a law department, and a faculty of arts. The medical department had in it three of the most eminent medical men in the United States, DR. DRAKE, of whom I have spoken, DR. GROSS, and DR. WILLARD PARKER. The last two are still alive; Dr. Gross, the most eminent surgeon in Philadelphia, and Dr. Parker, certainly one of the most eminent physicians in New York. The law school had been founded as a private institution, by two gentlemen of the bar, Edward King, Esquire, and Timothy Walker, Esquire. At this time, 1836, General King was dead, and the law school was composed of professors JOHN C. WRIGHT, JOSEPH S. BENHAM, and TIMOTHY WALKER. In these departments, however, I had less interest than in the literary faculty, of which I was a member. Of that I will relate some facts of interest at the time, but which may not now be remembered. The literary department of Cincinnati College ceased to exist after three or four years, for want of any endowment to sustain it. In that time, however, it excited great interest in Cincinnati, and was the center of all literary activity there. The faculty were composed as follows:

W. H. McGUFFEY, president, and professor of moral and intellectual philosophy; ORMSBY M. MITCHELL, professor of mathematics and astronomy; ASA DRURY, professor of ancient languages; CHARLES L. TELFORD, professor of rhetoric and belles-lettres; EDWARD D. MANSFIELD, professor of constitutional law and history; LYMAN HARDING, principal of the preparatory department; JOSEPH HERRON, principal of the primary department.

The president, REV. W. H. McGUFFEY, had been several years a professor of Miami University, Oxford, where he had acquired a high reputation, and after he left Cincinnati became president of Ohio University, at Athens, and subsequently professor of intellectual philosophy in the University of Virginia. In all this career his reputation was constantly increasing, his usefulness was great, and his ability in his peculiar department unsurpassed by any man in the United States. Mr. McGuffey entered Cincinnati College with the full knowledge that it was an experimental career, but he came with an energy and a zeal in the cause of education, and the pursuit of high and noble duties, which are rarely met with and are sure to command success. His mind was more analytical and logical than that of any one I have known or whose works I have read. In his discourses and lectures before members of the college he disentangled difficulties, made mysteries plain, and brought the abstruse and the profound within the reach of common intellects. Hence his Sunday morning discourses in the college chapel were always numerously attended, and his manner of treating metaphysics was universally popular. I thought then, and think now, he was the only sound and clear-headed metaphysician of whom it has been my lot to know anything. One reason of this was that he was a practical teacher of great ability. In fine, he was naturally formed for the department of philosophy, and in Cincinnati College put forth with zeal and fervor those talents which were peculiarly his own.

ORMSBY M. MITCHELL, professor of mathematics, has since acquired so broad a reputation as to reflect honor upon rather than have derived it from the chair he then held. He was a graduate of West Point, always distinguished for his love of mathematics and

astronomy. In Cincinnati he had been several years
a teacher, and no one ever taught more successfully.
In the college he took almost the sole charge of the
department of physical science, and for several years
taught large classes zealously and laboriously. He remained in the college while it was possible to hold it
together. Soon after the dissolution of Cincinnati
College, he commenced that career, both civil and
military, which has since made his name so distinguished and widely known. Of this I shall speak
again.

The Rev. Asa Drury, professor of languages, had
both the knowledge and the tact of an excellent
teacher, and both his pupils and colleagues gave tes-
timony to his worth. He was afterward professor in
the Baptist Seminary, Covington, for several years.

Charles L. Telford was not a common man. A
graduate of Miami University, he was a partner of Mr.
Groesbeck in the practice of the law, when he was
elected professor of rhetoric and belles-lettres. Tall,
erect, dignified, and of grave manners, he was of manly
carriage and commanding presence. Of him it might
be said, he was "without fear and without reproach."
He was a fine writer and a graceful orator, but died
young, soon after the dissolution of the college.

With such a faculty, I thought, as Dr. Gross did, of
the medical department, "we *should* have succeeded,"
and practically we did, for the college had at one time
as many as one hundred and sixty pupils, and certainly
received the encouragement of the community. But
it was entirely without endowment, and without any
revenue save that received from tuition. Experience
proved, after many trials, that a literary institution

can not be sustained without some endowment for its apparatus, library, and incidental expenses; the college, therefore, as a college, was dissolved. But having a very valuable lot, it still does a good work in the law school it has established, and in courses of lectures by able men. My own part in the practical teaching of the college was small, having no share in its class instruction. In one season, however, I delivered lectures on the *Law of Equity* and the Constitution, to the law class. And of that class several have since been distinguished in public life. I also delivered a series of popular lectures on the history of civilization. Aside from these I had taken part in the labors of the instituion. Meeting my colleagues in faculty meetings, and in social intercourse, we became intimate, and some of the pleasantest and most instructive hours I ever passed were spent in the intellectual and brilliant society of the professors of the Cincinnati College. We were all in the early prime of life, labor seemed light, care made no impression, and sorrow was lessened by the hopes of the future; we gathered knowledge from every passing event and pleasure from every opening scene. Such periods come but once, they make the golden thread of life, they give brightness to its days, and linger on through the years of memory. We never met without pleasure, nor ever parted without regretting the shortness of the hours. To have such meetings I regarded as no small blessing, and to have them no longer is among my deepest regrets. Connected in some measure with Cincinnati College was the establishment of the CINCINNATI CHRONICLE, of which I was editor. As this paper had much connection with the public interests, and did more than any other to promote the literary taste and talent of Cincinnati, I shall take some notice of its history and character. *The Chronicle* was founded in the year 1826. *The Chronicle* was published by the Messrs. Buxton, and edited at that time by Benjamin Drake, Esq. Mr. Drake was a gentleman of ability and literary taste. As a writer Mr. Drake did much for the public advantage and something for his own permanent reputation. In connection with myself he compiled Cincinnati in 1826. He wrote articles for the *Western Monthly Magazine,* the *Southern Literary Messenger,* and other periodicals. Besides these he wrote the " *Tales of the Queen City,*" " *Life of Black Hawk,*" and the " *Life of Tecumseh.*" He was thus one of the earliest pioneer authors in Cincinnati. *The Chronicle,* in the next twenty years, passed through many transmutations, having at one time ceased to exist in name, though not in substance. In 1834, it ceased as *The Chronicle,* and was amalgamated with a literary periodical called THE CINCINNATI MIRROR. In 1836, Drs. Drake and Rives, of the medical department of Cincinnati College purchased the " *Mirror* " of " Flash and Ryder," and re-established *The Chronicle* on its subscription list. They got a journeyman printer who knew nothing about publishing to print, and I, who was professor of history and law, to edit it. Both of us were equally ignorant of the modern art of getting up newspapers, and especially of the notable plan of printing the paper to puff ourselves. I doubt whether we ever mentioned ourselves, and we were in great fear when we mentioned the college, lest we should have the appearance of self-conceit. Happily, editors and publishers nowadays have got rid of this very imprudent modesty; and the generation of to-day is wiser than the generation which preceded it. The result of such a newspaper speculation, undertaken without any knowledge of the business, was the same as that of all similar undertakings. THE MIRROR had nominally two thousand subscribers, but at the end of six months, not one-fourth of them was left, and not one-half paid their subscriptions. The medical gentlemen became heartily tired, and sold the paper to Messrs. Pugh and Dodd—the former a member of the Society of Friends, and the latter a printer, who afterward became a well-known hatter. I remained editor, assisted by Mr. Drake, who was now a practicing member of the bar. In this new era of the *Chronicle*, we found ourselves with a new and unexpected embarrassment. It was the era of Abolition mobs. Just prior to this time, Dr. Bailey, afterward editor of the *National Era* at Washington, published an Abolition paper, of which Mr. Pugh was the printer. An anti-Abolition mob, composed chiefly of the most respectable young men, had torn down Bailey's press, thrown it into the Ohio river, and demolished the materials. The press was owned by Mr. Pugh, the printer, and now that the *Chronicle* had passed into his hands, the populace looked upon us with suspicion, and were disposed to visit us with a portion of their wrath. This made no difference with our course, but retarded the support and growth of the paper. It looks very strange now, in the great change which the public mind and nation have undergone, but it is true that the freedom of the press was in actual danger from the overawing influence of mobs. These mobs were instigated by men who believed that society was founded only upon trade, and like Demetrius, the silversmith, thought their craft was in danger, when the worship of the goddess Diana was abridged. The Diana of that day was slavery. The Cincinnati *Chronicle* was thoroughly anti-slavery, but not Abolitionist, so called. It was a Whig paper throughout its whole career, having the confidence and support of the most influential people in the city. It never hesitated to criticise and expose the conduct of the slaveholders or the political laws which maintained them, but did not think it necessary to establish a separate party for that purpose. In the meantime the *Chronicle* grew slowly, and managed by hard work to maintain itself. In December, 1839, it became a daily paper, having obtained the subscription list of the WHIG, founded by Major Conover, and then edited by Henry E. Spencer, Esq. The subscription list of both papers was small. The newspaper publishers of this day who inform the public (which the public very courteously believe) that they commenced with thousands and progressed with tens of thousands of subscribers, will doubtless be astonished to learn that we commenced the *Daily Chronicle* with two hundred and fifty and terminated the year with six hundred of what the world calls patrons. Mr. Pugh, the proprietor, and myself had a hard contest with the world against two prevalent ideas. One was slavery, and the other was liquor. We were utterly opposed to slavery in the day when two-thirds of the community were for it, and two-thirds of the remainder compromised with it. We both lived to see its entire destruction in this land of the free, as it is called, free in fact, standing out before the world the only successful republic. We both utterly opposed the liquor trade and the dram-shops. Pugh would not allow a single advertisement of any place where liquor was sold or drank. The consequence was a great loss of business from the liquor sellers and their friends. But in all other respects the *Chronicle* was popular and prosperous. We were warm Whigs—the friends and advocates of morals, religion, science, and literature. I think the first "Price Current" in Cincinnati was published in our office by Mr. Peabody, and Mr. Richard Smith began his long and honorable career as a newspaper man in our office. He soon after published the Price Current of the Merchants' Exchange, and became superintendent of that institution. This was a good practical education for the part he has so long held in the GAZETTE. At the same time Mr. Boardman, who has so long conducted the Highland News, was a printer in the office, and several other publishers of newspapers graduated from it.

The *Chronicle* had an able and brilliant corps of contributors, as the reader will readily see when I mention their names. MRS. STOWE, then Miss Harriet Beecher, published her first stories in it; Mr. (now DR) BLACKWELL wrote for it; so did JAMES H. PERKINS, MRS. SIGOURNEY, MRS. DOUGLAS, of Chillicothe, MARY DE FOREST, LEWIS J. CIST, and several others who have since been well known. As a paper, the *Chronicle* was a success, but it became involved in pecuniary troubles, and was at length merged in the *Atlas*, a paper begun by Nathan Guilford, and, after three or four years' existence, died. To edit the *Chronicle* was to me a pleasant business. It continued about fifteen years, and I look back upon my part in that paper as alike useful to the public and honorable to myself.

CHAPTER XVIII.

Southern Railroad—My Artic!e ana Speech—Public Meeting in Cincinnati—Drake—J. S. Williams— Judge Hall—General Harrison—Knoxville Convention—Ohio Delegates—Scenery on the Tennessee River —Cincinnati Mob—Court-house Meeting—Commercial Crisis of 1837—First Observatory at Ludlow Station—Mitchell's Observatory.

THE history of the Southern Railroad—a work which has recently excited much attention, and is still engaging the public mind—is curious and instructive. It is now more than forty years since the idea of such a work was formed and advocated, and yet while other works of far less importance have been constructed in various parts of the country, this great work remained unfinished. It is now time to give its history, that whatever of merit or demerit there may be in it may be traced to the originators.

Up to the year 1825, the only idea of great internal improvement in the West was that of canals. In that year, however (1825), the Liverpool and Manchester Railroad was completed, and a new and extraordinary era in locomotion began, which has revolutionized the modes of carriage, and given a new impulse to all the modes of commerce. In America, the new idea was taken up with zeal, and the construction of railroads began. Among the earliest of these were those attempting to pierce the Alleghany Mountains, and connect the cities of the Atlantic with those of the valley of the Ohio. Their progress, however, was slow. The Baltimore and Ohio Railroad, which was commenced in 1828, was only completed in 1853—a period of twenty-five years. The New York and Erie Railroad was begun in 1835, but only completed in 1852—seventeen years. In 1832–1833, the legislatures of Ohio and Indiana granted several charters for railroads, many of which have since been made. I became interested in this new mode of commercial enterprise, and in August, 1836, published in the WESTERN MONTHLY MAGAZINE, then edited by JUDGE HALL, an article advocating a railroad from Cincinnati to the South. My idea was to take the route to Knoxville, Tennessee, and thence by a road through Tennessee and Alabama to Mobile. That article was written before, but not published until after the first meeting held in Cincinnati on that subject. A meeting had been held at Paris, Kentucky, to take steps toward constructing a railroad from Cincinnati to that fertile region; but the plan of a railroad to the South Atlantic was first puplicly proposed at a meeting held in Cincinnati, and suggested by Dr. Daniel Drake. This meeting was held at the Commercial Exchange, Front street, in the summer of 1835, for the purpose of promoting the railroad to Paris, Kentucky. When the proceedings relative to that subject were concluded, Dr. Drake offered a resolution, which was unanimously adopted, to inquire into the advantage and practicability of a railroad to South Carolina. A committee of three was appointed, to report at a subsequent meeting. This committee consisted of DR. DANIEL DRAKE, THOMAS W. BAKEWELL, and JOHN S. WILLIAMS. This meeting, and the resolutions, were the initial steps in the plan of constructing the great railway between Cincinnati and Charleston, which is now being completed. The adjourned meeting of citizens was held at the Exchange, on the 15th of August, 1835, when Dr. Drake read an elaborate and argumentative report, placing the whole subject in a clear and conclusive light. His report was followed by speeches from Mr. John S. Williams and myself. I traced more in detail the route through Knoxville to Charleston. The proceedings, report, and speeches were ordered to be published, and I prepared a pamphlet, accompanied by a map entitled " Railroad from the banks of the Ohio river to the tide waters of the Carolinas and Georgia." A standing committee of inquiry and correspondence was apppointed by the meeting. That committee consisted of Gen. William Henry Harrison, Judge James Hall, Dr. Daniel Drake, Edward D. Mansfield, Esq., Gen. James Taylor, of Newport, Kentucky, Dr. John W. King, of Covington, Kentucky, and George A. Dunn, Esq., of Lawrenceburg, Indiana. I mention this committee particularly, because they did much to excite a zeal in this cause, both North and South, and diffused information concerning both sections through these wide and far separated regions of country. Being appointed secretary of the committee, I know that an extensive correspondence passed through their hands, and that they did no small amount of service in developing the knowledge of our resources, and awaking that zeal for public works which has ever since prevailed. It is well known with how much zeal and earnestness the citizens of Charleston, Savannah, and Augusta, and the states of South Carolina and Georgia adopted this scheme, and with what energy they carried it out. The great system of railways which now exists in those states had chiefly for its basis the construction of that great work, which should connect them with the great Valley of the Ohio. It is now forty-three years since this plan was conceived, and the public mind interested in the subject, and yet the Southern road is only now drawing toward completion. I was repeatedly asked if I thought this work was possible, and when it might be done. I uniformly replied that it was not only possible, but certain, and a necessity to the country. In 1863, a great Southwestern convention was called and held at Knoxville on this subject, in which were delegates from nine states, to wit: Ohio, Indiana, Kentucky, Tennessee, Virginia, North Carolina, South Carolina, Georgia, and Alabama. There was intense excitement in the country on this subject, and the convention was a numerous and able body. The delegates who attended from this region were Gov. Vance, Dr. Drake, Alexander McGrew, Crafts J. Wright, and myself, from Ohio; Gen. James Taylor, M. M. Benton, and J. G. Arnold, from Newport and Covington. The debates and proceedings of the convention at Knoxville were quite exciting and very interesting. The only serious controversy at that time was in regard to the termini at the South and at the Ohio river. The South Carolina and Georgia delegations each claimed, with great pertinacity, that they had the best route. But time has settled all these things. Each of these states, as well as Alabama and Tennessee, have completed their lines of railroad, so that they all concentrate at Chattanooga, on the Tennessee. Hence, when the city of Cincinnati determined the terminus of the Southern Railroad in the South, Chattanooga was preferred to Knoxville.

I must now return to my interesting journey through the South, with the condition and appearance of things in the South at that time. Six of us, including Gov. Vance and Gen. Taylor, left Cincinnati in a stage, passing through Lexington, Lancaster, and Crab Orchard, on what was called the Ridge road. We crossed the Cumberland river at Cumberland Ford, and Cumberland Mountain at Cumberland Gap. Nearly the whole of the country, except in the Blue Grass Region around Lexington, was thinly settled, and showed no signs of improvement. At Cumberland Ford I was struck by seeing coal banks of great thickness, but I soon found that this was nothing uncommon, for we were now in that great coal district which extends southeasterly from Trumbull county, Ohio, to Central Alabama, on the western slope of the Appalachian Mountains. We passed through Cumberland Gap, and then over Clinch Mountain; crossing the Clinch and Powell rivers, and arriving at Bean's Station, forty miles east of Knoxville. This was quite a noted place, being the night stopping place for the great stage line which passed through the valley of Virginia to the South. The change which has since taken place will be seen in the simple fact that this very route is now taken by the Great Southwestern Railroad Line which runs from Richmond, Virginia, to Mobile, Alabama. At Bean's Station, where we lodged at night, we found ourselves in a quandary. The stages on the Virginia line arrived, crowded with passengers, and could not take us to Knoxville. What was to be done? Some enterprising person in the party found that we could hire a six-horse wagon to take us into Knoxville, so, next morning, we embarked in the wagon with our trunks and valises on the floor with plenty of straw. We had fine horses, with a Tennessee driver more than six feet tall, with a red shirt. We talked and sang, told anecdotes, and looked with surprise on what has been called " The Switzerland of the South." Arrived at Knoxville, Dr. Drake, two or three others, and myself, were received into the house of a private gentleman, and hospitably entertained. That night we had a splendid exhibition of natural phenomena, in a violent thunder-storm. The vivid lightning lit up the hills and valley of the Holston, which were again plunged in utter darkness. After the convention, the party separated. Dr. Drake and myself took the stage to Kingston, on the Tennessee, about forty miles below Knoxville, where we found a small, new steamer ready to descend the river. We took passage in her, with two or three other passengers, and had a novel and delightful trip to Alabama.

I seldom see any notices of this region and its scenery, although the war has revealed to the country the immediate section round Chattanooga. I will, therefore, describe the Tennessee from Kingston to Triana, where we landed. What is now Chattanooga was then Ross' Landing of the Cherokees, who then occupied Northern Georgia. Ross was a chief of the tribe, as, I believe, his son is now. The Tennessee, for a hundred miles below Knoxville, passed through a mountain country, and in some places has forced its way through the mountains. Below Chattanooga, is Lookout Mountain, where Hooker fought his battle above the clouds. The river winds its way round the base of Lookout. On the opposite side, and below, are Walden and Raccoon Mountains. After passing the base of Lookout, about ten miles below the Tennessee seems to break through Raccoon Mountain, not unlike the Shenandoah at Harper's Ferry, or the Hudson at West Point. The stream here is rapidly compressed to seventy yards in width, and whirlpools are formed over the rocks below. This passage is called " The Suck of the Tennessee," and has always been regarded as a remarkable place.

It seemed as though there were no room for our little steamer to pass, but by skillful pilotage we glided through. Marvelous stories were told of " the suck " in early times. It was said that the water was so compressed that it would bear an ax. A few miles below this we passed out of the mountain scenery. Jefferson said that it was worth a voyage from Europe to see the passage of the Shenandoah, and if so, it is worth a great deal more to see the " Suck of the Tennessee." I have visited the most celebrated scenes in our country, and I think that the mountain scenery of Tennessee is fully equal to any other. Below "the suck " the river broadens and passes into a more level country. The horizontal limestone stratum begins to appear and is worn away at the base by the river, leaving little caverns, while the bank above is surmounted by foliage and flowers. This formation continues for a great distance, but when we reached Alabama, rock cliffs began to appear, which in some cases were colored red by the drippings of iron ore and presented a variegated appearance. Soon after this we got into the cotton country, and landed at Triana, whence we proceeded to Huntsville. It was then a small place, but in a very beautiful country, inhabited by pleasant and hospitable people. Here we remained two or three days, and the season being July, we visited the summer resort of the Huntsville gentlemen, MONTESANO. This is a high ridge, with a bluff termination, being apparently the southern terminus of the Alleghany Mountains. I had passed the Alleghanies in many places of their eastern range, and now stood on the southern end, where the mountains seemed to say: "I will go no farther, but rest in the contemplation of this beautiful country."

Here the gentlemen of Huntsville had built on the summit log houses, and enjoyed, in the midst of summer, cool air.

From Huntsville, we went by stage through Nashville and Lexington to Cincinnati. Arrived there, I was astonished to find a new form of modern civilization, and a new way to please the southern people. While we were at Knoxville, trying to secure the Union by links of iron, some of the young men of Cincinnati had made a mob, and, as I have before stated, tore down the abolition press of Dr. Bailey and thrown it into the Ohio. On this, the leading people of Cincinnati found themselves in a predicament. A mob was certainly not a way to recommend the community, and yet to tolerate abolition was not the way to please the South. So a great public meeting was held at Lower Market, just before we returned. The result of the meeting, however, was really nothing, the party of order not being able fully to denounce the mob, and the mob not being willing to defend themselves, so nothing was done. Soon after my return, Mr. Hammond, Mr. Chase, a few others, and myself, determined to hold a public meeting to vindicate our own opinions. We therefore called an afternoon meeting at the court-house. The affair was a curious one.

We did not expect to announce opinions for the whole city, but to give our own view of the subject. We did not, therefore, expect any interruption or opposition. What, therefore, was our surprise to find the court-house crowded, and among the crowd, the leading men of the city. We saw at once, that we were checkmated, and that like the market-house meeting, the result would be a neutral compound. A large committee was appointed to propose resolutions. I was upon that committee, and as I was almost alone in my views, I agreed to bring in a single resolution, condemning mobs in general terms, and the meeting passed off in an amiable mood. Since then I have thought that I wanted moral courage in that meeting. After the experience of forty years, I think the true plan would have been to have made a minority report, expressing fully my opposition to the pro-slavery movements of the day. This would have raised a storm, but it would have made discussion, and brought people to a full consideration of the subject. After events showed that there was no possibility of compromise, and we had at last to do what we should have done at first—to take an uncompromising stand against slav-ery; but Providence vindicated its own ways, as the history of subsequent events has shown. For the free states could not and would not conquer slavery in 1836 as they did in 1860–1865.

In the following year, 1837, Jackson's schemes of finance reached their climax, in the worst and most complete commercial convulsion which has ever been experienced in this country. We have already noticed his attack upon and overthrow of the United States Bank, but since the business of the government must be conducted through financial agents of some kind, he was obliged to find a substitute for the national banks. This he did in the state banks. He encouraged them to increase their loans; the natural consequence followed—state banks and corporate banks were multiplied; they had the government deposits, and they were on the high tide of prosperity, apparently. Speculation was rife in all departments of business. Soon after this, Jackson issued his specie circular, which required the receivers of land offices, at a time when the sales of public lands were great, to receive payment only in specie or its equivalent. The banks were then inflated to their utmost extent, and the effect of this circular was to alarm and endanger them. In the meantime there came another danger. In 1832, Clay and Calhoun, to avert the effects of nullification, made the compromise tariff.

The tariff was to be gradually reduced until it reached an average of twenty per cent. The process of reduction was going on from 1832 to 1837. The immediate result of this was to increase our imports of foreign goods, so that by 1837 the balance of trade had become greatly against us. Thus, the reader can see that the reduction of the tariff on one hand, and Jackson's experiment in finance on the other, had, brought to the country such a crisis that it was impossible to avoid commercial disaster. It came and brought ruin to thousands. It was of the same nature and brought on by almost the same causes as the great commercial convulsion of 1819-1822. At that time,

1819, Cincinnati was almost sold out to its creditors, but now, although hundreds were bankrupt, the city was in a better condition to bear it, and after a short time continued to prosper. The effect of the convulsion of 1837 continued until 1842, whan a protective tariff revived the industry of the country, and placed its commercial interests upon a more solid foundation. The commercial convulsion of 1837 and 1839 operated upon the country like violent medicine upon the individual. It gave pain and suffering, but it cleansed and purified the commercial system, so that when its revival came it was restored to greater strength and activity. The tariff being reduced to its minimum, foreign goods had overflowed the country, and the indebtedness to Europe caused a suspension of the banks, and almost a suspension of commercial credit. In this situation, necessity compelled the nation to adopt, as we have said, a protective tariff. All theories had to give way to practical experience. Under the new tariff, the business of the country rapidly revived. Notwithstanding the Democrats, in 1846, remodeled the tariff, they never reduced it to anything like its former low point. The tariff of 1846 was a horizontal tariff; that is, specific duties were abolished, almost all articles were placed in three or four great classes. The duties on nearly all articles which came in competition with American manufacturers, were respectively 25, 30, and 35 per cent. These were apparently sufficient, but, nevertheless, foreign manufactures, especially English, continued to be imported in large quantities. For the next twenty years, until the close of the late war, the contest between foreign and American manufactures, continued with doubtful results. The war tariff of 1862 gave a final blow to foreign competition, and now the industry of America is triumphant at home, and promises to gain an ascendency throughout the world.

In the meantime, just after the convulsion of 1837, say up to 1848, the growth of Cincinnati continued with great rapidity. Strange as it may seem, the commercial depression, and the want of money did not impede building, on the contrary, it aided Cincinnati.

Many emigrants from New York and Eastern cities came to Cincinnati to begin a new career, where they could live on less means and have an equal chance in the future. The prices of provisions and all articles for housekeeping had fallen very much, and it seemed like a return to primitive times. In this condition of things, the new emigrants required many houses, and the mechanics and lot-holders managed to build thousands of houses in three or four years, almost without money. Much of it was actually done by barter, the land-owners, the hardware men, the lumber men, mechanics, and grocers intertrading with each other, so that much less money was required. For several years the city grew rapidly. But when the general prosperity of the country seemed to be greater, the growth of Cincinnati was actually less, as the reader may verify by referring to the census returns.

Although not exactly in the order of time, I will here relate the history of the Cincinnati Observatory, because connected with something which occurred many years before, and also with the progress of science in this country. I have already related the appointment of my father as Surveyor-General of the

United States, and the object of that appointment, which was to establish meridian lines as the basis of public services. This could not be done except by a man of science, with suitable astronomical instruments. Thus it happened that the first real observatory in the United States was established in my father's house at Ludlow Station. The history of it was this: My father informed Mr. Jefferson that the meridian line could not be run without certain astronomical instruments, and that these instruments could not be had in the United States. Mr. Jefferson said that congress had made no appropriation for that object, but that he (the President) had a contingent fund out of which he would procure these instruments. Mr. Gallatin, then secretary of the treasury, wrote to Troughton, mathematical instrument maker, London, for the followingly instruments: First, a three-foot long reflecting telescope, mounted in the best manner, with lever motion; secondly, a thirty-inch portable transit instrument, which answered the purpose of an equal altitude instrument and theodolite; thirdly, an astronomical pendulum clock; fourthly, several astronomical books. These instruments and books cost $1,054, but would cost four times that now, for they were very excellent of their kind. They were ordered as early as 1803, but did not arrive until the autumn of 1806, and were set up at Ludlow Station in the spring of 1806. They were used in making a great number of astronomical observations and calculations not within the duties of the present surveyor-general, but then desired and ordered by the government.

Among other things, he observed and calculated the orbit of the great comet in 1807. This calculation was published in the memoirs of the Connecticut Academy of Arts and Sciences. He was directed by the government to ascertain the latitude and longitude of various places; and thus the United States surveys became the means of advancing astronomical science in this country. The instruments used have since been deposited in the philosophical department of the United States Military Academy at West Point, where they remain as memorials of the first observatory in the United States. In connection with this, I must mention the erection of the first Cincinnati Observatory. This was solely the creation of Ormsby M. Mitchell, who, having been a professor of mathematics and astronomy, and an active teacher, formed the idea of erecting an observatory on Mount Adams. He had a very superior mind, and was frequently thinking of various projects. He became enthusiastic about an observatory, and without any means save his own exertions, proceeded to work up that project. He talked and lectured until he got many people interested in it. He got the late Nicholas Longworth to grant him a site for a building on Mount Adams, and then got subscriptions for the building, The shares were at first $25 each, but the project was popular, and he finally obtained the means to buy the great telescope and erect the building. He went over to Europe to purchase the telescope. When there he found that the best makers of astronomical instruments were at the Franenhofer Institute, Munich. It was made by Messrs. Mertz & Mayer, and cost nearly $10,000. It was at that time the largest telescope in America—its focal length being 17¼ feet, and the diameter of the object-classes 12 inches. In the meanwhile Mitchell had the observatory building erected on the site given by Mr. Longworth. This whole work, of which Mitchell was the director and originator, was probably the first and *only* purely scientific enterprise literally carried out by the people.

When it was finished Mitchell determined to have a popular inauguration. To do this, he invited John Quincy Adams to pronounce an oration. He accepted the invitation, came to Cincinnati, and delivered a splendid discourse, of which only such a man was capable. An immense crowd and procession attended the inauguration, and it is, perhaps, the only instance in the world in which an observatory or any merely scientific work was made the occasion of a popular celebration. When the work was completed Mitchell resided there with his family, and for several years continued to make astronomical observations. In the meantime he invented two instruments to record the observations of right ascension and the difference in declination. They were very ingenious, and furnished observations of accuracy never attainable from any previous instruments.

Alas for Mitchell! He was one of those whom I have never ceased to regret. He was a man of genius and a man of worth. He was one of the earliest volunteers for the Union, and among the most successful officers, until he fell a victim to disease, at Beaufort, South Carolina. He was killed by that civil war, whose real authors have never been hanged, although, in all the records of time, there was never a criminal who more deserved to be.

CHAPTER XIX.

Political Campaign of 1840— *Van Buren— Washington Scandal—Break between Calhoun and Jackson—Van Buren's Success—Nomination of Harrison—Log Cabins and Hard Cider—Glee Songs—Defeat of Van Buren—Salt River—Lamentations.*

I SHALL now give my memories of the political campaign of 1840. Its results have entered into history; but not so the thousand incidents and singular scenes in that remarkable conflict. As a purely civil and political movement, it has no parallel in my memory, and was characteristic of what a free people, governed by law, can do without imperiling law or committing violence. It was at once amusing and serious, trifling and important. It was a whole nation enacting what was a comedy, but might have been a tragedy. It was not a conflict of great principles, such as resulted in the Missouri Compromise, nullification, secession, or a foreign war. It was really a conflict about the material interests of the people—in fact, about their pockets. The causes of this contest I have partly related in the account of the overthrow of the United States Bank, and the ultimate suspension of the state banks. But they can not be fully understood without going a little more into detail. I have narrated the overthrow of the United States Bank by Jackson; the encouragement given to the states banks to loan freely; the reduction of the tariff to a minimum of twenty per cent. ; the issuing of the specie circular, and the final suspension of all the banks, and the ruin of thousands of merchants.

Such was the state of things when, in March, 1837, MARTIN VAN BUREN became President of the United States. How he came to be so, and what he did, are important elements in the history of those times. Van Buren was, in brief, a sequel of Jacksonism, without the power to direct the storm which Jackson had raised. Jackson had sown to the wind, and Van Buren reaped the whirlwind. He was a New York politician, bred in the most corrupt school of politics which this country has ever known—a school which still continues its corrupt practices in that state, and whose last disciple and leader is Samuel J. Tilden, Esq. Mr. Van Buren was a man of respectability, of decided talents, and of good character. Yet his political career had neither dignity, respectability, nor virtue—I mean public virtue, for he had no private vices, and was deemed an estimable man. Let us, then, observe him from a public point of view. He was one of Jackson's chief supporters, and founders of the present Democratic party. In the conflicts of that day there was a social as well as a political conflict. It arose about Mrs. Eaton, wife of Secretary Eaton, Jackson's intimate friend, for reasons unnecessary to mention, and of no public interest at the present day. Mrs. Eaton was ostracised by the leading ladies of Washington, among whom were the wives of the Southern members of the cabinet. Mrs. Calhoun, Mrs. Berrien, and Mrs. Branch refused to call upon Mrs. Eaton. Eaton, of course, felt injured, and Jackson took his part. Van Buren sided with Jackson, partly, no doubt, because he was then a widower, and had no troubles of that sort. Jackson made it a personal matter with all of Eaton's opponents, and the result was a break up of the cabinet, the alienation of Calhoun, and the acceptance of Van Buren as the leader of the Jackson (then calling itself the Democratic) party.

In the meantime, there was a little political episode which ought to go into history. The reader, no doubt, remembers when Jackson, in the administration of Monroe, marched into Florida, and captured two men, named Arbuthnot and Ambrister, who, for some reason, either as spies or traitors, he executed. This was, doubtless, contrary to law, and his conduct was inquired into by congress. The administration, however, wished to defend its own commander, and in some way Jackson escaped punishment or reproach. The consultations which led to this result were held by the cabinet, of which Adams, Crawford, and Calhoun were members. In some way, probably by false information from the enemies of Adams, Jackson was firmly impressed with the idea that Calhoun was his friend and supporter in the cabinet, and that Adams and Crawford were opposed to him. In the end, and about the time of the Eaton trouble, it turned out, through some letter from Crawford, that Jackson's impressions were all wrong—that Adams had been his firm supporter, and Calhoun his opponent. Jackson became indignant, and looked upon Calhoun as a political intriguer and his own enemy. I state this to show the state of feeling among the public men in Washington at that time. It shows how completely Jackson had made the government a personal matter.

He put men out and in, quarreled with or supported them, for causes measured by his own feelings and interests. The government was as completely personal at that time as was the government of George the Third. So devoted were his friends, and so anxious the great body of politicians who formed the new Democratic party, to obtain power and patronage, that he was upheld in all his personal measures, and his administration maintained. But his successor, without his courage and daring, fell under the weight of popular indignation. The Eaton affair soon blew over. It was only a " tempest in a tea-pot." Berrien and Branch resigned ; new followers of Jackson were appointed to their places ; and the star of Van Buren became ascendant. Of course, Calhoun and his friends were opponents of Van Buren, but their efforts to stem the tide were unavailing. About this time, Van Buren was appointed minister to England. When the question of confirmation came up, the Whigs and the followers of Calhoun held a majority of the senate, and the appointment of Van Buren was rejected. There is no doubt but that this action was unwise and indiscreet, for Van Buren was entirely fit for the appointment—being a gentleman, and rich enough to perform the duties with dignity. This false action, turning wholly on personal feelings, led to consequences which, perhaps, would not otherwise have occurred. Van Buren was made president, and his party afterward signally defeated. Two months after the inauguration of Van Buren as president, every bank in the country had suspended, thousands of merchants failed, and the country was in a state of unexampled commercial distress. When congress assem-

bled, this was the sole topic of public consideration.
The president, of course, had to make it the subject
of his message. He stated the causes of this distress
very fairly—that it was overtrading (which I have
hitherto stated was caused by the reduction of the
tariff and the over-loaning of the banks), the inflation
of the banks, and the demand of specie for the government deposits. His remedy for this was an independent treasury. To understand this the reader will
remember that the government deposits, which are
always large, had been put in the United States Bank,
until Jackson destroyed that bank by his war upon
it; and that then he directed the deposits to be placed
in the state incorporate banks; and that at the same
time he recommended those bankers to accommodate
the people with loans. This commercial catastrophe
occurred, as we have seen, at the beginning of Van
Buren's administration. To avoid the evils dependent
upon the public deposits being placed in banks, Van
Buren recommended the independent treasury, or as
his opponents called it, the sub-treasury. The reader
will observe that, in theory, all the moneys of the
United States are supposed to be in the hands of the
United States Treasurer, but, as I have said, they were
really deposited in banks. The independent treasury,
as proposed by Van Buren, was to consist in keeping
the moneys by the treasurer, assistant-treasurer, and
certain public officers, who, for this purpose, were
provided with safes and other conveniences necessary
for keeping money. In other words, the independent
treasury meant to sever the treasury of the United
States from all banks or other moneyed institutions,
and put the United States money literally in its own

treasury. This scheme was at first violently opposed, not only by the Whig party, but by many Democrats. The consequence was that when first proposed to congress it was rejected, but at a subsequent congress was passed. In the meanwhile it became evident that the power of the Democratic party was broken. The votes in congress on the sub-treasury, and the local elections throughout the country, showed this conclusively. The great State of New York, under the able and shrewd management of William H. Seward and Thurlow Weed, aided by the Anti-Masonic excitement, had been carried by the Whigs, and politically revolutionized. For nearly thirty years it had been controled by Martin Van Buren and his able colleagues, who were called the Albany Regency. Seward had become governor, and the star of Van Buren had set for ever. The State of Tennessee, also, which seemed to belong to Jackson, had broken from its moorings, and throughout the country there was a state of excitement and indignation which augured the defeat of the Democratic party. Such was the real state of the nation in the administration of Van Buren, and the preparation for the political campaign of 1840.

The Democrats, of course, renominated Mr. Van Buren. The Whigs had before them three candidates for nomination. These were Mr. Clay, General Harrison, and General Scott. Under ordinary circumstances Mr. Clay would have been nominated, but before the Whig Convention met it became manifest that General Harrison had great popularity. In the previous election of 1836 he carried some states, such as Indiana, which Mr. Clay could not carry. There

was among many people the same fervor and enthu-
siasm for his military character which had been manifested for Jackson. Among politicians Mr. Clay was
far the strongest, for he was, in fact, the leader of the
Whig party, and supported by many friends with
great ardor. General Scott had also a good many
friends. But when the convention met the popular
feeling for General Harrison was so strong that he
was nominated, to the great regret, and almost grief,
of Mr. Clay's ardent supporters. It afterward turned
out that Mr. Clay could have been elected as easily as
General Harrison, for the country was in such condition that it required and must have a change. Among
the then Whig party of the South were many states
rights men, who had adopted, more or less, the ideas
of Mr. Calhoun. To conciliate these, and gain support in the South, John Tyler, of Virginia, was nominated as Vice-President. This proved to be a great
blunder; perhaps no greater mistake has occurred in
the history of the country. Mr. Tyler's doctrines
were those of the strict state rights school, and were
well known. Between those doctrines and those of
the Whig party there was an absolute antagonism.
The Whigs were for a National Bank, a strong tariff,
and internal improvements for the welfare of the
country. Mr. Tyler was opposed to all of these, and
the fact was well known at the convention. Yet, in
spite of this, the convention nominated Tyler, in the
vain hope, as it afterward proved, of conciliating the
faction which he represented. This blunder not only
defeated the Whig party several years after, but had a
most mischievous effect upon the whole country. After
the nominations were made, the " war-cry " of the cam-

paign became " Tippecanoe and Tyler, too !" General Harrison had fought and won the victory over the Indians at Tippecanoe, on the Wabash. The " Tyler, too," exactly expressed the fact that Tyler was a sort of affix—*addendum*—to the hero of Tippecanoe; nothing in himself, but a good deal when added to Harrison. " Tippecanoe and Tyler, too," became the chorus of every glee song, and was shouted through the hills and dales of this wide land. Among other incidents of this election, was a great paper ball, perhaps ten feet in diameter, on which was inscribed the names of states which, in the local elections of that year, had gone for the Whigs and Harrison. It was set going in some Eastern city, and is said to have been rolled through all the states of the Union. At all events, I saw that or a similar one in Broadway, Cincinnati, rolled through the city streets and on to the West. But the chief means of popular excitement were the glee clubs, which never before or since have been so effectually used. Songs were written specially for them of the most patriotic and exciting character. I recollect the first one I heard was from Chillicothe, led by a young man named Duffield, who, with a fine voice, a good club of singers, and new songs and airs, made the air thrill with popular excitement. The first song I heard had this verse :

> " What has caused this great commotion–motion–motion
> All the country through ?
> It is the ball a rolling on
> For Tippecanoe and Tyler, too !
> And with them we 'll beat little Van—**Van**.
> Van's a used up man."

This was sung in the afternoon of a warm August

day, and I never knew anything of that sort so en-
rage our political opponents, for they felt it was true.

Harrison being a pioneer and a farmer at North
Bend, was represented to the people as living in a log
cabin—living on corn-meal, pork, and hard cider.
The political processions were interlined with log
cabins, coons, and hard cider, while the glee clubs ac-
companying them shouted "Tippecanoe and Tyler,
too." I seldom went to these political meetings; but
in September, 1840, I attended the great convention
at Dayton—probably the greatest held in this country. I and my friend set out from Cincinnati in a
buggy, on one of the brightest of autumnal days. As
we ascended Walnut Hills, on or way to Dayton,
omnibusses, wagons, and buggies were before and behind us, while bands of music were playing. The
convention was to be held the next day, and at every
cross-road we met new companies swelling the great
throng to Dayton. I remember that at the present
village of Mason, in Warren county, we met a long
procession from Clermont county, with wagons, and
canvas, and people on horseback. At Centerville,
Montgomery county, we arrived at sunset, and, with
many other people, accepted the hospitalities of the
village. We found ourselves comfortably lodged in
the house of a friend, and next morning at daylight
proceeded to Dayton. The scene, just after sunrise,
entering Dayton, was very beautiful. Our road was a
descent from the east into the valley of the Miami,
and the city of Dayton and its surroundings lay below
us. Among other of the Whig devices, was to hang
out the flag at their great conventions, and, as we
looked down upon the city below in the bright sun-

light, Dayton was literally covered with flags. Every house seemed to have a flag, which waved in the breeze, while the bright sun shone upon it.

It was a beautiful and an animated scene. When we had reached the city, breakfasted, and arrived at the convention grounds, we were still more surprised. On the road from Urbana an immense procession was coming in. It was nearly all composed of wagons and men on horseback. It was said the procession numbered six thousand people, but that was probably exaggerated. In the midst of it was a great log cabin on wheels. On the top of the log cabin was a raccoon, and at the door was General Charles W. Anthony, of Springfield, representing the Western pioneer. Bands of music were playing. And thus procession after procession entered the convention grounds. The particular cause of this great assembly was that General Harrison was himself to speak. He did speak, but I, and I suppose thousands of others, could not hear him. While he was speaking I and Mr. Sam'l Forrer, who was a civil engineer, undertook to estimate the number of people on the ground. We were both competent to do it, and did not mean to exaggerate. As nearly as we could estimate, there were full fifty thousand people in the field where General Harrison spoke. When we returned to Dayton we found there were thousands of others in the streets who had not gone to the convention grounds at all. On the whole, I think there were sixty thousand people at the great meeting at Dayton, probably the largest political assembly held in the United States. For two months longer the campaign, at least in the West, went on in the same style and with the same excitement. Large processions, log cabins, hard cider, and Tippecanoe songs seemed to fill the country. With all this popular excitement for Harrison, and the active means employed, the Democratic party stood firm, and manifested an obstinacy as remarkable as it was creditable to the discipline of their organization. Few Democrats really changed their political opinions, but an immense vote was called out, which really determined the result.

The vote at the presidential election was nearly a million of votes greater than that at the previous election. This showed the popular excitement, but did not show any great change of parties. For example, the State of Ohio, with all this effort, gave only twenty-three thousand majority for Harrison, who had received nine thousand at the previous election. The increase of majority was fourteen thousand, and half of that, seven thousand, were all the votes actually gained from the Democrats. At times I was really doubtful of the result, though sanguine in feeling. It is the custom of political parties, to have a grand rally just previous to the election. These meetings are generally very large and interesting. I remember that two or three nights before the October election of 1840 (for the October elections determined the presidency), both parties were to have a grand rally, one—the Democrats—at the court-house, and the other—Whigs—at the Fifth street market place. The Democrats rallied their forces at the public landing at the river, and marched from there to the court-house. I was sitting in my mother's, on Third street, near Broadway, when I heard huzzas and the heavy tramp of feet going up Broadway.

Not remembering the Democratic procession, I rushed out to see what was the matter. It was the Democratic procession, marching by platoons to the court-house. The whole street seemed to be dark with them. Each man seemed to carry a club, which he struck against the ground, and hurraed for Van Buren. Many were Germans and many others Irish. "Hurra for Van Buren!" was constantly heard in deep guttural voices, which seemed to be earnest and determined. I had never before seen so large a procession moving in that way, and felt alarmed for the result. Going immediately to Fifth street market space I was undeceived; there I saw that large space filled with thousands of people. Four or five different speaker's stands were erected, and the most popular orators of the day were speaking to the multitude in animated terms. I returned home, satisfied that the Whigs would carry the day. Nevertheless, with all these hard efforts, Hamilton county was only carried by a bare majority. The day of the election presented other and different scenes. There had been not only great excitement, but a great many threats made. The Democrats, as I have said, carried clubs in their procession, and many of the Whigs, alarmed, carried pistols. The prudent men of the parties determined to keep the peace, and took all proper precautions. The grog-shops were all closed, the police were all armed and ready, and the polls so prepared that if possible there should be no trouble or difficulty. The polls opened at, I think, six o'clock in the morning. Long before that time people began to crowd around the voting places. The executive committees had taken the precaution to place a board walk from the window where the votes were received nearly across the street, so that the voters could proceed in order without collision. On each side of this board walk, and next the window, the challenging committees took their places, and challenged all voters who seemed to be doubtful. When I went to vote the line of voters extended entirely across the street, and it took considerable time to vote. Nearly the entire vote of the city was polled. The city of Cincinnati gave fifteen hundred majority, which, in a city of forty-six thousand inhabitants, was a large majority. The country townships were nearly all Democratic, so that the county of Hamilton only gave about one hundred Whig majority. I have given these details only to show the reader a picture of one of the most remarkable elections ever held in this country, and which made a profound impression upon all those who took part in it. The general election terminated, as history has recorded it, in the victory of General Harrison. He received the electoral votes of all the states but six. This, however, did not represent the true proportion of parties; for, while he received this great electoral vote, he received only one hundred and forty-seven thousand majority in two and a half million votes. Maine, Pennsylvania, and one or two other states had only given him three or four hundred majority. The general result, therefore, was, that while the triumph was complete, the real strength of parties was not materially changed. Let us now turn to those minor and amusing scenes which may interest the reader more than the historical result. Hundreds of these occurred, but a half dozen will show their nature. Among others was the celebrated slang

expression of O. K., which figured in every newspaper. It came about in this way: We received returns of local elections from many quarters, and
some of them from very illiterate persons. Most of
them were in favor of the Whigs, and the sender of
news would be often very exultant; one of them gave
a return of a Whig victory, and added " Oll Korect,"
and immediately the Whig editors adopted this sign
for their victory, O. K., and so it went through all the
country. Another term used then, and for several
years after, was " Loco-foco " and " Loco-focoism."
Nobody would know from these terms what they
meant, but it originated in this way: The Democratic
party in the city of New York, whose headquarters
was in Tammany Hall, and of which the Tammany
Society was the controlling element, never was, and is
not to-day, entirely united; there was a faction within
a faction. The differences arose from differences in
social condition. The working men could not then,
and can not now be altogether controlled. They are
always inclined to think that the evils of society are
owing to the rich and higher classes of society, and
to their influence in the government. The wealthy and
intelligent part of Tammany Society were undoubtedly conservative; but the working men were much
less so, and inclined to some new policy within the
Democratic party favorable to themselves. About
this time, or a little before, there had been an outbreak in the working man's class of the Democratic
party, and they ran an independent ticket of their
own. They got about ten thousand votes in the city
of New York, and this is about the proportion of
votes they get nowaday in the cities. During the

disturbed state of the business of the country a great
meeting was held in Tammany Hall, the object of
which I do not remember, but in which these opposite factions appeared in force and occasioned a remarkable scene.   One faction, I do not remember
which, not finding matters go to suit them, had prepared for this event by at once extinguishing the
lights and leaving the hall in darkness.   The other faction had anticipated something of the kind, and
brought with them the lucifer, or as some called them,
the loco-foco matches.   With these they immediately
relighted the hall, and carried out their proceedings.
The Whigs, who delighted in ridicule and nick-names,
immediately called the Democrats the "Loco-foco
party," and this name was attached to them for several
years.   "O. K. and "Loco-foco" figured in all the
Whig papers of the country.   The "Loco-focos did so
and so," and Whig victory was "O. K."   I have, by
these incidents, given some idea of that remarkable
political campaign, in which log cabins and hard cider
figured in processions, and "Loco-focos" and "O. K."
in the newspapers, and the whole was made musical by
the glee clubs, with "Tippecanoe and Tyler, too."   I
may close this account with two or three squibs, which
appeared after the election.   Among the types of victory or defeat was the rooster, either fallen on the
battle-field or crowing for victory.   In one cut was
seen, on the left the log cabin, and on the right a noble rooster crowing, with his foot on his fallen an-
tagonist, and underneath was this verse :

"Have you heard from all the Union,
Union, Union,
Good news and true;

Hundreds of thousands is the tune
For Tippecanoe and Tyler too,
Tippecanoe and Tyler too.
And with them we 've beat Little Van !
Van, Van 's a used-up man !''

Among others was a new version of " Cock Robin,"
published in the New York *American* by a young
lady :

"Who killed small Matty ?
We, says Tippecanoe,
I, and Tyler, too,
We killed small Matty.

" Who saw him die, oh ?
I, says O-h-i-o,
With my big Buckeye, oh !
I saw him die.

" Who dug his grave ?
I, says sturdy Maine,
And would do it, too, again,
I dug his grave !''

And other verses of the same kind. Another cut
represented a monument with a willow tree hanging
over it, and a woman weeping. The monument was
inscribed, " *In memory of Loco-focoism.*"

Several plates represented the departure of a steamboat and passengers for Salt river. Salt river was a
stream in Kentucky, and it was a common saying
when a person had been defeated or had met with a
misfortune, that he " was rowed up Salt river." Several wood-cuts in the newspapers represented Van
Buren and his cabinet as going up Salt river. One
of them was in the form of a newspaper advertisement. There was a cut of a steamboat and an announcement that : "The steamboat Van Buren, only

four years old, commander Amos Kendall, will leave
4th of March next for Salt river, *via* Kinderhook.
For freight or passage, apply at the White House,
Washington City, or at the captain's office." No less
a poet than Dr. Percival wrote a jubilee song, entitled
" Success to Tippecanoe." The last stanza was:

"Then let us all stand by the honest old man,
Who has rescued the country, and beat little Van.
The spirit of evil has gotten its due;
It is laid by the strong arm of Tippecanoe.
In the front rank our nation shall now take its stand;
Peace, order, prosperity, brighten the land.
Then loud swell the voice of each good man and true,
Success to the gallant Old Tippecanoe."

But notwithstanding all this excitement, this show
and parade, and this popular victory, the end was sad,
if not unfortunate, both to thousands of individuals
and to the entire nation. Harrison was inaugurated
on the 4th of March, 1841; his cabinet was an excellent one, and the country seemed on the verge of great
prosperity. As if to overturn this human vanity,
Harrison died in thirty days after his inauguration.
The nation was again agitated with new alarms. The
people began to see, though they did not then comprehend, the disastrous results of an administration
by a man whose principles were opposed to those of
the president elected and the party who elected him.
The thing to be remedied was the financial condition
of the country, and that could only be done by a national bank and a national currency, or, in other
words, the government taking control of the currency.
But to all this Tyler was opposed, and nothing could
be done. In consequence of this there was a violent

quarrel between Mr. Clay and Tyler. Clay was the leader of the Whig party, and the party followed him. The consequence was that the president (Tyler) was left with only five representatives in congress to support him. The Democrats could not support him, for they had opposed his election and had nothing in common with him. The Whigs could carry no measure on the currency, for Tyler was utterly opposed to their views. One thing favorable to the country was done. This was the passage of the tariff act of 1842–1843. This act, by encouraging American manufactures and supporting the industries of the country, really did good, and gradually the country in the next five or six years was reduced to its normal condition. I may here close this singular chapter of American history. The nomination of Tyler and the death of Harrison, both taught serious lessons. It taught, first, that no man should be nominated for vice-president who was not entirely fit to be president, and who was not in harmony with the party who elected him. And, again, Divine Providence taught, in the death of Harrison, the vanity of human hopes and the instability of human government.

CHAPTER XX.

The Newspaper Press—Its Origin, Character, and Purposes—The English Press—Public Writers—The " Morning Chronicle"—Fox and Sheridan—" Public Advertiser"—Junius—The American Press—Freneau) —Duane—Ritchie—Robert Walsh—" Evening Post" —Coleman—" National Intelligencer"—Gales—" New York Times"—Henry J. Raymond—Horace Greeley and Socialism—What should be the Tone and Character of a Newspaper?

IT will be seen from what I have related of my personal memories, that much of my life has been spent in writing for the public. My first newspaper article was published in 1824, at Litchfield, Connecticut. In the more than half a century which has elapsed, there has been no year in which I have not written for the press. In that time I became acquainted with many newspaper men and the newspapers in which they were engaged. Perhaps for this reason it is not out of place to give my views of the history and character of the press in this country. It is now about two hundred years since the newspaper press became established as one of the great features of society. It has become so great and important an element that it is quite as great as that of steam and locomotion. In one word, the newspaper press and steam comprehend all the great advance which society has made in modern days. Prior to newspapers, literature was wholly comprised in books, and these books could only be known to few persons. Now, the newspaper not only circulates its own news and information, but circulates the knowledge of books, so that the whole quantity, as well as value of literature, is much increased. Again, a writer for the daily press reaches a hundred readers where the bookmaker, pulpit orator, or public speaker can reach one. The public writer in the newspaper, therefore, if he has any information, thought, or idea that is valuable, can give it a weight or influence which no public speaker or other writer is able to do. This is the *real power* of the press. It is the power to give any thought or information a far greater range than any public writer or speaker can.

Is there anything valuable in the way of new ideas, inventions, or discoveries, the newspaper gives them ubiquity and makes them the common property of the people. Is there anything good in a book, a newspaper takes it up and gives it universal circulation. In one word the newspaper is the great forum in which all news, information, and discoveries are discussed and published. It is the great school-room in which more is taught than in all the school-rooms of the world. Such is the power of the press, which sends its sheets through the world, "thick as the leaves in Vallambrosa's vale."

The history of the newspaper press has had three periods, each distinct in character from the others. The first period comprehended more than half of the whole of newspaper existence. There was then no real freedom of the press, and, as a consequence, the newspaper was little more than a diary of the most ordinary events. The news given related chiefly to foreign affairs, with such accounts of murders and calamities as were publicly known. Domestic politics were not discussed, literary criticism was unknown, and there were no pains taken to produce news for the papers. In one word, a newspaper recorded many things which the public wanted, but was totally uninteresting as to any discussion on religion, politics, or literature. The first advertisement was inserted in 1648, and the first newspaper devoted to advertising and commercial intelligence was established in 1657. This period of the press continued for more than one hundred years. About the time of the American revolution, the newspaper assumed a new character, the restraints upon the freedom of the press in Europe and America were taken off. The newspaper then began to discuss religious, political, and literary questions with a boldness which has scarcely been exceeded since. In 1762, appeared " *The North Briton,*" edited by Wilkes, in England, who played a conspicuous part in consolidating the liberty of the press. Every reader of political history knows how Wilkes was prosecuted in libel suits; what celebrated trials took place ; how he was persecuted ; how the people sustained him, and how, at last, the liberty of the press was established. In 1766, appeared the *Englishman,* chiefly known as containing contributions from Edmund Burke. In 1767, the *Public Advertiser* published the first letter of Junius. Perhaps, no articles, before or since, in any newspaper, have attracted so much public attention. It was not merely the ability of the writer, but the peculiar state of English politics at that time, which gave these Junius letters importance. Parties had degenerated into

personal factions. The machinery of government
was made personal and often corrupt. In the midst
of these factions, George the III set up his own personal government. His adherents were called the
King's party. He undertook to rule by virtue of his
own prerogative; in point of fact, the royal prerogative was abridged by the death of Charles the I, and
abolished, substantially, at least, by the Revolution of
1689. William the III, though personally despotic,
paid great regard to his ministry and to parliament.
Ann, George the First, and George the Second, made
no pretensions to personal government. If, in their
time, there was any personal government, it was accomplished more through Caroline, wife of George
the Second, than any other person. She governed
through Sir Robert Walpole, who was prime minister.
George the Third, probably because he found parties
degenerated into personal factions, set up a King's
party, and in this he was as obstinate and injudicious as
he afterward was in the American Revolution. It was
in this state of things that Junius appeared in the columns of the *Advertiser.* If his own account be correct,
and his writings any indication of his true feelings, he
seems to have been a man of much real patriotism,
though probably with personal objects in view. He,
certainly, in the case of General Warrants, and the
special case of Wilkes, advocated what we should now
call the unquestionable rights of the people. He defended public justice and attacked public corruption.
He used the weapons of sarcasm, of invective, rhetoric,
and even of law and of facts with unsparing ferocity. He
had mercy on no party and no man, when within the line
of his attack. He attacked the king, the. noble, and

commoner with a caustic severity which has had no parallel in the press. In doing this, he spared neither pains nor labor with his compositions. He, himself, states this in one of his letters, and thought that the labor of his writing was a great task. This fact is well worth remembering by one who would write for the public. The most effective writers we have known have been painstaking and laborious in their early, if not in their later writings. Writing for the public is in itself an education, and the first person to be educated is the writer himself. It is only after years of habitual composition that a writer can afford to write with such facility as to make little or no correction. This ease and address is acquired only by habitual experience. It *may be thus acquired*, but is, like education itself, the result of time and labor. Junius used both these means, and, as a consequence, his writings rank among the finest compositions in the English language. I've heard it said, that Junius was only remarkable for invective and abuse. This is not true. He is remarkable for the best use of the English language, for strong sentiment, uttered in strong Anglo-Saxon. He had a good cause in asserting the rights of the people against royalty and corruption, and he used it with great effect. It is now one hundred years since he wrote his letters in the *Advertiser*, and there is probably no writer of his day better known than Junius.

The letters of Junius were among the many contributions to newspapers which mark personal influence in the press. For the next seventy or eighty years newspapers were influential according to the personal character and ability of their editors and contributors. In that period many remarkable men were connected

with the press of both Europe and America, of whom
I shall speak again. But within half a century after
the appearance of the letters of Junius, there began to
appear a class of papers, best described by the literal
term *news*papers. The first and greatest of these was
The London Times, which appeared under the title
of *The Universal Register;* it was a daily paper, and
its circulation only a thousand copies, while other
papers were far more numerous. Among them were
The Morning Chronicle, and *Morning Post*, which
had great literary and political importance, especially
on account of their celebrated contributors. Mr.
Stuart was editor of the *Morning Post*, to which
Coleridge, Southey, Lamb, Wordsworth, and Macin-
tosh contributed. Mr. J. Perry was editor of the
Morning Chronicle. Fox and Sheridan were his
personal friends, and contributed to the ability and
influence of the *Chronicle.* In the meanwhile *The
Times*, which was published by John Walter, was
steadily gaining ground. Its remarkable success
since then is due to several causes. It was free from
party ties. It was conducted with great business care,
and used steam power for its printing press. On the
morning of November 29, 1814, the readers of *The
Times* were informed that "the journal of this day
presents to the public the practical result of the greatest
improvement connected with printing since the dis-
covery of the art itself." This was the application of
steam to the printing press; but, after all, the greatest
improvement, and the greatest success of the *Times*
was in the collection of news. *The Times* was, I
believe, the first newspaper which employed special
couriers and private expresses to get the news in ad-

vance of the mails. In this they were successful, and
the public became accustomed to looking to the
Times for the earliest intelligence of any important
matter. This increased its circulation, but *The Times*,
and other newspapers, continued to add to their
facilities. On January 29, 1829, *The Times* came out
with a double sheet, composed of eight pages of
forty-eight columns. At the same time it increased
its domestic intelligence, and gave minute accounts of
trials, crimes, accidents, etc. Reporting, as now understood, especially parliamentary proceedings, began at
a very early day, but was so imperfect and unreliable
as to be unimportant. The speeches were never reported as spoken, and could not as reported be relied
on as correct. Even as late as Dr. Johnson's time, he
was said to have written himself the speeches in parliament, some of which have become famous. Every
boy in college remembers the attack of Walpole upon
Pitt, and Pitt's famous reply: "I am charged with the
atrocious crime of being a young man!" But it is said
they were both written by Johnson. The business of
reporting for newspapers has now arrived at a perfec-
tion which was not then dreamed of. The speech of
the orator now is not only reported accurately, but
literally, word for word, and the portrait of the orator
in thought and speech is now laid before the public.
This brings us to the last of the newspaper epochs.
In one word a newspaper is now strictly and literally
a *news*paper. It is no longer a mere record of foreign
and commercial intelligence. It is no longer a mere
personal representative, dependent on the ability of its
writers. Ability of the highest order it *must have*, and
it would soon sink without it; but its great character-

istic is the diffusion of universal intelligence; in this there is nothing too high or too low for its observation. We hear of the march of great armies, but also of the thief at midnight. We hear of the great orator, but also of the petty street wrangler. We hear of the earthquake that shakes half the globe, and also of the falling of a small house. We hear of the death of a renowned captain, and also of the suicide of a poor girl. In one word, we hear of both the great and the minute, of the social and the solitary, the good and the bad; in fact, the eye of a great newspaper is now upon the whole world. There is nothing hidden that is not brought to light, and nothing so obscure that it is not made lucid. Every art, science, and talent of the modern world have been brought to the aid of the newspaper. From the steam press which throws off its tens of thousands of sheets, to the locomotive which carries its express messenger; from the steam ship which carries its reporter to the remotest regions, to the telegraph which flashes its news, all arts and inventions aid the newspaper. Thus aided by modern inventions, the newspaper is making the human mind ubiquitous. Nations correspond and discuss affairs, as individuals did in times past. Thus nations are brought together, and the world is filled with universal intelligence. This progress of the newspaper has been the work of the last half century, and is certainly not the least of those evidences of progress which characterize the present age. I shall not stop now to describe it further, but shall return to notice some of the most distinguished editors and writers who marked what I have termed the *personal* period of the newspaper. I have already mentioned some of the great

names which have distinguished the English press.   I
will now proceed to notice the *personelle* of the United
States press.

Philip Freneau was one of the first journalists who
attracted attention in this country.   He was more of a
poet than a journalist.   He graduated at Princeton
College, New Jersey, and was the room-mate and personal friend of James Madison.   He began his literary
career by writing a poetical history of the Prophet
Jonah.   He was the author of the Indian ballad, beginning :

> " The sun sets at night and the stars shun the day,
> But glory remains when their light fades away.
> Begin, ye tormentors!   Your threats are in vain,
> For the son of Alknomack shall never complain!"

The first couplet ought to give fame to any writer.
It contains one of the most beautiful images in nature.
This ballad was attributed to an English lady, but it
has been satisfactorily ascertained to be Freneau's.
Upon the establishment of the Federal government at
Philadelphia, he was appointed French translator in
the department of state under Mr. Jefferson, and at
the same time became editor of the *National Gazette*.
That paper was made the vehicle of bitter attacks on
the administration of Washington ; but it was said
Freneau was not responsible for them.   He himself
said that the most severe of them were dictated by
Jefferson.   That paper was discontinued in October,
1793, and two years after Freneau started a paper at
Middletown, New Jersey, which continued but a short
time.   Freneau is now little known, but he was a true
poet and an able writer.   Several editions of his poems
were published in his lifetime.   Scott and Campbell

borrowed whole lines from him, and Jeffrey predicted that his poems would be as well known as Hudibras.

William Duane was one of the most noted editors in the United States. He was born in New York; learned the art of printing, and went to India to seek his fortune. There he edited a paper called the *World*. Having offended the government, he was seized, sent to England, and his property confiscated. There he edited a paper called *The General Advertiser*, and sided with a faction headed by Horne Tooke. In 1795 he returned to America, and became editor of the *Aurora*, published at Philadelphia. This paper became the most influential organ of the Democratic party. Jefferson attributed his election to its influence. At that time party spirit was higher than it had ever previously been in America. Philadelphia was a Federal town, and the Federalists distinguished themselves by a black cockade. The office of the *Aurora* was mobbed, and my father (then teaching in Philadelphia) was one of a party of Democrats who defended it. When the seat of government was moved from Philadelphia to Washington, the *Aurora* declined, but Duane continued to edit it until 1822. He was not a fine writer, but a powerful political advocate. One of the most noted political editors in this country was Thomas Ritchie. He was born in Virginia, and edited the Richmond *Enquirer* from 1804–1845. He was the leading, and perhaps most influential, Democratic editor at that time. There were in these days two political centers, Albany and Richmond, Va. The managers of the Democratic party in those places were called the Albany and Richmond "Juntos." At Albany the chief manager was Martin Van Buren, and at Richmond, Ritchie, Madison, and others of the Virginia clique held sway.

In the forty years in which Mr. Ritchie was editor, these juntos held supreme control in the Democratic party, and through that over the country. When Ritchie left the *Enquirer* to edit the *Union*, in Washington, Polk was elected president, the western influence began to assert itself, and the juntos of Albany and Richmond ceased to be supreme. In 1849 Ritchie retired, after a long and successful editorial career. He was a strong writer, a distinguished man, and, through the Virginia dynasty, exercised a great influence on the politics of the country.

William Coleman was for nearly thirty years a leading editor in the Federal party of New York. He was born and educated in Massachusetts. He was bred to the bar, and was for a short time a partner with Aaron Burr in the practice of the law. But, in 1801, Hamilton and other leading Federalists set up a daily paper in the city of New York, and selected Coleman, who was a warm Federalist, to conduct it. This paper was the now well-known *Evening Post*, and, in the nearly eighty years of its existence, has been conducted for most of that time by Coleman and Bryant. When Coleman first began his career, party contests were very hot, and Coleman was involved in several personal conflicts. Nevertheless, he and the *Post* maintained their ground. The *Evening Post* has survived hundreds of papers which have flourished and died since it was established. Soon after Coleman left it, Bryant became editor, and for more than forty years maintained and increased the reputation of the paper. The next editor I shall mention was perhaps more successful than any I have noted. This was Joseph Gales, editor of the *National Intelligencer.* His father was an Englishman, who had edited a paper in England; came to the United States, and edited the *Raleigh Register,* of North Carolina. Joseph Gales was himself born in England, but in 1800 came to Washington, and began his career in the *National Intelligencer.* This was a Republican paper; for the reader will observe that the old Democratic party never called itself Democratic, but was officially known as the Republican party. The reader who will refer to the old files of the *National Intelligencer* will find that every caucus held by congress was called the Republican caucus. In fact, it was not until Van Buren's time, as we have learned, that the Democratic party called itself Democratic. The *Intelligencer* survived fifty years, and died during the war of the Rebellion.

The only other editor of the last generation I shall mention is Robert Walsh. He was, in every respect, a noteworthy person; he was born in Baltimore, and died in Paris. He was, during his life, both a political and literary character. He was a Roman Catholic; studied law with the celebrated Robert Goodloe Harper, and traveled in Europe. Naturally inclined to literature, he did little at the law, but began writing for the "*Portfolio,*" edited monthly by Joseph Dennie. From this time forth, he was nearly half a century a public writer. He had, from his travels in France, formed his own opinions and opposed the policy of Napoleon, and published strictures upon it which met with great public favor in England. He made two strong but unsuccessful attempts to establish an American Quarterly. In 1819, he published

"An Appeal from the Judgments of Great Britain," respecting the United States of America. The occasion of this was a continual abuse and criticism upon the American action of all kinds, by the press of Great Britain. To look back upon it now, it seems a surprising example of the weakness of human nature, manifested in the jealousy of a great nation. I have already, perhaps, mentioned that while we were living at Mill creek, a man called on my father, who gave his name as D'Arville, but whose real name was Thomas Ash, an Englishman. He cheated Dr. Goforth out of the skeleton of a mammoth, and published a book in England abusing America. The book was profitable, and from that time, to Mrs. Trollope and her successors, abuse of America continued to be popular in England. Walsh took the matter up and his "Appeal" was a useful and able work. One of the British quarterlies had sneeringly asked : "Who reads an American book?" To put that question in contrast with the present re-publication in England of all noted American books, is decidedly amusing. More than forty years ago, Dr. Dwight published his " *Theology*," a work which Scotch and English critics pronounced the best modern work upon that subject in the English language. In 1821, Walsh became editor of the *Philadelphia National Gazette*, one of the ablest and best papers in the United States. It was strongly conservative, sustained the Whig party, and probably had more literary readers than any paper in the country.

After some fifteen years' existence, the paper declined, and Walsh was appointed consul to Paris. There he was the Paris correspondent of the *National*

Intelligencer and *Journal of Commerce.* Of Thurlow Weed, in Albany, Benjamin Russell, of Boston, William L. Stone and Nathaniel Carter, of New York, it is unnecessary to speak ; they are well known. Of Charles Hammond, I have fully spoken in my notice of Cincinnati. Of Horace Greeley also, I make no special notice, because he is well known to all readers of newspapers. To Henry J. Raymond notice is due, because he was one of my friends and one of my earliest newspaper acquaintances.

He was born in Western New York, graduated at the University of Vermont, and began the study of the law, but both his tastes and his necessities obliged him to resort to something else. He began his contributions to the *New Yorker* in 1840, and the next year, when Greeley established the *Tribune,* he became the assistant editor. In 1843, he entered the staff of the *New York Courier,* then edited by James Watson Webb, where he remained the next seven years. In the meantime he had become noted as a reporter ; he had remarkable ability for work of this kind, which has, since then, become very important.

During his connection with the *Courier,* he had a controversy with Horace Greeley on the subject of socialism, as advocated by Fourier. Greeley was always eccentric, and in nothing more than his attachment to socialism. He was always making schemes to reform society, by law or organization. The socialistic schemes of Fourier were attempted in this country by several associations, and were all failures. In my day, I have seen this socialistic idea attempted in several different ways, from the Society of Rapp, in Pennsylvania, to that of New Harmony, in Indiana. From that of Robert Owen to Fourier and Shakerism. Sometimes they have succeeded in making a peaceful, quiet community, as that of the Shakers, but have never succeeded in being either useful or profitable to the same extent as the same number of persons in general society. It is not in accordance with the principles of Christianity. Christianity does not propose to reform society by law or organization, but to bring forth the peaceful fruits of righteousness by reforming the heart. Raymond was said to be a *born* editor, and he was one. He was one to whom editing and managing a newspaper was as familiar as the elements around him. In 1841–1842, when I was editing the *Chronicle*, he was, for a short time, a correspondent of the paper.

In 1850, having had a disagreement with Webb, he left the *Courier*, and, in 1851, founded the *New York Times*. This was an important event in journalism, for the *New York Times* has become one of the most important newspapers in this country. Raymond was attached to the Whig party, and naturally a radical, but he kept the *Times* in fact conservative, for he well knew that a great paper in New York city must derive its chief support from the conservative element in society. He knew what a newspaper should be, and gradually brought up the *Times* to his ideal standard. On the formation of the Republican party, he took an active part, and made speeches for Fremont, and at a subsequent period he was elected member of congress, and lieutenant-governor of New York. In all this, however, he took less interest than the *Times*. Before his death, he ceased to hold office or political aspiration. He told me, himself, that he thought holding office was injurious to his paper. He died too young, not merely for himself, but for the public interest. I will mention here some of the characteristics of editors and newspapers. It is somewhat remarkable that, excepting Mr. Raymond and Mr. Walsh, who was consul, hardly any of the noted editors of the United States have held office. It was not for want of ample opportunity. Ritchie, Gales, Hammond, and probably others, refused office. Nearly all editors of leading newspapers have realized, what is certainly the fact, that their position had more influence than any office could confer. Besides this, all public writers acquire a strong taste for that pursuit, and there are few instances of anyone being diverted from it.

I now come to the question of what is the proper tone and character of a newspaper. I am asked: *What should* a newspaper be ? I answer, first of all, it should be a *newspaper.* But this includes many things, positive and negative; and, as far as observation and experience enable me, I will give my views upon that subject. First of all, a newspaper should be impersonal. We have noticed three periods of newspaper existence. The first was barren of anything but commercial and foreign intelligence; the second was noted for the ability and influence of its writers; and the third, in which we now are, is that of the real newspaper, in which *news* is the main point, but in which great ability in all departments must be manifested in the discussion of all questions—for this fresh discussion is in part news, being later and much more fresh than any books or dogmatic learning. When I say that the main business of a newspaper is *news,* I do not forget that the ablest articles on all topics of the day do and ought to appear in newspapers, but the editorship of a newspaper, that department which assumes to say " we," should be impersonal. Nothing is more common, or generally more disgusting to the reader, than the personal controversies of John Robinson and Joe Thompson, as newspaper editors. Contributors to the French press generally sign their names, but they do not enter into personal controversies. The practice of signing names to articles by contributors, is commendable, when the writer is known, and no special object in concealment. On the other hand, there is no objection to the " anonymous." Some most absurd things have been written upon this subject. It is claimed that every writer should sign his name to his articles. This is absurd ; for, it may be, the things written may be important and useful to be known, and yet the writer become obnoxious by stating them. The things he has said are true, and ought to be stated, but there is no reason why he should expose himself to obloquy by signing his name. His name, however, should be known to the editor, and then the paper will stand between him and the public. A most remarkable instance of this was in the case of Junius. Woodfall, the publisher of the "*Public Advertiser,*" acknowledged that he had seen Junius, and knew him, but his name was never disclosed, and probably never will be. From this something may be inferred about Junius. That is, that Junius was a man of wealth and influence, or Woodfall would never have accepted his guarranty against the dangers he encountered.

The anonymous has its uses, but whether it shall be permitted or not must be left to the discretion of the editor. The next, and, in one respect, the most im-

portant part of the paper, is to employ able contributors, who can discuss any particular question in the
fullest and most complete manner. This is done by
all the large city papers, and must be done by all papers which expect to attain reputation and influence.
We have seen that this has been done by the great
English papers. Burke, Sheridan, Johnson, Coleridge,
and many others of like rank, were, as we have already said, contributors to London papers. In the
United States, John Quincy Adams contributed to the
National Intelligencer; Hamilton and Madison contributed to other papers. There can be no good
reason why a newspaper should not employ the ablest
pens in literature, politics, or science, in the same manner as publishers of books. They have a great advantage in this, as their publications can be, at the
same time, fresh, instant, and popular. In one word,
a newspaper should be in advance of all publications,
on the greatest as well as smallest subjects of thought,
discussion, or fact. In this department, also, the
newspaper should be absolutely free. It should allow contributors to discuss all sides of any subject,
provided it be done in a decent and temperate manner.
In this respect most religious and political papers have
made a mistake. They usually adopt the side of a
particular party or sect, and allow no other opinions
to be expressed in their columns. This diminishes
the general interest of a paper, and certainly its fair-
ness. Of course there *are* limits to free discussion.
Treason should not be permitted to be published—
neither treason to faith or to government. A Christian
paper should not permit infidel attacks upon Christianity to appear in its columns. A political paper

should not publish attacks on the foundation of a Republican government, for such attacks are, in reality, treason. Within these limits, however, a great newspaper has a wide and useful range of discussion. Absolute freedom of the press is an essential element of a great newspaper. Now I come to a point on which there has been much difference of opinion between readers of newspapers and their publishers. This is relative to the duty of a newspaper to advocate, at all hazards, certain great principles of morals, religion, or politics. The individual reader, let us say—whom we may suppose to be a just and good man—insists that his paper should advocate certain good measures, just as he sees them. In this he mistakes the office and purpose of a newspaper. Unless a paper is established for the express purpose of advocating a particular cause, that advocacy is not its business or necessarily its duty. Its office, as I have described it, is to diffuse intelligence, to sell to the people information and intelligence on all subjects which they need information upon or are interested in. In doing this its material support depends upon that sale, and not upon the personal integrity of its editors and publishers. Undoubtedly, as upright men, they could not publish what is against a good cause, but, on the other hand, unless they are required to be martyrs, they can not sacrifice to any abstract opinions either their paper or their usefulness. On this subject, however, I may boldly claim for the newspaper press, that it has done and suffered as much for a good cause, as any other business or class in the community.

There is another point—so much can not be said for newspapers. This is the publication of improper or immoral advertisements. This is done to a great extent by publishing medical advertisements, and those of saloons and public places of resort, which are known to have an immoral tendency. The excuse for this is that advertising is a business, and a profitable one to the paper, and that a newspaper is a public forum. This is a good excuse as far as it goes, but it goes no farther than is allowed to conduct in the public streets. It is well known that public opinion, and even the law itself, does not permit certain conduct in the streets. Why should a newspaper be more privileged? Yet we often find in the columns of newspapers advertisements, especially medical advertisements, containing words and ideas which would not be permitted expression on the public forum. Happily this practice is being abandoned, and I have seen several first-class papers which do not contain them. We may now see, from what I have said, in what the real power and influence of a newspaper consists. Taken in its collective character, it is the only organ of general intelligence. Books fail in this, because they are partial and read by few. Schools fail in this matter, because, except in universities, they never reach the high thought and discussion on important questions, especially practical and commercial, which is found in the great newspapers of the present time. In fine, the newspaper diffuses universal information. It has given ubiquity to intelligence, freedom to discussion, power to thought, by impressing it upon the minds of millions. The newspaper is to mind what steam is to matter—gives locomotion to ideas, as steam does to persons. Both are characteristic of the present age—monuments to the progress of invention, of learning, and of freedom.